# Cyber

## Dictionary

### Your Guide to the Wired World

# For Knowledge Exchange

CyberDictionary photo/illustration credits:

pg 4     ©1996 PhotoDisc, Inc.
pg 7     Logo courtesy of ARPA
pg 11    Text and artwork ©1996 by YAHOO!, Inc. All rights
         reserved. YAHOO! and the YAHOO! logo are trade-
         marks of YAHOO!, Inc.
pg 43    Photo courtesy of Avis, Inc.
pg 49    ©1996 PhotoDisc, Inc.
pg 61    ©Cameron Clement/Spots on the Spot!
pg 79    ©Robert Neubecker/Spots on the Spot!
pg 82    ©John Clark/Spots on the Spot!
pg 83    ©Bryan Friel/Spots on the Spot!
pg 89    ©Randy Verougstraete/ Spots on the Spot!
pg 90    ©John Dykes/Spots on the Spot!
pg 91    ©Peter Hoey/Spots on the Spot!
pg 95    ©Robert Neubecker/Spots on the Spot!
pg 108   Courtesy of Virtual Research Systems Inc.
pg 122   ©M.E. Cohen/Spots on the Spot!
pg 131   Credit: Chris Wren. ©Chris Wren. Courtesy of the MIT
         Media Laboratory.
pg 134   ©1996 Sony Signatures Inc.
pg 136   ©Peter Alsberg/Spots on the Spot!
pg 140   Images courtesy of Apple Computer, Inc.
pg 146   Logo courtesy IEEE.
pg 157   Photo courtesy of Apple Computer, Inc.
pg 173   Photo courtesy of Apple Computer, Inc.
pg 174   ©John Dykes/Spots on the Spot!
pg 176   Media Lab (of MIT). Wiesner building. Credit: Bea
         Bailey. ©MIT Media Lab.
pg 176   Media Lab (of MIT). David Koons, Advanced Human
         Interface Group. Credit: Hiroshi Nishikawa. ©Hiroshi
         Nishikawa.
pg 181   Two views of a complex microchip from LSI Logic
         Corporation. The chip packs over a million transistors
         into an area smaller than that of a postage stamp. It
         forms the heart of interactive, satellite and cable tele-
         vision set-top boxes, enabling up to 500 television
         channels tobe viewed. Photos courtesy of LSI Logic
         Corporation.
pg 182   Photo of Pentium® chip courtesy of
         Intel Corporation.
pg 190   ©Peter Hoey/Spots on the Spot!
pg 201   NetWare screen capture courtesy of Novell.
pg 223   Photo courtesy of Apple Computers, Inc.
pg 223   ©Paul Schulenbury/Spots on the Spot!
pg 227   Screen capture courtesy of Kodak.
pg 231   ©Christoph Hitz/Spots on the Spot!
pg 251   Logo and photo of Sonic courtesy of
         Sega Corporation.
pg 271   Photo courtesy of Peter Cahoon, MAGIC, University of
         British Columbia.
pg 286   ©Robert Neubecker/Spots on the Spot!
pg 289   Screen capture of Adobe's illustrator 6.0 for the
         Macintosh, a vector-based image-building application.
         Logo and screen capture courtesy of Adobe Systems,
         Inc. All rights reserved.
pg 247   Photo courtesy of NASA Ames
         Research Center
pg 302   ©Robert Neubecker/Spots on the Spot!
pg 305   Photo courtesy of Sun Microsystems, Inc.
pg 309   ©David Wink/Spots on the Spot!
pg 313   Courtesy of The Net magazine

| | |
|---|---|
| President + CEO | Lorraine Spurge |
| Chairman | Kenin M. Spivak |
| Editor | Freude Bartlett |
| Design Firm | Sussman/Prejza & Company, Inc. |
| Creative Directors | Deborah Sussman Debra Valencia |
| Graphic Designer | Natalie Rosbottom |
| Production | Sylvia Park |
| Cover Illustrator | Marty Gunsaullus |
| Diagrams | Cate Bramble |

The following original illustrations were prepared by Cate Bramble: pg 22 (asynchronous transfer mode), pg 32 (bandwidth), pg 35 (bitmap graphics), pg 40 (bus), pg 48 (CD), pg 52 (cellular telephone), pg 56 (coaxial cable), pg 86 (digital satellite system), pg 94 (electromagnetic spectrum), pg 110 (facsimile transmission), pg 111(fiber optics), pg 115 (firewall), pg 156 (ISDN), pg 163 (kiosk), pg 169 (local area network), pg 185 (modem), pg 217 (open systems interconnection), pg 220 (packet switching), pg 230 (point-to-point protocol), pg 236 (public data network), pg 246 (router), pg 256 (simple network management protocol), pg 265 (switched multimegabit data service), pg 276 (token ring), pg 281 (twisted-pair cable), pg 295 (virtual circuit).

## In association with Wordworks Inc., Boston, Massachusetts

### Knowledge Exchange, LLC
### 1299 Ocean Avenue, Suite 250
### Santa Monica, CA 90401

Printed in the United States of America.

# Cyber
## Dictionary
### Your Guide to the Wired World

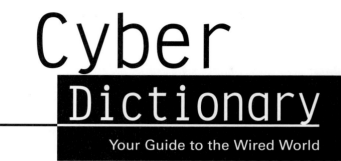

*Edited and introduced by*

# David Morse

KNOWLEDGE EXCHANGE

# Table of Contents

# Using CyberDictionary
## *Text Page*

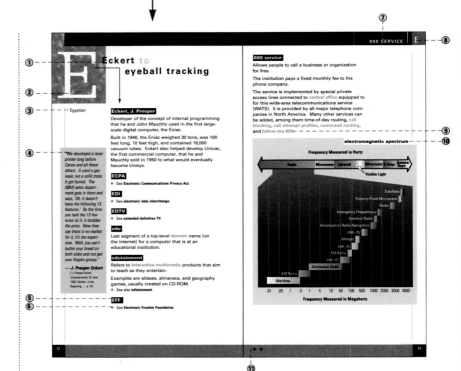

① **Section title range**
The alphabetical range of subjects per section

② **Sample font**
A typeface reference per alphabetical section

③ **Font name**
The name of the typeface shown for each alphabetical section

④ **Quote**
A quote pertaining to definition

⑤ **Word**
Word to be defined

⑥ **See also**
For more information…

⑦ **Section word**
Indicates which definition starts off on page

⑧ **Alphabetical section**
Indicates which section the reader is in

⑨ **Hot word**
Indicates a word with it's own entry

⑩ **Illustration title**
Title for illustration indicating the word it applies to

⑪ **Arrow**
Indication of how many essay pages follow

# *Essay Page*

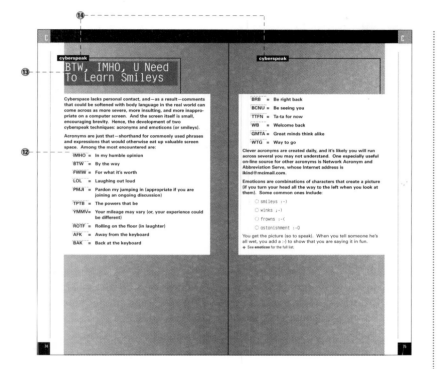

⑫ **Callout**
Definition for
abbreviations, words,
or symbols

⑬ **Essay title**
Subject of essay

⑭ **Word**
Word that essay refers to

# Foreword

**I**n one 24-hour period in July 1995, the global computer network known as the Internet grew by 770 sites—"channels" you could tune in to get news, conduct research, find medical advice, hear audio, see video, and argue with people over current events. The number was not unusual. The next day, 547 sites made their debuts. The pace has not slowed since.

The breadth of new information made available that one day, alone, is astounding, and takes every form from the sublime to the ridiculous: the winners of the 1995 Pulitzer prizes; the Byron Poetry Server, where readers can submit their own poems or comment on works already posted; the World Wide Arts Resources directory, with information on 150 art museums; the Teesside Business School, one of the United Kingdom's largest and most diverse; Pacific Holiday Villages, "maker of hand-crafted, portable recreation cottages"; U-Mar Racing, "America's only on-line, off-road racing team."

Not to mention five employment services; one credit union; two optometrists; *Derniers Nouvelles d'Alsace*, the daily newspaper for Strasbourg, France; and 13 individual résumés.

The Information Revolution—the convergence of communications and computers—was going full-tilt. Yet on the same day, Bell Atlantic officials in Dover Township, New Jersey, were conceding that their interactive cable pilot project had fallen into a quagmire. They wanted to build and operate a system to deliver interactive cable television and local and long-distance phone service to homes over a single fiber-optic cable. In two years, fiber-optic cable had been laid to only 8,000 of Dover's 38,000 homes. Another two years would be needed just to finish the cabling.

Technical issues had raised their ugly heads. Engineers testing the system had transmitted both picture and sound—but they did not arrive at the customer's TV set at the same time. "It looked like a badly dubbed foreign movie," admitted Lawrence Babbio, Bell Atlantic vice chairman. What's more, the cost of wiring a single home was twice the $1,000 initially estimated. And Bell Atlantic had managed to sign up only one commercial customer for its interactive services. In this case, the merger of computer and communications technology was moving at a pace only Judge Lance Ito could appreciate.

Make no mistake. Convergence is on the way. It is the coming together of the computer and communications industries, their services, and their products. It is the model on which telephone companies such as Bell Atlantic, AT&T, MCI, and Sprint, as well as cable TV giants such as Time Warner, Cox, and Tele-Communications Inc. have built their optimistic projections.

But as happens at the start of all new eras, some activities are racing along while others stumble. It is a complex transformation. Convergence is rocket science—the Internet grew out of a Defense Department project to make sure America's defense could survive ballistic missile attacks from Russia. And convergence is the subject of this guide.

The Internet—and its graphics-oriented, commercial World Wide Web—is the best evidence that convergence is rapidly under way. It will have such a great impact on society and business that the Clinton Administration—and the rest of the Washington establishment—have already embraced the Infobahn. The 1996 Presidential candidates all prepared "home pages" on the Web where voters can read about the officials' good deeds. Republicans campaigning in New Hampshire mention their on-line E-mail addresses almost as often as their desire to cut spending.

The politicians have come to recognize that the navigation of cyberspace is a required core competency for the years ahead. And if they have accepted it, the rest of us are probably already living it. But to survive in cyberspace, you have to know the language. Without this understanding, you will not be able to access the databases you need, or subscribe to the services you want, or find the newsgroups on which your research depends. The thrill of finding yourself on the frontier of the Convergence Age will quickly turn to frustration if you do not know the lingo. Once you do, to paraphrase Timothy Leary, you'll be able to log on, link in, and let loose.

In preparing this guide, we have created several levels of information that will help you do just that. First, you get basic definitions for more than 900 key cyberspace words, phrases, and names. Second, you will find a slew of definitions expanded to yield greater detail on the importance or implications of a word: how, what, why, where, or when the term might apply. Third, you will see dozens of intriguing sidebars that give you revealing background, colorful insights, and a few startling surprises. They're also just plain fun to read.

It is the nature of the high-tech beast for one term in a guide like this to lead you to several more. So for easy cross-reference, we have identified in bold blue type the terms used in one entry that are more fully defined in another. Where appropriate, we have also pointed you to additional entries that offer related information.

As these pages help you unlock the meaning of more and more terms, we are sure you will find yourself soaring ahead through that exciting and amazing zone called cyberspace.

# Introduction

## By David Morse

All of a sudden, it seems we have a new and fast growing communications medium. It combines the best of radio, TV, and the telephone with the interactivity of the personal computer. It is a result of advancing computing and communication technologies coming together. It is evolving every day and it is so new it doesn't really have a name. Consider its capabilities:

You can access your local newspaper and many magazines whenever you want from your home or office.

You can get instantaneous stock/bond prices from around the world.

You can communicate and have a discussion on almost any subject any time with interested parties all over the world—sports, politics, movies, cars, fashion, you name it.

You can get information on most subjects of interest delivered to you almost instantaneously.

What do you need to take advantage of these capabilities? A computer, a modem, and a connection to the Internet.

There's a revolution going on out there. Rapid technological progress in computers and communications is transforming how we work and how we play—how we lead our daily lives. And the language of cyberspace is no longer spoken only by those creatures with pocket protectors. Our world—and the words we use to describe it—have changed dramatically. If you don't hop on the cyberexpress, you're going to be left at the station.

CyberDictionary is a lot more than a dictionary. It's your guide to cyberspace—your companion. Sure, it has got the definitions that will take some of the mystery out of our rapidly changing world. But we also hope we've conveyed some of the excitement we feel about this cyberage we're living through. We want cyberspace to come alive for you.

That's why we've presented the personalities, the issues, the current developments—the flavor of cyberspace. We take you for a visit to a cybercafe, teach you the proper use of smileys and other emoticons, warn you about the do's and don'ts of etiquette, bring you up to date on network design, give you a glimpse of cybersex, and explain how the computer was born (no relation to cybersex).

When I started Amiga Computer in 1982, the personal computer had limited usefulness. After initially appealing to hobbyists, the PC's market broadened considerably with the introduction of the IBM PC in 1981. Spreadsheets, word processing, and entertainment were the primary uses.

At Amiga, we thought that by adding strong graphics capability to a PC, many additional uses would emerge. That proved to be the case and another class of users for the PC emerged.

Later, networking—initially on a local basis and eventually by way of wide area networks—began the development of the PC as a communications medium.

Now computers talk to other computers, and all types of information—audio and video, as well as data—can be sent across the world in seconds or minutes. As the infrastructure develops, further capabilities will emerge.

Most of the innovations in the PC business have come from small start-ups: Microsoft, Apple, Novell, Oracle, Cisco, Sun, America On-Line, and Netscape were all started by entrepreneurs with a vision of what could be someday.

My own fascination with computing and technology began when I was a graduate student at Dartmouth. One of my personal heroes, John Kemeny, had as much to do as anyone with the invention of personal computing. Dr. Kemeny, who at the time headed the math department and later became president of the college, brought the first personal computing experience to the campus. A big mainframe computer was connected to teletype machines all over campus. A simple language was required, codeveloped by Kemeny, called BASIC. It was clunky, slow, and totally text-based, but for the first time the average person could actually use a computer.

The world of technology and computing has come a long way since then. Some of the most creative and innovative people have been attracted by its potential and have created new uses and applications. This process is continuing. We invite you to take advantage of the information and insights—and humor—contained in CyberDictionary to launch your own journey into the future.

# access to avatar

## access

To get into a computer system, dial-up service, or network, by retrieving data, dialing a phone number, or logging on a network such as the Internet.
✚ See also **access site**.

## access control

Ways to protect confidential data in a computer or computer network from unauthorized access.

Protection is a big issue for everyone. The first line of defense is the password. Operators can control access to their system by choosing a password that is difficult to crack. Passwords may be a combination of upper- and lowercase letters, numbers, and keyboard symbols such as & and $. Passwords can keep most people out, but a hacker may use a computer program to quickly test millions of possible passwords.

High-level security—often imposed by government agencies, multinational corporations, and research laboratories—requires encryption, which is a process for scrambling data. The mishmash can be decoded only by an authorized user who has the decryption device or software.

## access site

Location on a network where users can find data or programs.

Each site has a unique name. For example, at Washington University State Library, there is an archive database stored on a particular computer. It can be accessed by someone who has logged onto the Internet and entered the name "wuarchive. wustl.edu." A woman in Florida or a man in Beijing can each retrieve the files they need from the database. A site's address generally says something about what kind of organization is offering the data.

## access time

The time it takes a device to retrieve stored data. Technically speaking, access time is the time interval between the instant a computer calls for data from a storage medium (a hard disk, say, or a CD-ROM) and the instant the data is delivered. This can be a matter of minutes on an old magnetic computer storage tape, or just microseconds from a computer's Dynamic Random Access Memory (DRAM).

✚ See also random access.

## ACD

✚ See automatic call distributor.

## acoustic coupler

Forerunner of the modern modem, an acoustic coupler is an electronic cradle the size of a dictionary, with two rubber cups, wired to a computer.

When a user wants to send data from the computer, he or she turns on the acoustic coupler, picks up a telephone handset, and inserts it into the cups. The coupler then transmits the data over a phone line. The acoustic coupler was the first means of communicating digital information from computers over phone lines. It is still useful in places that do not have a modular (RJ11) telephone jack.

✚ See also analog-to-digital and digital-to-analog.

## acronym

Word formed from the initial letters, or groups of letters, of a phrase or name.

The best acronyms are catchy, so not only the nerds can remember them. You are likely to know what a CD-ROM is, but if your friend said, "I just bought a computer with a Compact-Disk Read-Only Memory," you might congratulate her and walk away stunned.

Acronyms are popular in electronic media like E-mail and the Internet because they reduce the amount of typing required. They also often signify who's an insider. If you use *TAT* for *turnaround time*, you will be perceived and accepted as a savvy Internet sophisticate. And when you begin every other sentence with IMHO (in my humble opinion), you are really demonstrating that you belong to the in crowd. A favorite in this guide: WYSIWYG.

## active display

Information on a monitor that you can access or alter.

On your computer, it is the screen you are looking at. On your trendy TV, it is the little "status" box you can use with your remote to change color, contrast, and so on. At the dinner table, it's the expression on your kid's face when you tell him he has to eat liver.

## adaptive differential pulse-code modulation (ADPCM)

Technique for translating speech or other analog sound into a digital format.

ADPCM is accomplished with circuitry that takes rapid samples of the sound and translates them into binary code (1s and 0s). Because it eliminates errors in transmission, it is used on transcontinental phone lines to prevent noise from building up along the long connection, and for communications from satellites and space vehicles, where the layers of the atmosphere often disturb analog signals. ADPCM also requires less computer memory for the equivalent unit of sound; it is therefore used in CD-ROMs so images, data, and sound can be combined on one disk. The drawback: Transmission is slower than a direct analog link.

✚ See also **compression** and **sampling**.

## active matrix display

✚ See **liquid crystal display**.

## A/D converter

✚ See **analog-to-digital converter**.

## address

Combination of letters, numbers, and/or symbols that identifies a location where information is stored.

Cyberspace addresses come in all shapes and sizes:

- Telephone numbers (connect you to a particular person).
- Time codes or frame numbers (identify the location of video and/or audio material on a tape or disk).

- Sets of numbers (identify a location in a storage medium such as a computer's hard disk or floppy disk).

In E-mail, an address links you to someone else's computer. A typical address on Internet consists of three parts: the individual's mailbox name, the E-mail service he is on (which always begins with the symbol @), and a suffix designating the type of system. For example: "president@aol.com" is the E-mail address for the (1) "president" of (2) America Online (aol), which is a (3) commercial (com) organization. A period (or "dot") separates parts of the address not separated by the @ symbol.

In a network, the address links you to a site where you can access information, bulletin boards, chat lines, or newsgroups. These addresses vary in format. For example: "sci.bio.microbiology" gets you in touch with professors conducting research in microbiology. If that doesn't tickle your fancy, "rec.humor.funny" probably will; it's a site where users swap jokes.

The addresses for the World Wide Web, the graphics-oriented lane on the Internet superhighway, get complex. They begin with the prefix "http://www" and may go on at length.

Some neat ones:
"http://www.whitehouse.gov"
(information on Presidential initiatives);
"http://www.digiplanet.com/hackers/index.html"
(images from MGM/UA's movie "Hackers")
✦ See also **alphanumeric**.

## addressable

A TV reception box that can be controlled by the service provider; e.g., a cable company.

## addressable programming

The process in the cable television industry whereby you order and receive a pay-per-view event or movies-on-demand.

If you want to watch the next Mike Tyson fight, you call a special phone number provided by your cable company. The company checks your account and, if you have good credit, sends an encrypted message along the cable line to your set-top box, which then unscrambles the channel playing the desired event. The fee will show up on your bill.

# Guessing An Internet Address

Millions of newcomers log on to the Internet monthly, and the lack of a comprehensive directory system has posed an occasional headache. Not that Newt Gingrich needs the dial-up address for World of Flashdancers at his fingertips. But for Internet surfers, it is hard to find people if you do not already know their address. There is just no equivalent to a phone book or the ubiquitous telephone information number 555-1212. The come-on "What's your URL?" (the electronic address of a site on Internet's World Wide Web) may soon replace the Age of Aquarius pickup line "What's your sign?"

So what is an addressless, love-starved, or information-needy Net surfer to do? Search-software engines like YAHOO (Yet Another Hierarchical Officious Oracle) can find sites that contain a "keyword" you give it. However, you might end up with a long list; if you search for a friend named Marilyn, you might find an index of amusing Marilyn Monroe and/or drag queen sites—and you won't find Norma Jean.

The alternative is an address-finding software utility. One of the most widely used is NETFIND. Once it is downloaded in your computer, you dial-up Telnet (which links your computer to the Internet) and connect yourself to any of the following sites and log in as NETFIND:

- ○ bruno.cs.colorado.edu
- ○ eis.calstate.edu
- ○ mudhoney.micro.emn.edu
- ○ netfind.sjsu.edu

These sites will work with the NETFIND program and attempt to locate the person you are trying to reach.

WHOIS and FINGER are two other utilities that can help. Accessible through Telnet in the same way, WHOIS can find some individuals based on the user's name. FINGER requires a domain **name, too (the name of the Internet access site where the user's address resides).**

**Coming up with the user's name is pure guesswork. Try the person's last name. For the domain, try the name of the company or institution where the person works. You can narrow down the choices by also specifying the type of network the person is on, which forms the last three letters of the address. Here is a guide:**

| | | |
|---|---|---|
| edu | = | educational institutions |
| mil | = | military sites |
| gov | = | nonmilitary government sites |
| com | = | commercial network providers |
| net | = | special network services |
| org | = | other organizations |

**When trying to locate a person or site in another country, you might also add an abbreviation at the very end of the address. Sites in Canada, for instance, end with "ca," and those in Australia end with "au." Some sites may help you by providing what is called a mail** server—**essentially, a directory of persons and sites at that institution. The address for these begins with the letters "mail." For example, if you want to find someone at Auburn University, contact "mail.auburn.edu" and you will get a listing of everyone who is** on-line **there.**

**The frustrating part is that all these detective tools are limited. Many addressees refuse to be listed. For individuals, there's the privacy issue. For administrators, there's the traffic issue; an interesting site can attract thousands of sightseers a day. Directories of addresses are beginning to hit the market; whether or not they can keep up with the blazing pace of new sites remains to be seen.**

## ADPCM

+ See **adaptive differential pulse-code modulation**.

## ADSL

+ See **asynchronous digital subscriber loop**.

## advanced intelligent network (AIN)

A scheme for routing calls that is used by telephone companies to design their networks for the 1990s and beyond.

With an intelligent network, when a phone company initiates a new service for a customer, it does not have to rewire or change central processors, a process that can be slow and costly. Instead, it sends an inaudible signal along the customer's voice channel that tells a central computer to route the call through the processor or database where the service is performed. AIN handles large database services such as credit-card calling verification, call forwarding, caller-ID, 800 service, and 500 service—the first personal, universal phone number system.

+ See also **personal communication service (PCS)**.

## Advanced Research Projects Agency (ARPA)

The agency of the Department of Defense that developed the Internet.

+ See also **Defense Advanced Research Projects Agency (DARPA)** and **Usenet**.

## agent

A software program that sorts through information on electronic networks.

It goes network to network, seeking and organizing data in a form that is useful to a human. A clipping service, for example, uses an agent; you request information on, say, Alzheimer's Disease, and the agent searches medical journals, organizes what it finds, and puts the tidy file in your electronic mailbox.

An intelligent agent, which can make certain judgment calls about the information it finds, is known as a "softbot." An agent designed to leave havoc in its wake as it penetrates systems is called a virus.

## AI

+ See **artificial intelligence**.

> "What happened next was a sort of "big bang." In 1989, 80,000 computers were on the Internet. Today, there are more than 30 million users and 2 million computers on the Internet."
>
> — **Wired Magazine**
> [Clyde Ellis, "In the Beginning...," *Wired*, June 1995, p. 20]

Logo courtesy of ARPA

# The Evolution Of The Net

Our wonderfully eclectic information superhighway was actually born of 1960s Cold War. The country's military leaders were worried that the Russians would bomb key military installations, crippling the U.S. defense system's ability to communicate. So in 1969 the Department of Defense (DOD) started to build an electronic network that would link military installations. It would be called Arpanet. With sites connected in network fashion, the defense system could survive regardless of which sites were destroyed.

Even now, one of the characteristics of the Internet is that alternative routes can be found between point A and point B. Russian bombs may no longer be a threat to phone lines, but the ubiquitous backhoe certainly is.

The prototype "wide-area network" was built in 1969 by Bolt Beranek & Newman (BB&N), a Cambridge, Massachusetts, company, under contract to the DOD. BB&N engineers first designed interface message processors—today known as routers. These processors could identify and distribute individual messages bundled and sent in a single high-speed data stream over a telephone line. The processors, installed at three California colleges and the University of Utah, were activated on September 2, 1969.

By the early 1970s, the Usenet linked 20 university and military sites, and demand soared. So the network was broken into two parts: Milnet, which had the military sites, and Usenet for the rest. The two networks remained connected, however, thanks to a communications protocol that enabled them to talk to each other. This "internet protocol" (IP) would eventually become the namesake of our beloved Internet. The IP depended on a suite of standards that enabled physical networks to exchange data, published in 1974 by engineers Vincent G. Cerf and Robert E. Kahn. In 1978, the network proved it was independent of the hardware used: A van on a California highway was able to communicate via packet radio with a local host computer, and—after transcontinental and transatlantic transmissions—with a second computer in London.

In 1982, using Usenet as a testbed, defense-funded researchers built a prototype Internet. Top computer scientists at universities and corporations had access to it through yet another burgeoning network, the Computer Science Network (CSnet), sponsored by the National Science Foundation. Meanwhile, by 1983, all military installations nationwide had been linked by Usenet.

Foreseeing the future, the National Science Foundation in 1988 funded the building of a high-speed wide-area network called NSFnet. For starters, it linked the country's five supercomputer sites. But it was clear that demand would grow like crazy, and by 1990 NSFnet was opened up to the public as the Internet. So much military computer traffic had shifted to NSFnet that the original Usenet was decommissioned the same year.

The National Science Foundation continued to manage NSFnet, the backbone of Internet in the United States, until recently, when it was taken over by a University of Michigan consortium. With that transfer, the trunk of the Internet tree became funded by nongovernmental sources.

**AIN**

✤ See **advanced intelligent network**.

## algorithm

A set of rules or instructions for solving a problem in a finite number of steps.

Algorithms tell software programs how to compute numbers, databases how to organize entries, and electronics how to control everything from your microwave to the mix of air and fuel in your new automobile's engine.

## alias

An alternative name for software, hardware, or user that points to the real name.

For example, on your computer, you can name your hard drive Thelma instead of the insipid manufacturer identification, like Q540. An alias applied to a software program will allow it to be opened via different names or icons in different windows. Most E-mail providers allow you to choose an alias in place of your real user name on the network, so a message addressed to joesmith@smith.com will get to a user registered as mjsmith.

## aliasing

Unwelcome visual or audio effects on a computer screen.

The peculiar effects take many forms; one of the most common is jagged edges along what is supposed to be a smooth curved surface—say along the letter O or S—and diagonal lines on the screen that look like stair steps instead of a solid line. Aliasing can be the result of several causes, usually related to difficulty in translating computer code into actual signals or movements delivered to the screen, or interference between two frequencies of signals being directed to the screen.

✤ See also **anti-aliasing**, **artifact**, and **jaggies**.

## alphanumeric

Made up from the letters, numbers, punctuation, and symbols found on a standard keyboard.

## alt.

Prefix that indicates an "alternative" site on the Internet.

Although there is nothing radical about an alt. site by definition, many alt. sites, like alternative music groups and the alternative press, harbor an antiestablishment bias—not surprising, given that many of the early sites were created to bypass the standard, relatively rigid requirements for beginning an on-line newsgroup.

As might be imagined, alt. sites are where you find the most eclectic fare: conspiracies, erotica, people who like UFOs (alt.paranormal), and Barney haters (alt.barney.dinosaur.die.die.die).

**alt.**

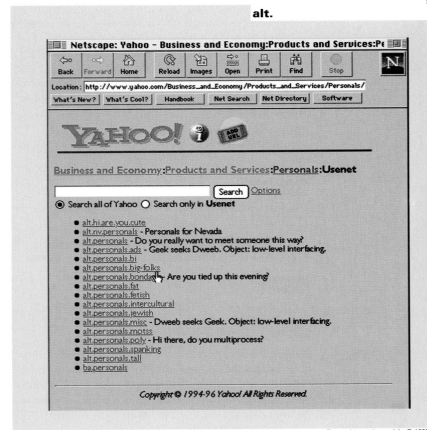

## American National Standards Institute (ANSI)

Independent industry organization in Bethesda, Maryland, that publishes technology standards for American industry.

ANSI (rhymes with fancy) is the U.S. member of the International Standards Organization (ISO) and the International Electrotechnical Commission (IEC), the preeminent global standard-setters. ANSI standards are voluntary, but virtually all businesses conform to them to endure compatibility. ANSI publishes thousands of standards on everything from how your computer terminal is controlled to the impact resistance of bike helmets.

0 1 0 0

10110110

## American Standard Code for Information Exchange (ASCII)

Code of ones and zeroes that all personal computers use to represent text.

11100110

In ASCII (pronounced "ask-key"), each alphanumeric character on a keyboard is represented as a series of seven 0s or 1s, which make up binary code. For example, the letter "c" is represented as 0010011; the number "3" is 0110011. Computers that are not compatible can usually still transfer pure "text-only" files between them because they both use ASCII to define the characters.

11110111

01110110

ASCII characters also serve as the "paint" for a school of art popular on the Internet (but not yet in major museums of modern art).

11000110

### amplitude

The distance between the high point and zero value of a waveform, or signal.

This determines how loud or strong the signal is.

+ See also **adaptive differential pulse-code modulation (ADPCM)**.

### analog

A system or device in which the input, output, or data are represented by a continuously changing variable, such as voltage or current.

Analog information flows and changes continuously, in contrast to digital information, which is either "on" or "off" and is sampled at regular, short intervals through time. Analog devices are characterized by dials and sliding mechanisms.

In old car stereos, one would turn a knob to find a station. Turning the knob caused a metal bar (usually red) to slide from left to right, along a small strip of metal inside the radio (which one did not see). As the bar slid, it gradually and continuously changed the frequency the radio was supposed to tune in. If one wanted "Live 105.5 FM," one had to slide around the 105–106 area until the reception was acceptable. With a digital radio, one simply enters the exact call numbers, and a microchip instructs the radio's electronics to pick up that frequency.

✛ See also **digital**.

## analog-to-digital (ADC)

The conversion of data or signal storage from analog format, like the continuous electrical vibrations triggered by a voice on a phone, to the on-off digital format of computer code.

An example is converting a tape recording into a compact disc (CD).

✛ See also **analog-to-digital (A/D) converter** and **digital-to-analog**.

## analog-to-digital (A/D) converter

A circuit that changes a continuously varying signal into a digital one.

A/D converters, despite sounding obscure, are key components in many of our most-used technologies. Telephone companies use them to convert your voice, which is a continuously varying series of bursts of air coming from your mouth, to a stream of on/off (digital) light signals that can be carried over a fiber-optic cable.

Bought a CD of the Beatles or Elvis lately? Old analog recordings (a.k.a. "records") can be transformed into digital CDs thanks to A/D converters, which sample the continuous electrical vibrations transmitted by a needle on a record player 44,100 times per second.

✛ See also **sampler** and **sampling rate**.

## ANI

✛ See **automatic number identification**.

## animation

A series of still images (drawn or computer-generated) displayed in rapid succession to create the illusion of motion.

This illusion arises from the phenomenon known as persistence of vision—the brain retains a single image for a moment after the image is out of sight. Once images are delivered at a rate of more than 15 or 16 per second, one no longer sees the separation between them; one sees continuous motion. Animation works best at 24 frames per second in film and 30 frames per second in video.

✛ See also **computer animation**.

## anonymity

Cynic's view of the social fabric fostered by the Internet and other electronic networks, which allow people to exchange information and discourse without any personal interface.

The anonymity allows people to build new (and misleading) identities for themselves and carry out hoaxes and frauds. A married person with four children can flirt as a swinging single and take advantage of a trusting, lovestruck innocent.

## anonymous file transfer protocol (FTP)

Method for **downloading** files on the **Internet** to your computer from directories or databases where you don't have an account.

Anonymous FTP lets you get documents, files, programs, and other archived data from public directories anywhere in the Internet. You simply enter "anonymous" as your **userid** (user identification) and your **E-mail** address as the password.

A search engine called **Archie** gives you a list of anonymous FTP sites and files that are available. Anonymous FTP can be a cost-effective method for finding information about a particular subject or getting shareware programs and upgrades for your computer in a matter of minutes.

✦ See also **file transfer protocol (FTP)**.

## anonymous posting

Message placed on a **bulletin board**, **E-mail**, or other **network** that does not identify the person who sent it. Chicken!

## anonymous server

On the **Internet**, an **interface** server—acting as a **gateway** or conductor of information—that is independent of a particular **access site**.

It expedites the flow of information and can be used to preserve security for the sender and receiver.

## ANSI

✦ See **American National Standards Institute**.

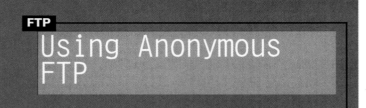

**FTP**

# Using Anonymous FTP

When you access files using anonymous FTP, you are actually running another person or company's computer, to get files listed in directories. To do so, you have to give it commands. They include

| | | |
|---|---|---|
| ls | = | list files in current directory |
| page | = | display contents of a text file |
| cd | = | change directories |
| get | = | transfer file to local computer or server |
| quit | = | close the connection |

At most FTP sites, one subdirectory labeled "public" contains all the files an outsider will be able to access. On many FTP systems, each directory includes a text file called README or INDEX, which will summarize the contents of the directory. The *page* command will display these files. Once you have found a file you want, the *get* command will download it to your local computer.

Popular FTP sites may be difficult to access; you might be referred to another site that holds the same files. Try them. Or try back later. The easiest access tends to be after business hours where the FTP site is located. Transfer speed can be slow depending on your hardware, the hardware of the site, and the amount of traffic on the Internet. If the file you are seeking has been archived, it has probably also been compressed to take up less hard disk space and so it can be more quickly transferred. The name of compressed files will end with a suffix like ZIP, ARC, SIT, TAR.Z, or GZIP. An unarchiving program is necessary to unpack a compressed file; the programs can often be found for free on the Internet.

## anti-aliasing

A software technique used in imaging systems to make curved or diagonal lines look smooth and continuous.

✦ See also **aliasing**.

## applet

Bomblets are tiny bombs; applets are tiny computer applications.

These bits of software are part of the Java programming language. You download them from Java sites on the Internet and use them on your own computer to create little animated or interactive routines for your own World Wide Web home page.

## application program interface (API)

Software that enables an applications program to communicate with another program or the operating system.

If you are putting together a newsletter for your garden club, you might lay out a blank front page, then get a text file about petunias, and a photo of a petunia, and put them on the page. The API lets you retrieve the writing and graphics and paste them into the layout.

The API is also used to initiate contact between your computer and network services, and between computers that are linked on a local network, such as all the computers within a company.

## applications program

A computer program or set of programs that performs a specific job such as word processing or accounting. Also called *applications software*.

This contrasts with an operating system, such as DOS or Windows, which manages how your computer performs tasks, and utilities, which perform a single task in all applications, such as spelling checkers and word finders.

## ARC

✦ See **Augmentation Research Center**.

## arcade games

Coin-operated game machines designed for use in public entertainment areas.

There's Pac-Man, Indy Racer, Street Fighter, Donkey Kong, F-16....

## Archie

A software program that searches Internet files for information on a particular subject.

In operation, a user connects to a nearby Archie server and requests a particular file. Archie then puts together a directory of the file transfer protocol (FTP) archive sites worldwide that can be browsed to find the required information. Veronica, Jughead, and WAIS are other programs that search Internet files.

## architecture

(1) For hardware, a computer's components and the blueprint by which they interact. (2) For software, the operating system and programs that control peripheral devices such as printers, and the blueprint by which they interact.

The major hardware component is the central processing unit (CPU)—"The brain, Igor!" Other major components include the storage medium (hard drive and disk drive) and input/output devices that connect to peripherals. "Open architecture" refers to systems—such as the IBM PC and compatibles and, recently, the Macintosh—that allow you to add peripherals and internal enhancement cards from other hardware manufacturers. "Closed architecture" systems—such as the Sega and Nintendo game cartridges—are "all-in-one-box" products; you cannot add peripherals or use cartridges from other vendors.

## archive

(1) Backup of a file or files on some storage medium, such as a floppy disk or tape. (2) Related files grouped together and stored under one name.

## archiving

The process whereby you prepare data for storage.

Typically, archived files are compressed to reduce their size and then decompressed when there is a need to restore the file to its original size.

# The Interactive Test Track

Visit a state-of-the-art arcade today and you may find yourself surrounded by folks who appear to be caught in an enraged hypnotic trance—head and arms flailing—as if battling for their lives. What fun!

The arcade game has introduced computer software to the masses in a way that Tom Watson, who led IBM for 45 years, could never have envisioned. Computer graphics have virtually replaced the arcade games of old, such as pinball machines and air gun and ball-rolling games. They first infiltrated candy stores, bars, theme parks, and movie lobbies but now have a place all their own—the so-called location-based entertainment (LBE) site. You know, those dark noisy caves in shopping malls and along city streets where wild-eyed youth, not to mention executives on lunch break, go to do electronic battle.

The first successful computer-generated arcade game was Pong, a two-dimensional Ping-Pong game produced by Nolan Bushell in 1972. Since then, arcade games have soared in complexity, using buttons, joysticks, trackballs, or steering wheels, and full 3D effects. Video images stored on laserdisc create photographic-quality illusions.

Arcade games have always pushed current technology to the limit. Indeed, computer companies often use the arcade world as the unofficial testing ground for future interactive media. A product that first appears in an arcade game will often later show up in the home, playable on a PC or a dedicated game system such as Nintendo. Arcade games—and the theme parks and LBEs where they are found—are also where new computer-consumer interfaces emerge, such as the head-mounted helmet displays used in virtual reality.

The convergence of virtual reality and arcade video games is likely to develop next into virtual theme parks. Instead of going to Las Vegas, Six Flags, Disneyland, or the Jersey Shore boardwalk, you will be able to dial up high-powered systems and on-line interactive games networks and display them on your big screen at home. You may even pit your jet flying, car driving, and kick boxing skills against a competitor in another city, in another country. Forget Tom Cruise; you'll be your own Top Gun.

## area code

A telephone company's three-digit code that designates a "toll" center, used when callers dial long distance.

✚ See also **exchange**.

## ARPA

✚ See **Advanced Research Projects Agency**.

## Arpanet

A network that connected Department of Defense research sites across America. Although it formed the foundation of the Internet, it was decommissioned in 1990.

✚ See also **Advanced Research Projects Agency (ARPA)**.

## artifact

An unwanted graphic, usually small, that remains on a screen after an image is distorted by a mistake, omission, or limitation in graphics software or hardware.

Artifacts may cause pixels to be dropped or to clump together.  Other types of artifacts occur when the quality of a videotape is poor (if metal particles flake off the tape, for example) or when decompression is faulty.

✚ See also **aliasing** and **noise**.

## artificial intelligence (AI)

Computer hardware and software packages that try to emulate human intelligence in order to solve problems using reasoning and learning.

One of the earliest and most successful applications were computer programs that could play chess, even at the Grand Master level.  Most practical applications of AI are for so-called expert systems, which aid human decision-making.  Two of the most advanced expert systems are those that help doctors diagnose diseases based on a patient's symptoms, and automatic pilot systems that help Air Force pilots in dog fights.

## ASCII

✚ See **American Standard Code for Information Exchange**.

## aspect ratio

The ratio of a computer, TV, or movie screen's height to width.

# Coding America

The telephone companies assign area codes to different regions of the United States. The first digit is any number from 2 through 9. In the past, the second digit was always a 0 or 1. That is changing, however, because the designers of the numbering system never anticipated the rampant proliferation of fax machines, pagers, and cellular telephones. There just aren't enough area codes, so other numbers must serve as the middle digit. This, in turn, has created havoc for large companies with computerized phone systems that will not place long-distance calls unless a 0 or 1 is the second digit.

Some three-digit codes—900, 800, and 500—indicate a particular kind of service rather than a particular region.

The aspect ratio of most modern motion pictures varies from 3:5 to as wide as 3:7. These "wide screen" ratios have to be adjusted when motion pictures are transferred to the more square-shaped television screen, which has a typical aspect ratio of 3:4. Proposals for high-definition television (HDTV), sometimes touted as the next generation of home television technology, include an aspect ratio of approximately 3:5.

## assembler

A program that translates a symbolic language like Fortran or C (the computer instructions people write) into machine code—the 1s and 0s a computer can read.

✦ See also **language**.

## assembly language

A symbolic language that enables people to write programs using words, letters, and numbers.

This assembly language is translated into machine code by a translator called an assembler. It takes several lines of machine code to accomplish the same thing as one line of an assembly language.

## assets

In computerland, any copyrighted intellectual property such as an audio, video, game, text, or graphics program.

## asynchronous digital subscriber loop (ADSL)

Transmission method that improves the delivery of a signal, making it possible to transmit a data-intensive signal such as video over ordinary copper phone wires.

With ADSL, you can send and receive voice, data, and video files from a house or office over the standard, old-fashioned copper telephone wires. Phone companies are steadily laying fiber-optic cables that can easily support video and the most data-intensive computer transmissions.

## asynchronous transfer mode (ATM)

Type of fast packet switching that will be the basis for most telecommunications by 1997.

This technique enhances the already great capacity of fiber-optic lines to carry data, and at greater speed. Gradually being implemented by phone

## asynchronous transfer mode

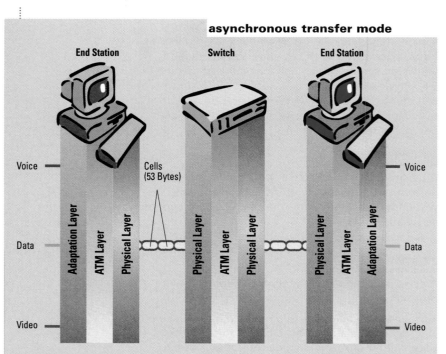

The **Adaptation Layer** inserts/extracts information into 48-byte Payload (IP data). The **ATM Layer** adds/removes 5-byte Header to the Payload.

The **Physical Layer** converts to appropriate electrical or optical format.

## ATM Cell Architecture

Cell (53 Bytes)

| Cell | | | | | |
|---|---|---|---|---|---|
| Header | | | | | Information |
| Generic Flow Control | VCI/VPI Field | Payload Type Indicator | Cell Loss Priority | Header Checksum | Payload |
| 4 bits | 24 bits | 2 bits | 2 bits | 8 bits | 48 bits |

**Generic Flow Control** maintains the traffic entering the network. If traffic is too high, it will limit the amount of data entering the network. **VPI/VCI Field**—VPI identifies the particular path the cell takes on the network. VCI identifies the exact channel the virtual path will take.

**Payload Type Indicator** distinguishes between user cells and control cells.
**Cell Loss Priority** indicates if a cell can be dropped during congestion.
**Header Checksum** protects the header field from transmission errors.
**Payload** is the IP data.

companies as they upgrade their switches, ATM will connect the local and global networks of the late 1990s. It will make possible the long-awaited **broadband integrated services digital network (B-ISDN)**, which will be able to deliver voice, data, fax, **E-mail**, full-motion video, **video conferencing**, and **multimedia** to any home or business user.

✦ See also **asynchronous transmission**.

## asynchronous transmission

A **telecommunications** method that sends one character at a time between computers.

This is the basis for all **modem** calls, **E-mail**, and links to **networks**. Communications software tells the receiving computer when the transmission of each character starts (called a start bit) and stops (called a stop bit).

Contrast this with **synchronous transmission**, in which strings of multiple characters are continuously transmitted. These strings are preceded and followed by a synchronization character that aligns the sending and receiving devices' clocks, so they can track the position of each character. Synchronous transmission can be four times as fast as asynchronous, but it is more expensive.

✦ See also **network**.

## AT&T Consent Decree

Legal document ordering the breakup of the AT&T monopoly by 1984.

✦ See also **Bell operating company (BOC)** and **regional Bell operating company (RBOC)**.

## ATM

✦ See **asynchronous transfer mode** and **automatic teller machine**. Your choice.

## audio

(1) Sound humans hear, normally ranging from 15 to 20,000-**Hz** range. (2) The audio portion of a television show, film, video, or multimedia program.

## audio frequency

The number of times per second a sound impulse vibrates, creating sound heard with normal hearing.

Sound travels through gasses (air), liquids, and solids. The greater the frequency, the "higher" the pitch. For example, an earthquake sends shock

# The Making Of Telecom's Brave New World

Until midnight of December 31, 1983, when the consent decree took effect, AT&T was the dominant telephone carrier, although GTE, Contel, and several other large companies also provided telephone services and equipment in the United States. There were also more than 1,000 small, independent phone companies providing service to limited local areas. At the time, telephones were available only from Western Electric, owned by AT&T. Local telephone service was primarily available only from the Bell operating companies, also owned by AT&T.

The decree was negotiated in 1982 by William Baxter, head of the Justice Department's Antitrust Division during the early days of the Reagan Administration. The agreement successfully separated local and long-distance service. It was seen by many legal experts as a sound application of settled antitrust principles designed to prevent the abuse of monopoly power.

In 1984, as a result, the Bell System was divided into seven separate regional Bell operating companies (RBOCs), known as the Baby Bells. These include such companies as NYNEX in the Northeast and Pacific Telesis in the West. The Baby Bells own 22 smaller Bell operating companies (BOCs), each of which has a monopoly for local service, such as New York Telephone, Indiana Bell, and Northwestern Bell.

The decree allowed any company to try to compete for long-distance service. MCI and Sprint quickly rose to the challenge.

It also allowed any company to make consumer telecommunications products such as telephones. On the flip side, the decree lifted regulations that restricted AT&T from making computer equipment. In the beginning, many expected AT&T to make a run at IBM in computer, and IBM to make a run at AT&T for telecom equipment. Both diversifications were started, but neither panned out. Subsequent deregulation now allows competition for local service, too.

Rulings in 1995 have made it possible for cable TV companies to offer phone service, and phone companies to offer television service. Bell Atlantic (an RBOC) has already announced plans to offer a wireless cable system by 1998, and video dial-tone service as soon as federal approval is given. Sprint has formalized an agreement with Comcast, Tele-Communications, and Cox Communication to package long-distance, local telephoning, and cable services to consumers. And MCI is launching access to the Internet and electronic shopping, and pushing into the local phone market.

Ambition, however, may be outrunning accomplishment. While Ameritech (an RBOC) hoped to connect more than a million customers to an interactive video network by the close of 1995, the *Wall Street Journal* reported that fewer than 200,000 were expected to be connected. "None of us realized the complexity of building an interactive network," Bell Atlantic Chief Technical Officer John Seazholtz confessed to a reporter in July 1995.

waves that create vibrations through the earth's crust at the lowest frequencies audible by man (about 15 Hz) and even lower frequencies that we cannot hear. The highest note on a violin begins to reach the upper frequencies of human hearing. Dog whistles emit a pulse into the air at a frequency that is too high for humans to hear but still within a dog's range.

So is that vibration considered a "sound," if we can't hear it?

## audiotex

Voice-response systems that allow phone callers to access information or leave messages, without the aid of a live person.

Audiotex technology creates the experience of dialing a phone number and hearing a machine present several options. This service is often called voice mail (sometimes voice jail). The caller may or may not find this satisfactory: "Hello, you've reached Flora. If you are rich, hit 1... If you are handsome, hit 2... If you are Bob, hit the road."

## Augmentation Research Center (ARC)

Lab at the Stanford Research Center in Palo Alto, California, for computer research.

ARC was set up in the 1960s by Doug Engelbart, the visionary perhaps most responsible for today's style of visually organized interactive personal computing. It was funded by ARPA. Engelbart believed that the computer exists to augment the human mind. He developed the graphical user interface (GUI) tools—mouse, icons, and the hypertext system—that were expanded at Xerox PARC and, 20 years later, became the basics of the Macintosh computer and operating system.

ARC also developed ideas about teleconferencing, E-mail, and workgroup processing tools.

*"The computer was something on the same order as writing, the printing press, agriculture...People need a new eloquence and skill. They need to be able to explore new areas of process knowledge...I made a conscious decision at the age of 25 that money would be secondary to what kind of contribution my work would make. Sometimes, though, I think I've overdone the pro bono idea. You get way out on the frontier*

## authoring

Preparing a computer program, often with an authoring language or authoring system.

Authoring allows users without formal computer programming training to prepare applications programs for computer or videodisc-based systems.

✦ See also **scripting language** and **C++**.

## authoring language

Specialized, high-level, plain-English computer language that permits nonprogrammers to program basic functions of computer, interactive CD-ROM, or videodisc programs.

In authoring languages, the program logic and program content are combined, providing a faster development path but fewer capabilities than the fundamental authoring system a professional programmer would use.

## authoring system

(1) Specialized computer software that helps its users design interactive programs using everyday language, without the painstaking detail of computer programming. (2) System that separates logic and content, allowing greater flexibility in design.

## automatic call distributor (ACD)

Specialized telephone system that automatically directs incoming calls to available personnel.

ACD serves large organizations such as telemarketing centers, airlines, and hotels as well as smaller companies that receive many incoming calls. An automatic call distributor can also track calls, providing management with information about the arrival of incoming calls, how they are routed, if they are abandoned (callers put on hold who do not wait), and from where the calls originate.

ACDs can be programmed to read the incoming caller's telephone number via automatic number identification (ANI). The call is then directed to a specific customer service representative while the host computer retrieves and displays the customer's record. So next time you call your credit card company with a question, they will have your record in front of them before you tell them your name.

## automatic number identification (ANI)

Function that determines an incoming caller's telephone number and displays it on the recipient's telephone or computer screen.

ANI is made possible with an integrated services digital network (ISDN) connection. Some feel ANI is a violation of privacy, and suggest it will discourage calls from runaway children and people who want to leave anonymous tips concerning criminal activities.

## automatic teller machine (ATM)

On-the-street banking machine that dispenses money and accepts deposits.

ATMs are linked to a central computer through telephone lines and a multiplexed data network. The computer compares information on the user's ATM card with bank records to see if the user enters the correct personal identification number (PIN) into the ATM. If so, it allows that customer to withdraw or deposit money in his or her bank account, or check a balance. ATMs have been the first exposure for many people to the concept of a computer network.

## avatar

A digital "actor" (like a chess piece, fish, or penguin) used in virtual reality markup language (VRML) as a surrogate for a person communicating on-line in three-dimensional chat lines such as World Chat on the World Wide Web.

In plain English, if you want to chat and there is no one else on-line, you can talk to the fish.

# b-channel to byte

## b-channel

Bodoni

Connection between users on an integrated
services digital network (ISDN) system that
provides simultaneous voice and data service.

## B-ISDN

✚ See **broadband integrated services digital network**.

## backbone

A central high-speed communications corridor that
connects disparate networks or clusters of computers over hundreds, even thousands, of miles.

It's the trunk of the tree, the interstate of the road
system, the backbone of your skeleton (ah, that's
where the name came from!).  Note that the
backbone (in all these systems) doesn't connect
two points; it enables all points to connect to
each other.

✚ See also **Internet**.

## bandwidth

(1)  Range of signal frequencies, or amount of data,
a carrier can handle before it is maxed out.

A phone line can only transmit so many calls
at a time.  A highway can only hold so many cars
at a time.

(2)  In cyberspace, slang describing how
multiskilled and superintelligent a person is.

✚ See also **carrier, compression, and spectrum**.

## basic rate interface

An ISDN standard governing how desktop
terminals and telephones can be connected to
an ISDN switch.

Specifically, it's by two b-channels that provide
simultaneous voice and data service, and one
D-channel that carries call set-up information and

# The Emerging Importance Of Bandwidth

The marriage of computer and communications technologies will have to be conducted in the church of bandwidth. In defining the capacity of a communication channel, bandwidths have become both politically and economically important.

Why? Consider this. The Internet was originally designed to link computers working with ASCII text and numbers. Today, Net users often send and receive high-resolution graphics and video. This demands that more data be transferred over the same physical wires or satellite channels-requiring greater capacity, or bandwidth.

The channels also need different kinds of bandwidth, which can transfer different frequencies of data. For example, high-resolution images are transmitted at high frequencies, about 6 megahertz (6 million cycles per second), while audio is transmitted at only 44 kilohertz (44,000 cycles per second). A wideband circuit that can carry one television channel could carry 1,200 voice telephone channels. Transmissions are classified as broadband (greater than 3,000 hertz), voice band (300-3,000 Hz), and narrowband (below 300 Hz).

Because the information superhighway demands a high bandwidth infrastructure to carry all forms of communication, the

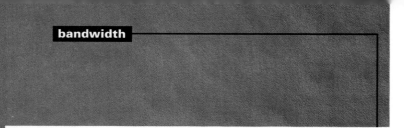

decision by a regulatory body as to whether cable television and telecommunications companies should provide fiber-optic or copper cable networks is not simply a technical one. That choice determines what services can or cannot be provided over those networks. Fiber-optic cables can handle broadband transmission; copper wire can't.

Private companies—industry experts now realize—are not willing to invest in building expensive fiber-optic networks without the assurance of profitable returns. And (they assert) profit can only be achieved if they are allowed to carry a wide range of services.

Nevertheless, regulatory bodies restrict telecommunications companies to carrying a narrow range of services with the rationale that restrictions serve to foster competition between the telecommunications, computer, and entertainment industries that offer network services.

The same debate exists regarding the division of the broadcast frequency spectrum that will accommodate new cellular telephone and cellular radio and new channels for television and digital radio.

# bandwidth

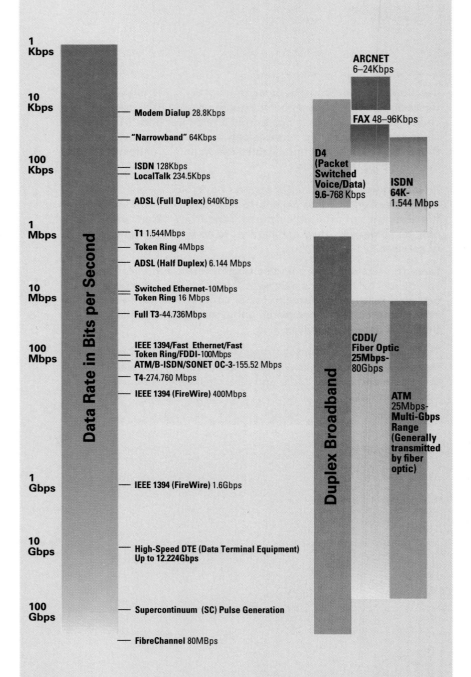

**Data Rate in Bits per Second**

| | |
|---|---|
| 1 Kbps | |
| 10 Kbps | Modem Dialup 28.8Kbps<br>"Narrowband" 64Kbps |
| 100 Kbps | ISDN 128Kbps<br>LocalTalk 234.5Kbps<br>ADSL (Full Duplex) 640Kbps |
| 1 Mbps | T1 1.544Mbps<br>Token Ring 4Mbps<br>ADSL (Half Duplex) 6.144 Mbps |
| 10 Mbps | Switched Ethernet-10Mbps<br>Token Ring 16 Mbps<br>Full T3-44.736Mbps |
| 100 Mbps | IEEE 1394/Fast Ethernet/Fast Token Ring/FDDI-100Mbps<br>ATM/B-ISDN/SONET OC-3-155.52 Mbps<br>T4-274.760 Mbps<br>IEEE 1394 (FireWire) 400Mbps |
| 1 Gbps | IEEE 1394 (FireWire) 1.6Gbps |
| 10 Gbps | High-Speed DTE (Data Terminal Equipment) Up to 12.224Gbps |
| 100 Gbps | Supercontinuum (SC) Pulse Generation<br>FibreChannel 80MBps |

**ARCNET** 6–24Kbps

**FAX** 48–96Kbps

**D4 (Packet Switched Voice/Data)** 9.6-768 Kbps

**ISDN 64K-** 1.544 Mbps

**Duplex Broadband**

**CDDI/ Fiber Optic** 25Mbps- 80Gbps

**ATM** 25Mbps- Multi-Gbps Range (Generally transmitted by fiber optic)

customer data and access to slower-speed networks, like videotex.

+ See also **primary rate interface (PRI)**.

## baud

Measure of transmission speed for data communications.

It's the number of data elements that can be transmitted each second. For example, a 9,600-baud modem transmits a data element 9,600 times a second. Baud rate is often equated with bits per second (bps), but the two are not necessarily equal. If your modem is sending a single bit of data at a time, then 9,600 baud will transfer 9,600 bits of data a second. But if your 9,600-baud modem is transmitting 8 bits at a time (a byte), it is sending 76,000 bps.

+ See also **bandwidth**.

## BB&N

+ See **Bolt, Beranek & Newman**.

## BBS

+ See **bulletin board system (BBS)**.

## Bell operating company (BOC)

Local phone company that was created as the result of the 1984 breakup of AT&T.

+ See also **AT&T Consent Decree and regional Bell operating company (RBOC)**.

## benchmark

Standardized task used to measure how well a device or system operates.

There are many types of benchmarks. A benchmark for a microprocessor is a certain calculation. Different microprocessors can be rated by giving them the same benchmark calculation to perform, and comparing the speed and accuracy with which they find the result. Manufacturers often run benchmarks on their devices under ideal conditions, which may not indicate how well the device will perform in the real world. Wags like to joke, "In the computer industry there are three kinds of lies: lies, damn lies, and benchmarks."

## big iron

Cyberslang for a large mainframe computer.

In the early days of IBM and DEC, these would fill entire rooms.

## binary

System for counting and computation in which every value is represented as either the number 0 or 1.

## binary digit (bit)

The smallest unit of information recognized by a computer.

A computer is made of circuits. In each circuit, an electric signal is either present or absent. Since the circuit has only two states, it can be instructed to change or remain the same by computer code written using 1s and 0s. A 1 indicates a circuit should be on, 0 indicates off. Any form of information can be represented in code as a combination of 1s and 0s; therefore, any data can be stored in a computer as a combination of on and off circuits. Computers are so accurate because a bit is a clear, unambiguous signal.

It takes about 80,000 bits to represent the text on a single page of double-spaced, typewritten text; 56,000 bits to represent one second of speech; 10,000,000 bits to represent one second of TV video.

✚ See also **analog, byte,** and **digital**.

## binary file

Contains data or instructions written in terms of 0 or 1.

## biosensor

Device embedded in a piece of clothing, or attached on or under the skin, that gives feedback to a computer about a person's biological conditions, such as skin temperature, brain waves, or subtle muscle movements.

✚ See also **virtual reality**.

## bit

✚ See **binary digit**.

## bitmap graphics

A digital representation of an image on a computer screen.

A bitmapped letter "C" or a bitmapped image of a cat is displayed on a computer screen as a pattern of thousands of glowing dots (pixels) on the screen's surface. Graphics programs manipulate bitmapped images by moving the dots around, changing the relationship of the dots to each other.

✚ See also **vector graphics**.

Bitmap Graphic

Vector Graphic

## bits per second (BPS)

The number of bits of information transmitted per second.

A kilobit (kb) is 1,000 bits; a megabit (Mb) is a million bits.

✚ See also **baud**.

## BOC

✚ See **Bell operating company**.

## bogus newsgroup

A network site set up to look like a topic-oriented newsgroup on Usenet but actually created to sell a product or exploit the naive and the uninitiated.

## Bolt, Beranek & Newman (BB&N)

Cambridge, Massachusetts-based computer network and software technology company that helped pioneer the development of the Internet in 1987 under contract to the Advanced Research Projects Agency.

BB&N operates Nearnet (a service of the Net operating in New England and New York) and has continued to develop network data transmission and analysis products, including network switches for simultaneous large-volume data and voice video transmission. BB&N is under contract to AT&T to develop proprietary access applications to the Internet.

## bookmark

Tidy little computer routine that automatically links you to a network site you have already checked out.

When you use an on-line file search program like Gopher, a bookmark sends you to a specific menu or file that interests you, without your having to jump through all the usual connection hoops. Put a number of these bookmarks together and you will have your own personalized "booklist" or menu of your preselected information sites. Sort of like a net surfer's black book.

## Boolean logic

A system of math that uses operators such as "and," "or," "not," "if...then," which permit computation.

The system is named after George Boole, an English mathematician who introduced the logic in 1847. Simple programming languages like Basic use the Boolean logic operators. Network databases also use a form of this logic to enable keyword searching. Telling an on-line database to search for "cats and dogs" will result in a long list of articles that contain both these words. Searching for "cats not dogs" will yield every file containing the word "cat" and no mention of "dog." "Adj" stands for "adjacent" and is used when a searcher wants to find two words that appear next to, or very close to, each other, such as "virtual adj reality."

## BPS

✦ See **bits per second**.

## branching

Property of an interactive story or instructional sequence that lets the user select among two or more paths or destinations—the proverbial fork in the road.

The most common logic diagrams for interactive story lines are described as "tree" structures and are said to "branch" at user-driven-or system-driven-decision points.

## BRI

✦ See **basic rate interface**.

## bridge

A connection between geographically close and similar networks (those that use the same protocol) so that they look like one large network.

A bridge is an efficient handler and monitor of traffic, allowing a local area network to be expanded to include more workstations.

✦ See also **gateway and router**.

## broadband channel

High-speed, high-capacity transmission channel.

Broadband channels are carried on coaxial or fiber-optic cables that have a wider bandwidth than conventional telephone lines, giving them the ability to carry video, voice, and data simultaneously.

The quality of a broadband channel is enhanced by empty spaces called guardbands between channels that ensure no interference. This makes them ideal for cable television, considered the "classic" broadband channel because it carries many channels simultaneously. Local area networks at businesses and universities may also use broadband channels.

✚ See also **broadband network**.

## broadband integrated services digital network (B-ISDN)

Very high-speed telecommunications service able to transmit multimedia over the phone line.

Based on the synchronous transfer mode, it runs over optical fiber, operating at speeds surpassing the rates of transmission on a narrowband integrated services digital network.

✚ See also **bandwidth** and **integrated services digital network (ISDN)**.

## broadband network

High-speed, high-capacity transmission network with greater bandwidth than conventional telephone lines; carries data, voice, and video over long distances.

✚ See also **broadband integrated services digital network (B-ISDN)**.

## broadcast address

All the user addresses on a particular network service to which information can be sent.

For example, a company can use a broadcast address to send a message to every employee on its E-mail system.

## broadcast storm

Network meltdown. More specifically, a chain reaction caused when an incorrect packet broadcast on a network forces most hosts to respond at once, shutting down a network.

## broadcasting

Sending information to more than one receiver at a time over radio waves, a network, or via satellite.

✦ See also **high-definition television (HDTV), narrowcasting, and interactive broadcast TV**.

## browser

An applications program that provides tools for searching out information on a network.

Popular browsers include Mosaic and Gopher because of their user-friendly features.

## browsing

Using a software program known as a browser that allows a user to find and access documents from various sources on the Internet.

You can preview all the available files before selecting the ones of interest. Browsing software lets you view but not manipulate the information.

## bug

Error, mistake, goof; usually refers to a software problem.

A bug ain't a glitch ain't an artifact ain't aliasing. Leave it to the computer industry to have a specific name for each kind of mistake!

## bulletin board system (BBS)

A network site that provides on-line services such as E-mail, chat lines, forums about special interests (from sports to parenting), games, and more.

Most BBS's are small and confined to a local geographic area of users, and are often free. But some can get bigger. Usenet is a monster.

## bus

Circuitry, wires, or other hardware that transmits data between integrated circuits, computer components, or computers on a local area network.

The central processing unit (CPU) in computers has become so fast that the speed with which data can be input or output across the bus is now often the critical bottleneck in computer systems, especially in multimedia and high-resolution applications.

✦ See also **peripheral component interconnect (PCI)**.

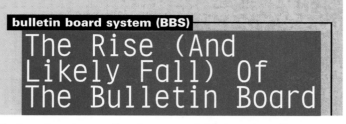

**bulletin board system (BBS)**

# The Rise (And Likely Fall) Of The Bulletin Board

Bulletin board systems often have special-interest audiences who share the same points of view on religion, politics, technology (IBM PC users and Apple Macintosh users), and so on. The reach of a particular BBS, however, is generally local, because most users spend significant time on-line, and long-distance charges would become prohibitive.

Bulletin boards are often run as entrepreneurial home businesses, the most successful commanding as many as 250 telephone lines. They typically offer—for a nominal fee—scores of games, programs, and graphics files that users can download, occasional Internet access, and local E-mail. But programs now being introduced to facilitate navigation of the Internet may put a dent in the popularity of BBSs. More information can be accessed on the Internet at less cost than on a BBS. And, via the Internet, a user can communicate with special-interest groups around the globe instead of just in one area code.

Bulletin board systems have come under attack, too, for harboring adult-only material that is easily accessible to minors. The content can range from prankish (an image of the President's head superimposed on a nude bodybuilder's torso) to deviant (images of sexual activity between adults and animals). Deviant bulletin boards spurred the House of Representatives and the Senate to pass legislation criminalizing the creation, distribution and availability of obscene material or indecent communications to minors. Opponents of the Communications Decency Amendment—signed into law February 8, 1996, by President Clinton—argue that it violates the Constitutional guarantee of free speech and that it may be difficult to enforce.

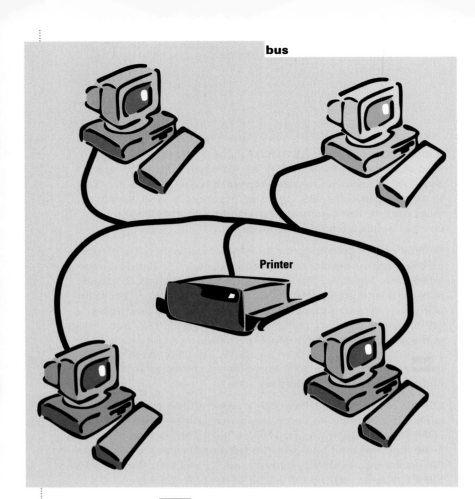

**bus**

Printer

### byte

Set of eight bits.

Data are often packaged in bytes. One byte, for example, represents one character, such as S or 5 or *.

In the land of computation, nomenclature can get tricky. A bit is abbreviated with a lowercase b; a byte with a capital B. To make matters worse, although the prefix "kilo" means 1,000, a kilobit (kb) is actually 1,024 bits; a kilobyte (kB) is actually 1,024 bytes (because the label actually represents 2 raised to the 10th power). A megabyte (MB) equals 1,048,576 bytes, or 2 to the 20th power. A typical floppy disk used in a personal computer can hold 1.44 MB of data. A computer hard drive with a capacity of 540 MB can hold 540 megabytes of data.

# C++ to cyberspeak

Cathedral

## C++

The most robust version of C, one of the more recent programming languages that can be used with most computers.

First used to implement UNIX, C is popular for systems and microcomputer applications and for computer graphics. C++, unlike C, can perform object-oriented programming and has been adopted by several major software vendors—Apple chief among them—as the standard in-house programming language.

## cable

Your basic wire.

Metal cables can carry power or communications signals. Cables made with glass fibers that can transmit light can carry only communications, but at much higher densities. Communications cables operate at lower voltages and higher frequencies than electric power cable. Multiple telephone conversations can be carried on a single strand. To transmit television signals, cable must be able to carry even higher frequencies than telephone. Cables are designed for the least amount of interference for the type of frequency passing through them.

There is a fundamental problem facing communications companies that want to bring interactive communications to individual American households: Ninety percent of the country's telephone cables— the most common linkage—is made of twisted-pair copper wires, unsuitable for carrying the large amounts of data required to transmit images. It is estimated that replacing the 2.7 million miles of copper cable will cost about $120 billion.

✚ See also **coaxial cable, copper cable, fiber-optic cable, twisted-pair cable** and **network**.

## cable modem

A modem attached to a coaxial cable television system.

Cable modems can transmit data at 500 kilobits per second, much faster than the typical computer modem that sends signals over telephone lines.

## Cable Reregulation Act of 1992

Legislation passed by Congress that reversed the Cable Television Act of 1984 and forced the Federal Communications Commission to reregulate cable television.

When Congress noticed that local cable operators were acting essentially as monopolies, it decided the cable industry had to be regulated. Subsequently, the FCC forced the industry to lower its rates by 10 percent in 1993 and by 7 percent in 1994.

## cable television

System in which television programming is sent over coaxial cable to viewers (for a fee) instead of being broadcast (free) across the airwaves.

A television station sends its master signal from a satellite or a microwave tower to receiving stations (or head-ends) spread around the country or world. These stations then retransmit the signals over local coaxial cables to individual homes.

## Cable Television Act of 1984

Legislation, spurred by deregulation, that left the Federal Communications Commission with virtually no jurisdiction over cable television.

The act did away with state control over cable rates, resulting in a 50-60 percent rise in rates. However, the bill was superseded by the Cable Reregulation Act of 1992.

## CAD

✦ See **computer-aided design**.

## cafe

(1) Often termed Internet cafe, or cybercafe, a public eating and drinking establishment where the principal entertainment is on-line access through terminals at individual tables.

So you grab a trendy bottled water or espresso, maybe a veggie burger, and log on at your seat while you eat.

(2) A chat line designed to emulate a cafe.

## CAI

✚ See **computer-aided instruction**.

## call attempt profiles

A service, available to people and businesses that have 800 phone numbers, that provides a record of the number of attempted calls made to the number.

Among other things, the profiles let you know if you need more phone lines or staffers to handle the incoming calls.

## call blocking

A service, available to people and businesses that have 800 phone numbers, that allows them to block calls coming in from specified area codes or states.

This prevents calls from potential customers in areas you cannot accommodate.

## cancelbot

A program sent to eliminate certain postings in Usenet newsgroups.

## car navigation system

A small computer, mounted on the dashboard of an automobile, which helps a driver choose the best routes to set destinations.

Photo courtesy of Avis, Inc.

The system communicates with the global positioning system (GPS) a satellite system that tells it where the car is located on the earth—to within 100 feet! The car navigation system then accesses maps stored on CD-ROMs, and tells the driver about the best route to get to a target destination. It can also suggest alternative routes so drivers can avoid traffic. While the technology is still experimental, car rental companies have begun limited use of it in some markets.

## carpet bomb

A message that swamps a network, going to every subscriber whether they want it or not. Usually they don't.

# Hanging At The Cybercafe—One User's Perspective

In Seattle and Spokane, Internet surfers visit coffeehouses on special nights to go on-line on computers brought in for that purpose. On the streets of Manhattan, five espresso-cum-Internet joints with names like "@Cafe" and "Cyber Cafe" opened their terminals between April and July 1995. Through the summer of 1995, the network access provider Prodigy listed 60 cybercafes pouring coffee and bytes nationally.

One, at Harvard Square in Cambridge, Massachusetts, boasts a 48-station "electronic environment." One user's report:

"I open the door of the 4,600-square-foot room and find a rack of glossy magazines. Inscribed on the staircase are encouraging words from mid-sixth century BC: 'I hear and I forget. I see and I remember. I do and I understand.'—Lao Tsu.

"Encouragement, apparently, for on-line neophytes. All ages are at the 50 tables with players and monitors that will zoom you into Cyberspace. There are a surprising number of father-son combinations. For them, multimedia Mitsubishi warrior games seem to have the broadest appeal.

"Access is promised to the following: the Internet, networked games, Women's Wire, CompuServe, E-World, Prodigy, America Online, Smitty's On-line Cafe, and software that lets you create a digital self-portrait. To get anywhere, you purchase a pre-paid calling card that costs $0.175 a minute, or a little less than

twice the going rate of Sprint's special national long-distance calling plan.

"If necessary, you can seek help from a 'technical advisor' roaming the room. I do. 'Bob Dylan,' I tell him, and the advisor shows me where to type Dylan's name on the search screen of the Yahoo, a directory that can access World Wide Web pages, FTP sites, and bulletin boards without having to know the Internet address. From there, it's a matter of clicking. I feel like Dorothy in red slippers, able to travel anywhere in this Oz of information.

"Unfortunately, my access card's time soon expires. And, before it does, I want to download some of this stuff. No luck. Technical problems, I'm told. Possibly commercial problems, too. Such as, should there be a separate charge?

"In another section of the cafe, two virtual-reality pods (nearly $1 a minute here) host disoriented middle-aged men trying to collaborate with each other on a simulated hunt-and-shoot game. 'I'm confused,' whines one, unable to adjust his body movements to the inevitable delays resulting from the technology's inability to feed spatial data in real time. 'Max, I can't figure out how to orient.' Max, absorbed in his own pod, happily blasts away, oblivious to the fact that he's now vulnerable to a virtual surprise attack. I sip my coffee, and decide to wait for the game's next generation."

Carpet bombs are sent via a broadcast address. Often, they are sent by a commercial vendor who sees this as clever mass-marketing tactic, but it has been proven ineffective because what it does, primarily, is raise the ire of dedicated network users.

## carrier

(1) A company that provides local or long-distance telecommunications services. (2) An electric signal at a single frequency, which is altered to carry information.

When you make a phone call, you complete an electrical connection that is maintained at a single frequency. However, a separate signal modifies that connection to indicate whether the phone you called is ringing or busy. The initial connection is the carrier. The ringing or busy signal you hear is produced by phone company equipment that alters that carrier's frequency. The process of altering a carrier signal is called modulation.

## Cartesian coordinate system

A system to plot the position of a point on a two-dimensional plane (such as graph paper) or in three-dimensional space.

Invented by René Descartes in the 17th century, it is now an essential standard for describing the fabrication of any shape or object in computer graphics programs.

✦ See also **computer-aided design (CAD)**.

## case sensitive

When it matters if letters are typed uppercase or lowercase.

Some computer programs and network services are case sensitive: "XYZ" is considered different data than "xyz." Some Internet users are case sensitive, too: It bugs them if they receive messages typed completely in CAPITAL LETTERS (it's the visual equivalent to listening to screaming).

## cathode ray tube (CRT)

A picture tube, with a screen.

Most computer monitors and television screens are CRTs. Phosphors line the inside front surface of the tube, and when a beam of electrons from the back of the tube hits them, they radiate light. An image is created by scanning the beam from top to bottom in hundreds of horizontal bands and refreshing the image on the screen every thirtieth of a second.

Each frame of video is really two scans that are interlaced, one set containing the even raster lines, the other containing the odd ones; thus, video has 60 fields per second. Most colors in the visible spectrum can be represented using combinations of red, green, and blue phosphors on the CRT.

## CAV

+ See **constant angular velocity**.

## CCITT

+ See **Comite Consultatif Internationale de Telegraphique et Telephonique**.

## cd

A DOS command for changing the current directory to a specified directory.

For example, if you type cd:\purple when you are in a general directory, you will be able to access the directory called "purple."

## CD

Stands for compact disk; refers to a 4.5-inch diameter disk containing digital audio or digital computer information that is read by a laser-equipped player. It was originally developed by Philips and Sony and introduced in the early 1980s as an international format for delivering extremely high-fidelity audio. The specifications for the CD have been adopted universally. Most CDs can only be played, not erased or changed.

The fastest-growing consumer technology ever launched, compact disks virtually eliminated vinyl records overnight. Today, CD players number in the tens of millions. For many interactive media, CD is the audio format used.

## CD-DA

Stands for compact disk-digital audio; refers to sound stored digitally on a CD-ROM.

The sound may be music that was originally recorded with analog technology or it may have been recorded digitally and transferred to a CD. On the

CD, the sound cannot be changed, only played. Stereo sound is sampled, and each sample is described with 16 bits of binary information. The resulting information encoded onto a compact disk produces less background noise and a greater dynamic range than an analog recording.

## CD-I

Stands for compact disk-interactive; refers to a CD-ROM that holds not only information, but audio and graphics, and lets the user interact with the program material.

The CD-I player incorporates a high-speed processor and a friendly interface that encourages users to make choices and "play" with the material. CD-I is marketed as multimedia for the home-couch potato-ware for the masses.

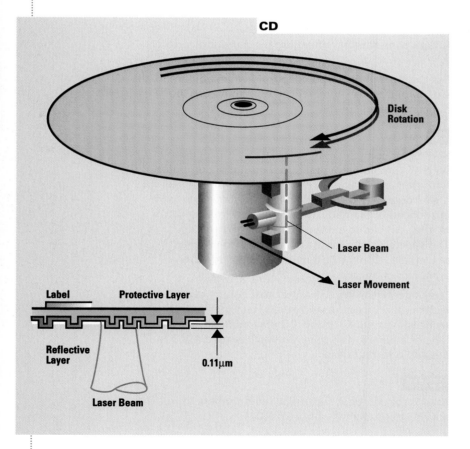

CD

Disk Rotation

Laser Beam

Laser Movement

Label     Protective Layer

Reflective Layer

Laser Beam

0.11μm

## CD-M

Stands for compact disk-MIDI; refers to a compact disk system on a computer that connects to an electronic musical instrument.

When the instrument is played, the system displays graphics related to the instrument's tempo and tone. CD-MIDI also enables prepared musical scores to be played "live" by electronic instruments. It enables a musician to add and remove tracks and change the orchestration, tempo, and tone as desired. Beethoven might feel violated. MIDI users feel like Beethoven.

MIDI stands for musical instrument digital interface.

## CD-R

Stands for compact disk recordable; refers to technology that enables you to "write over" (i.e., change) the information on a compact disk.

## CD-ROM

Stands for compact disk-read only memory; refers to a form of optical storage in which data are stored on a disk similar to a musical compact disk.

© 1996 PhotoDisc, Inc.

CD-ROM codes data digitally and, like its audio equivalent, is accessed with a laser-equipped drive. One CD-ROM can hold the data for 100,000 pages of text. The documentation for a jet fighter weighs several tons, yet it can be stored on a single disk. CD-ROM has become the delivery vehicle of choice for multimedia.

> *"CD-ROM technology is not a vacuous thing. I realize that. But it's stuff that can happen without you having to participate, like Jerry Garcia's ties. I'm just a singer and performer. The other stuff can sponge off that. It doesn't need any of my input. I wouldn't know how to use it if I had to."*
>
> **— Bob Dylan**

## CD-ROM XA

Stands for compact disk-read only memory extended architecture; refers to a CD-ROM format with both audio and graphics capabilities that allows extended storage of a particular type of data.

Kodak, for example, uses CD-ROM XA for its Photo CD, which digitally stores and displays photos you have taken.

# From Directory Assistance To Multimedia: The Growth Of CD-ROM

Initially, CD-ROM was used exclusively to distribute extensive databases, such as telephone directories covering large areas of the United States. Large corporations, the product developers correctly believed, would save millions of dollars in directory assistance calls using the CD-ROM directory. But as the cost of CD-ROM players and disks came down, consumers started to buy them for the home, even though there weren't many disks around.

When interactive encyclopedias were offered in the late 1980s, everything changed. The encyclopedias offered quick and easy access to stores of information, and enhanced the text with sound, music, illustrations, and photographs. Parents wondering what to do with the hardware they'd proudly bought for Christmas had their anxieties relieved. CD-ROM became a staple of the home PC market.

By the early 1990s, advances in compression techniques and the new chips for decompression enabled faster loading and smoother motion video on CD-ROMs. With exciting new images, CD-ROM became the central medium for the distribution of multimedia software, which has proliferated rapidly. Today, "bundles" of multimedia CD-ROMs, typically containing an encyclopedia, sports disk, games disk, and computer utilities are often offered with the purchase of a new PC that has a CD-ROM drive.

On-line services are also popping up that will enhance the value of a CD-ROM. For example, there is a baseball CD-ROM with pictures and backgrounds on the Major League players; if you activate it, then dial up a certain network, you can obtain the latest statistics on a favorite player. Businesses have begun to offer CD-ROM versions of their catalogs, with pictures of all their merchandise and a program that enables you to order items on-line. Major growth in CD-ROM publishing is reflected in greater and greater venture capital investment, and the entry of media giants into the field.

## CDV

Stands for compact disk video (CDV); refers to audio CDs that also deliver up to five minutes of video.

These were launched by Philips in 1986.

## cell

+ See **cellular telephone**.

## cell-net

+ See **cellular radio network**.

## cell relay

A transmission system using small cells of uniform length called packets to transmit data across networks at high speed.

Cell relay is a packet-switching technology that can divide information, say in a piece of E-mail, into fixed-length packets. It transmits the cells over various routes, then puts the pieces back together when they reach their destination. This improves on other packet-switching modes, such as X.25 or frame relay; in those systems, the packets (or frames) vary in length, so the network must constantly adjust the timing and flow of the packets.

## cellular radio network (cell-net)

A network of radio transmitters, organized into cells, that is used for mobile communications such as cellular phones. A cellular mobile radio in a car or other vehicle communicates with a local transceiver. The area this transmitter covers is a cell. As the car moves from one location to another, a master computer hands the signal off from cell to cell. The system is expandable by subdividing the cells and adding more transceivers. Alternatively, new digital compression techniques can pack more and more transmissions into existing cells.

Remember Dick Tracy's wristwatch? It was a two-way radio that existed only in the comics. By the late 1980s, the portable pocket telephone was almost as small. Now personal communications systems can track user's locations and route incoming telephone calls to them. The revolutionary value of wireless technology is found in portability and connectivity.

+ See also **wireless network**.

## cellular telephone

A telephone transmitting voice or data on low-powered radio frequencies, independent of telephone cables, and typically functional only within range of a cell site.

The cellular telephone industry divides urban areas and corridors along major highways into cells. Each site transmits signals within a finite radius. As a user talks while driving, one cell picks up the transmission from the previous cell. Initially, these phones were used by businesspeople. But now, increasingly smaller phones and lower prices have encouraged the use of cellular telephones everywhere, from cross-country skiing terrain to the boardroom.

**cellular telephone**

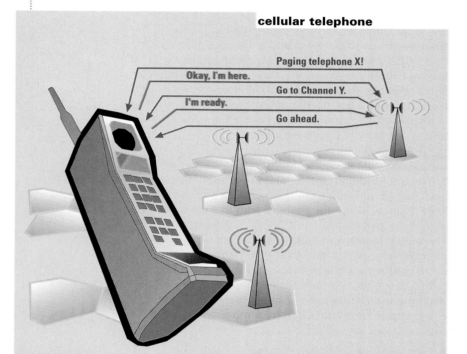

A mobile telephone looks at the dedicated control channels and tunes to a suitable paging channel. It assumes "idle" mode, monitoring the data being transmitted. If the signal level falls as a result of the phone moving through cells, the telephone again scans for another suitable paging channel. Before an incoming call is received, a paging call is transmitted from all base stations in the cell phone's current traffic area. When it receives the page, the phone moves to the access channel where it is allocated a voice channel. It returns to the voice channel and the connection is made. The base station sends an alert message to the telephone, which in turn causes it to alert the user to an incoming call.

*Information courtesy of **AirTouch Cellular***

Criminals, however, might use the old pay phone. Because the conversation is broadcast to the cell, it is easy to eavesdrop with radio equipment. Cell telephone conversations have been used to track criminal deals and the recordings have been used in court. They have also helped bring down a royal family member or two.

+ See also **cellular radio network (cell-net)**.

## central exchange (centrex)

A service offered by the phone company that links the many telephones in a business or office.

Because of centrex, we have intercoms, call forwarding, conference calls, direct interoffice calling, and other handy features. The functions are similar to those of a private branch exchange (PBX).

## central office

The phone company's switching facility, which handles all the telephone lines in the vicinity.

Your telephone is connected to the nearest central office. These offices communicate with one another over cables and satellites to form the telephone network.

## central processing unit (CPU)

The brain of the computer.

In a personal computer, the CPU is usually a single microprocessing chip (microprocessor), which manipulates all data and performs all calculations.

## centrex

+ See **central exchange**.

## Cerf, Vincent

President of the Internet Society (ISOC) and cocreator (with Bob Kahn) of the transmission control protocol/Internet protocol (TC/IP), which enables computers to talk to each other over the Internet.

To test the Defense Department network's fortitude in 1973, Cerf and Kahn simulated its breakup and "glued" it back together, using mobile radios in Strategic Air Command aircraft. This proves that a network could reconfigure itself so that no communications would be lost.

*"The Information Superhighway is sort of the moon shot of the '90s, except that it's a lot less clear or understandable. The objective of putting somebody on the moon was pretty simple. Everybody understood what that meant."*

*— Vincent Cerf*

## CERN

The European Organization for Nuclear Research in Geneva—a high-energy physics lab where, believe it or not, the World Wide Web was developed.

For purists among you, it stands for Conseil Européen pour la Recherche Nucléaire.

## CERT

✤ See computer emergency response team.

## CGI

✤ See common gateway interface.

## channel

One-way communications path where data such as voice, fax, television images, and digital information are transmitted.

✤ See also internet relay chat (IRC).

## chat

✤ See chat line and internet relay chat.

## chat line

A site on a network where any number of computer users can type in messages to each other in real time, creating an on-line conversation.

Most chat lines have a particular focus. For example: /macintosh is for Macintosh users, /initgame is an ongoing game using the initials of words, /russian is for people who want to communicate in, well, Russian. The chat line /hottub is the basic free-for-all, and a crowded hot tub it is.

## chip

(1) Industry term for an integrated circuit. (2) Snack made of potato. (3) Name given to preppy yuppie child.

## chroma key

A video technique that lays one electronic image "on top" of another.

It's what is used when the television meteorologist stands in front of the weather map with the storms swirling behind him.

✤ See also video graphics.

## CISC

 See **complex instruction set computer**.

## CIX

+ See **commercial Internet exchange**.

## Clari

A Usenet hierarchy with some 240 newsgroups, provided by Clarinet.

This service gives you access to a wide array of edited and prepackaged published news reports from newspapers and wire services. It covers a variety of subjects, including commodities, lawsuits, international economics, mergers and acquisitions, as well as the remarks of renowned columnists and humorists.

## Class A, B, and C networks

Three kinds of networks certified by the Federal Communications Commission (FCC).

Each one has a certain bandwidth, and hence a different speed for data transmission.

## client-server

An architecture whereby one computer can get information from another.

The client is the computer or workstation that asks for access to data, software, or services. The server is a program on a host computer—anything from a mainframe to a personal computer connected to the Internet—that processes and sends the requested material to the client. In cable television, a client is the TV or channel-box that asks the cable provider for a particular program.

+ See also **server**.

## Clipper chip

A microchip for encoding information.

Originally intended for the telephone, the Clipper chip was designed to create some measure of security by encoding information; only people with the correct decoder could listen in. If it were deployed by phone companies, however, it would include a

*"Apart from the unpleasant Big Brother implications of such a system, the Clipper chip idea is also untenable—you can double-encode information and thus render the trap door useless quite easily."*

*—Douglas Rushkoff,* author of Media Virus! Hidden Agendas in Popular Culture.

trap door—a master code that would let the government listen in to track criminal activity or actions threatening national security.

The federal government endorsed this system and tried to promulgate a standard for it, but backed off when civil libertarians questioned the wisdom of letting the Feds hold the keys to everyone's secret transmissions.

✚ See also **Digital Telephony Act, encryption, intellectual property** and **key escrow.**

## CLV

✚ See **constant linear velocity.**

## coaxial cable

High-capacity cable widely used in telephone and television systems.

Coaxial cable is very effective at carrying many analog signals at high frequencies. In cable television networks, it stems from the local provider to your TV set. In phone systems, it reaches the pole or drop nearest your house, and a twisted-pair cable comes into the house and to your telephone.

The physical cable has two conductors. The outer one (a woven metal sheath) completely surrounds the inner one (a more solid wire). (They both run along the same axis; hence the name coaxial.) A signal to your home is sent in one direction on the outer sheath and returns on the inner metal core. Insulation separates the two concentric conductors, and a hard casing protects the entire cable.

In contrast to twisted-pair wires, coaxial has a much higher bandwidth to carry more data, and offers greater protection from noise and interference.

✚ See also **fiber-optic cable, twisted pair,** and **copper cable.**

**coaxial cable**

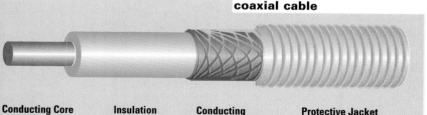

Conducting Core     Insulation     Conducting Mesh or Sleeve     Protective Jacket

▶

**Clipper chip**

# What Would George Orwell Say?

Should there be a federal standard for encoded messages on computer networks and telephone lines that would let the government listen in if it felt necessary? The issue came to a head in the 1993-94 debate on the proposed use of the Clipper chip. The Clinton administration, in particular the National Security Agency (NSA), envisioned this microchip as a replacement for the existing federal encryption standard, DES. With the Clipper chip, government officials felt they could both stop the rampant spread of multiple nonstandardized encryption techniques and crack down on criminals' use of coded information.

Objections were quickly raised by civil libertarians, especially the American Civil Liberties Union and the Electronic Frontier Foundation. Despite the government's insistence that the microchip's decoding keys would be held in escrow until such time as a court might order a chip's key to be released to law-enforcement agencies, opponents said the potential for abuse of the escrow arrangement was high. Moreover, they noted, a United States software industry had been built around encryption programs, and the Clipper chip would have to stand as the only such legal program in order to be effective.

Cyberpunks—anarchic young programmers—meanwhile were announcing on the Internet their intentions to create and distribute free encryption technology, further muddling the debate.

For its part, the government maintained that, when a court does approve a wiretap or other form of legal eavesdropping, law-enforcement officials must have a way to understand what is being communicated.

The battle wound down in 1994 when a Bell Laboratories researcher went public with the news that he had found a flaw in the microchip, an error that could let experts encode messages that security agents would not be able to read even with a decoding key. AT&T said the researcher had made an error himself, but the Clinton Administration quickly backed off its insistence that the microchip establish a national standard. Then, in 1995, the government said that, while it would not set a single standard, powerful decoding software of any type could be exported only if the decoding key was placed in escrow.

## code

(1)  A system of characters and rules for presenting information to a computer.  (2)  Colloquial term for a computer program.

+ See **language**.

## coder-decoder (CODEC)

Device that  (1)  translates analog signals into digital ones so they can be understood by a computer and sent over a digital network, and (2)  translates received digital signals back into analog ones.

Video signals are digitized for transmission over ISDN telephone lines with a CODEC.

## com

The domain name given to commercial providers on the Internet.

For example, a subscriber to America Online has an E-mail address that ends in com, such as anonymous@aol.com.

## Comite Consultatif Internationale de Telegraphique et Telephonique (CCITT)

The international setter of voluntary standards for telecommunications equipment, systems, networks, and services.

CCITT is now known as ITU-TS (for Telecommunications Sector within the International Telecommunications Union).  It is headquartered in Geneva.

## command routing

Telephone service from 800 number providers that allows the user to change the call-routing scheme at any time.

A company can, for example, route calls to a different location when the first is overloaded.

## Commercial Internet Exchange (CIX)

System that routes traffic between commercial Internet providers.  (Pronounced "kicks.")

## common carrier

Company that provides telecommunications or transport services to the public.

A common carrier is generally licensed by a state or federal agency and is obligated to "carry" customers at prices and conditions outlined in a public tariff filed with the government authorities. Long-distance telephone carriers are now called interexchange carriers.

The term common carrier has become synonymous with "the phone company," but it applies just the same to railroads and steamship lines. Perhaps carrier pigeons would qualify, too.

## common gateway interface (CGI)

A program that allows an Internet user to interact with the World Wide Web.

## communications satellite

Earth-orbiting spacecraft designed to receive and send data.

The satellite receives signals from, and sends them to, earth stations or other satellites. The signals may carry voice, facsimile, data, or video. Communications satellites are usually positioned in a geostationary orbit—that is, they remain in a fixed position over a point on the earth, and at a fixed altitude of 22,300 miles (35,000 kilometers) above the earth's surface. A satellite in that orbit can communicate with about one-third of the earth's surface. This area is called the satellite's footprint. Three satellites properly spaced in geostationary orbit can blanket the globe.

The average life-span of a satellite is seven years. There are hundreds of inoperable satellites circling the earth.

✚ See also **geostationary satellite (GEOS)**.

## comp

One of seven world newsgroup categories on Usenet, covering computer hardware and software topics.

## compact disk standards

Published technical standards for the digital-optical formats.

They were pioneered and developed by Philips (which owns the laser patents) and Sony, whose Toshi Doi invented the CD-player. Philips publishes the standards in a set of books: The Green Book specifies CD-I standards; the Red Book specifies CD-DA; the Yellow Book is for CD-ROM; the Orange Book for CD-R; and the White Book for CD-Video.

## competitive access

Rules set up as part of the AT&T divestiture that gave long-distance carriers an equal opportunity to compete for customers.

✦ See also **AT&T Consent Decree**.

## compiler

Software that translates programs written in a high-level programming language into assembly or machine language.

For example, a programmer would use a compiler to translate a program written in FORTRAN into machine language, which is made up of the binary digits 1 and 0. Contrast a compiler with an assembler, which translates assembly language into machine language.

## complex instruction set computing (CISC)

A programming technology enabling a CPU to carry out multiple simultaneous instructions-albeit slowly.

Older Apple Macintosh and IBM-compatible computers are CISC. The faster technology of RISC-based computers is now becoming prevalent.

## component video

A video technology (like super VHS) that distinguishes between color (chrominance) and brightness (luminance) and transmits them via separate wires.

Component video has higher resolution than composite (regular) video because it eliminates the signal degradation that occurs during normal signal encoding and decoding.

✦ See also **composite video**.

## composite video

An analog technology that mixes together brightness, color, and synchronization signals in one electronic package.

It is the common standard of the video signal, used in consumer VCRs, NTSC, and PAL television systems, and video cameras. Composite video must be converted to digital format for use in multimedia applications.

✦ See also **component video**.

## compressed files

✦ See **compression**.

## compression

An encoding process that squeezes data into a file that requires only 1/2 to 1/200th the storage space it ordinarily would need.

Compression lets you store and transmit files more efficiently. After downloading a compressed file, you can look at the last three letters of the file's name to determine what software you will need to decompress it. Common suffixes are ARC, GZIP, SIT, TAR.Z, and ZIP.

## computer

You know.

The electronic wonder on the 20th century has changed the way the modern world lives and works and will continue to do so.

The computer and its attached devices are called hardware, and the instructions that guide its working are called software.

*"It would appear that we have reached the limits of what is possible to achieve with computer technology, although one should be careful with such statements, as they tend to sound pretty silly in five years."*

— ***John von Neumann***, 1949

## computer-aided design (CAD)

A program used by architects, engineers, and others who want to visualize and manipulate the objects or spatial environments they are designing.

CAD translates two-dimensional drawings of plan (as seen from above) and elevation (as seen from the side) views of a structure into a three-dimensional graphic representing the composite structure.

© Cameron Clement/Spots on the Spot!

## computer animation

Using the computer to make graphics or cartoons move.

Before computers, 15 to 30 drawings had to be made to create one second of smooth-motion video. With the help of computer animation programs, an animator can draw just the key frames that start and

# Fitting Big Files Into Small Spaces

Compression minimizes the memory space a computer needs to represent the data in a file. The data are compressed through use of an algorithm that substitutes markers for common information. For example, in binary code, every letter is represented by a string of seven 1s and 0s. In compression, a common letter like "e" may be represented by a single marker requiring only one bit instead of seven. In decompression, the marker is translated back into its original state.

Standards of compressing video are still evolving, but MPEG is now widely used. MPEG-2 will likely be the standard for digital cable television. Other video compression systems used today in multimedia computing are Cinepak and Indeo. Another technique, fractal compression, can achieve compression ratios of up to 200:1 for full-motion video.

Compression is essential in the transfer of certain dense information. Without compression, a minute of full-motion broadcast-quality video would take up 1.5 gigabytes of memory; twice the entire storage space of a fairly hefty PC. As both memory and compression get better, CDs and other digital storage devices will surpass the use of videotapes for recording and storing video.

Transmission of data, voice, or video on cable and wireless networks also benefits from compression. For instance, one cable television channel can carry up to 10 television signals by using compression. Compression expands the abilities of all kinds of interactive multimedia programs, from video games to telemedicine. It is crucial for effective videoconferencing and broadband network communications.

✦ See also **joint photographic experts group (JPEG)**.

finish each new sequence, and the computer draws the frames in between. It saves hundreds of hours of drawing time.

The process of animating with a computer is analogous to tacking up string: The more detail wanted, the more thumbtacks—or key frames—needed. Lighting, color, and other effects may be programmed to change and move over time. The techniques can produce dramatic, sophisticated imagery. Morphing—now a staple of Hollywood action and horror films—is a popular animation program that interpolates between one image and another to give the illusion of transformation. One person's face changes into another's, or a tiger's, or an alien's.

Computer animation can also be created by entering signals from sensors on a moving live person or on an object being moved in space by a live person. Those signals then define the motion of a computer-generated image of an object, creature, or person.

✚ See also **real-time animation**.

## computer-assisted learning (CAL)

Incorporating computers into the educational process, where programs increase and test students' understanding.

✚ See also **distance learning**.

## computer-based instruction (CBI)

✚ See **computer-assisted learning**.

## computer emergency response team (CERT)

Government-financed security organization that watches for and issues advisories about threats to the Internet.

## computer graphics

Still images, generated on a computer.

Computer graphics are everywhere. They may include architectural drawings, photographic collages, or (most typically) graphics and illustrations achieved with the help of drawing, painting, and 3-D modeling software.

Computer graphics software includes the graphics tablet, which enables artists to render in a natural and painter-like style; ray-tracing programs, which produce reflections of surrounding environments on

> "If the automobile had followed the same development cycle as the computer, a Rolls Royce would today cost $100, get a million miles to the gallon, and explode once a year, killing everyone inside."
>
> —**Robert X. Cringely**
> in InfoWorld, 1995

# How The Computer Was Born

The computer was described by John von Neumann, a Princeton mathematician, who in 1945 outlined the basic structure of digital computers. Von Neumann's vision was realized by the first all-electronic computer, ENIAC, constructed at Harvard's Aiken Computer Laboratory just after World War II.

**Von Neumann envisioned the computer with five basic units:**

○ An arithmetic unit to perform calculations.

○ A central processing unit (CPU), which tells the other units what to do and when to do it.

○ A memory unit, which stores both data and instructions.

○ An input unit for receiving data and instructions.

○ An output unit for presenting results.

**Little did von Neumann know that, a half-century later, computers much as he described would be almost as ubiquitous as telephones and tea cups.**

The basic premise behind von Neumann's vision was that the computer would process instructions in series—one at a time, but very quickly. This serial architecture forms the basis for almost all current computers. Alternative architectures have been theorized, and a few have been built. The leading option is a parallel processor, which processes many instructions simultaneously, although each one is processed more slowly than in a serial machine. For certain problems that use many variables, or require the comparison of many factors, such as a weather prediction, parallel processing gives a faster answer. Some of today's supercomputers are built as parallel processors.

any shiny three-dimensional object; and fractal-generating programs, which give an edge of realism to the representation of natural objects.

To render complex images with these programs requires powerful processors and fast storage devices, or lots of time. Images created with computer graphics programs may be used in animation sequences, as seen in many animated television logos.

✦ See also **video graphics**.

## Computer Supported Cooperative Work (CSCW)

✦ See **groupware**.

## constant angular velocity (CAV)

Rotating a disk at constant speed for recovery of data.

This is the reading mode used with a floppy disk, hard disk, and a laserdisc. Retrieval of data gets faster as the read/write head nears the center of the disk because the diameter gets smaller. The fastest CAV on a disk is 54,000 frames per second. With such fast frame retrieval, you can display a perfect, still frame. Laserdiscs are the best choice for interactive video and interactive programs needing high-resolution still frames or high-quality full-motion video.

Compare with constant linear velocity (CLV).

## constant linear velocity (CLV)

Varying the speed at which a disk rotates so that the read/write head retrieves data at a steady pace.

With CLV, the disk slows down when the outer tracks are accessed and speeds up for the inner tracks. This provides a way to increase the capacity of optical disks by keeping the linear—or bit—density constant.

Compare with constant angular velocity (CAV).

## content provider

Any business providing information or entertainment in exchange for a fee.

The telecommunications companies see their role in a fully wired and deregulated future as content providers as well as service providers.

*"Computers make it easier to do a lot of things, but most of the things they make it easier to do 'don't need to be done.'"*

— *Andy Rooney*

## convergence

The merger of the telephone, computer, and cable television/entertainment industries into a single industry.

The term is derived from the way in which we see: left-eye images and right-eye images fuse to create a single, three-dimensional image.

The three key areas comprising convergence are content, distribution, and technology.

- Content is all the "stuff" that is accessed electronically and created by the consumer. This includes information, games, movies, virtual shopping malls, and on-line communities.
- Distribution is the "shipping" of digital information.
- Technology is the enabler. It includes processing and display hardware, authoring tools, navigation tools, and complex transaction-processing systems.

Convergence is creating physical, social, and economic changes in the global communications infrastructure. The development of fiber-optic networks, the establishment of high-bandwidth information superhighways, and the creation of interpersonal communications via cellular networks and satellite systems point the way to a digital communications revolution that will transform our world as dramatically as the telephone, automobile, and television have.

## copper cable

Used in both twisted-pair and coaxial cable; the most common telecommunications cable.

Copper cable is unable to carry as much bandwidth as fiber-optic cable.

## copyright

Legal protection of the expression of an idea from being copied or used without the permission of the author.

Copyright has been virtually unenforceable in cyberspace, where thousands of perfect copies of an author's writing or software can be mass-mailed to thousands of people with a few effortless keyboard commands.

Most software agreements require a separate purchase for every computer that the program will be installed on. Large software vendors have successfully sued large corporations for pirating—illegally copying software. Nevertheless, since copying programs is quick and easy, many users have not abided by the rules.

The spread of digital transmission and the consequent difficulty of preventing copyright abuse have challenged creators to develop new ways of minimizing the unpaid use of their works.

Copyright and patents are referred to as intellectual property.

## core

(1) Computer memory that can be directly addressed by the computer's central processing unit (CPU). (2) Allocation of limited memory (RAM and ROM) for programs and data to be permanently or temporarily stored, as well as for working storage. (3) As in: Core War, a game played by two or more programs (and vicariously their authors) that run on a virtual computer called a Memory Array Redcode Simulator.

The object of Core War: to cause all processes or the opposing program to terminate, leaving your program in sole possession of the machine.

## CPU

✦ See **central processing unit**.

## crackers

People who take pride and joy in outwitting security systems designed to keep them from breaking into a computer network.

Their goal is to view, alter, or steal restricted data and programs.

## Cray, Seymour

Creator of supercomputing and chairman of Cray Computer, a spin-off of Cray Research.

Cray introduced chips made of gallium arsenide, instead of the standard silicon, into computers in 1979, dramatically increasing the speed with which they could process information. The new

> *"People who develop circuits without knowing about computers... make rules that make it very hard to make computers. Thank heaven for start-up companies or we'd never make any progress. People who get unhappy with structure in companies can move on and start their own, take the big risks, and occasionally find the pot of gold."*
>
> — ***Seymour Cray**, Chairman, Cray Computer*

speed led to supercomputers, that brought radical advances in engineering, solid modeling, and complex simulations.

## cross platform

Hybrid computer that can speak and understand different operating systems.

Cross platforms are increasingly popular in a world of proprietary systems.

✚ See also **platform**.

## cross-talk

Interference in reception of audio or video.

In audio, it can refer to bleed-through of one channel's signal to an adjacent channel. So you tune in one radio station and hear bits and pieces of another. In laser videodiscs, it is a meshing of transparent, wormy lines that drift across the picture you see. This is caused by inaccurate focusing of the laser beam on the disk surface, the warping of disks, or dirt in the system.

✚ See also **noise**.

## CRT

✚ See **cathode ray tube**.

## cryptography

Secret writings made with codes and ciphers.

✚ See **encryption**.

## cuecon

✚ See **icon**.

## cyber

✚ See **cybernetics**.

## cybercrime

Criminal activities in cyberspace.

It can be theft of R&D secrets from a computer on a network, or the vandalization of networks by letting loose a virus. Cybercrime's destructive power is derived from the very efficiency and usefulness of networks. By breaking into the secret "vaults" of a network, crackers can access and manipulate vital information for their own benefit or vandalize systems by crashing them, clogging them, or infecting them.

*"The Panther Moderns allowed four minutes for their first move to take effect, then injected a second carefully prepared dose of misinformation. This time, they shot it directly into the Sense/Net building's internal video system. At 12:04:03, every screen in the building strobed for eighteen seconds in a frequency that produced seizures in a susceptible segment of Sense/Net employees. Then something only vaguely like a human face filled the screens...."*

— ***William Gibson***, *Neuromancer*

Crackers use various techniques, including

- Sniffers—programs that capture passwords as they travel over the Internet.

- Spoofers—similar to a program used by cracker Kevin Mitnick to break into the U.S. Navy's Command Control Ocean Surveillance Center in San Diego, California. Spoofers fool a system into believing it is being accessed by an approved user.

- Human engineering—where a cracker simply walks into a business, steals an internal telephone directory, and calls back at an odd hour, pretending to be an employee with priority access. The cracker then pressures the person he has reached into disclosing a high-level password under threat of being fired.

Concern over the theft of research and development secrets has prompted the scientific and business communities to adopt encryption techniques. The widespread threat of cybercrime also has led to a new kind of policeman—the cybercop. Using computers, cybercops pursue purveyors of electronically transmitted pedophilia as well as telephone company freeloaders and Internet marauders.

Cybercops are not always people—they may be intelligent agents—programs designed to seek out suspicious behavior. Whether human or not, cybercops face staunch resistance from many in the Internet community who do not want to be under surveillance.

Common criminals—scam artists, fencers of stolen property, pushers of bogus investment schemes— are also honing in on cyberspace, broadening cybercrime's definition once again. The worldwide reach of the Internet, coupled with easily accessible first-rate graphics, can give a local con man unwarranted national credibility. Mainstream access providers such as CompuServe and America Online already have internal security personnel reviewing on-line content for scams.

**cybercrub**

Obscure and opaque tech-talk; the computer equivalent of bureaucrat-speak.

## cybernetics

Term coined by Norbert Weiner to mean the science of human control functions, and mechanical and electrical systems to replace them.

Developed in the 1940s by a group of scientists and engineers led by Weiner, cybernetics studies the similarities between person and machine and their differences. It is critical to the design of large, complex computer systems.

✦ See also **cyberspace**.

## cyberpunk

(1) Science fiction genre centered on the culture of high-tech and underground attitudes. Also called the '80s Wave, Mirrorshades Group, Outlaw Technologist. (2) Lifestyle characterized by computer games, net surfing, designer drugs, and an attitude.

Cyberpunk is glorified in novels like those by William Gibson—Neuromancer, Count Zero, and Mona Lisa Overdrive—and movies of the late 1980s and 1990s like Mad Max.

✦ See also **cyberspace** and **cyberspeak**.

## cybersex

On-line communication between two or more people leading to a virtual sexual encounter or act.

When the telephone company said "Reach out and touch someone," it didn't mean cybersex. Yet people always seem to find ways of exploring sex with any new communications technology, and communicating on-line is no exception.

The allure of sex through a keyboard is absolutely safe sex, no self-consciousness about your physical body, and complete privacy from your daily world. All you need, in fact, is an on-line connection and a vigorous imagination. Cybersex can be an escape for a paraplegic, an outlet for lovers who are separated by long distances, or a chance for a lesbian to experiment in the straight world. The danger is the ease with which a person of harmful intent can lie and convince his or her victim to meet off-line.

## cybersexism

Tendency of male-dominated mores to influence on-line communication and etiquette.

# The Continuity Of Cyberpunk

Novelists plumb its depths. Pop stars glorify its rebel-with-a-mouse attitude. Hollywood has climbed on board, and sometimes led the way, with slick futurist fables like *Blade Runner* and *Johnny Mnemonic*.

From magazines (Mondo 2000) to video games (System Shock) to electronic 'zines (Line Noiz), the cyberpunk subculture is alive and well wherever Netheads hang. In many ways it is the evolutionary successor to the beatnik, hippie, and punk movements that preceded it in the '60s, '70s, and '80s.

Each generational warp adopted an aggressively antiestablishment posture. Each spawned its own distinctive literature, art, music, fashion, and drugs of choice. Each got tagged with a generic label that takes in a wide variety of looks, attitudes, and lingo.

What differentiates cyberpunk from its cultural forebears is technology—and the ability to manipulate it. The techno-bohemians are a new breed indeed, combining the wizardry of the MIT artificial-intelligence geek with the alienation of James Dean and Johnny Rotten. Attitude is good. An Intel Pentium microprocessor is better.

Cyberpunk's literary avatars include William Gibson (Virtual Light, Count Zero), Neal Stephenson (Snow Crash, The Diamond Age), David Brin (Earth), and Bruce Sterling (The Difference Engine), all of whom dwell in the fictional realm where futurism meets computer technology. Patron saints run the gamut from LSD guru Timothy Leary to sci-fi master Philip K. Dick to interactive anchor Max Headroom, the hyperbolic star of the futuristic, if short-lived, network television series by the same name.

Gibson is generally credited with coining the term cyberpunk— in his landmark 1984 novel Neuromancer, a postapocalyptic thriller starring a renegade band of teenage hackers. Gibson himself disavows this, claiming that an unnamed journalist actually came up with the term to describe characters in Gibson's novels. Whatever its precise origin, however, cyberpunk has become a mass-media buzzword liberally applied to the vast computer underworld and its myriad denizens.

As technology has advanced, so has cyberpunk's influence on pop culture—often to the dismay of hard-core hackers who proudly resist being mainstreamed. Many innovations have been breathtaking, though. Last year Inverse Ink introduced its Reflux series, billed as the first live-action graphic novel. Running on Windows CD-ROM, it combines live-action footage, morphing, and 3-D storytelling to create multiple-perspective narratives that push the cyber-envelope significantly.

"I'm not really sure what it means," Gibson admitted to one interviewer when asked to define cyberpunk. Like many at the core of this loosely defined movement, Gibson presumably knows it when he sees it.

On-line communication may exemplify the democratization of free speech, but on-line forums mimic real life in subtle and unintended ways. The number of men engaging in on-line communications far outnumbers women. Therefore, being a woman on-line—that is, having a female name and describing yourself as a woman—can be like walking into a room of teenage boys. You may get harassed simply because your name is Miranda or Carmen.

The beauty of on-line communications is the ability to change those names to Myron or Cody and get directly to the conversational point without reference to gender. Conversely, men have changed their "gender" on-line, passing as women, not always for devious "pick-up" purposes but to experience what it's like to be treated as a woman.

## cyberspace

Where all media converge: audio and video, telephone and television, wire and satellite.

The term cyberspace was coined by science-fiction writer William Gibson, who defined it as a "consensual hallucination...a graphic representation of data abstracted from the banks of every computer in the human system."

Thirty years ago, Marshall McLuhan predicted an interconnecting telecommunications web that would become "the electronic extension of our central nervous system." And that may yet come to pass. Without thinking about it, we deal with cyberspace every day: when the ATM gives you money, you hold a three-way phone conversation, order merchandise from a home shopping network, order a pay-per-view cable TV program. Unfortunately, cyberspace also raises concerns about personal privacy, data-record security, copyright protection, computer crime, and the controlling power of governments and corporations.

But, optimistically, the access that cyberspace provides will enable millions of people to share information, experiences and activities, thereby crossing barriers of space, time, race, language, culture, and, ultimately, creating McLuhan's "global village."
✦ See also **convergence**.

## cyberspeak

The language (often jargon, slang, and acronyms) of cyberspace; the preferred method of communication in a world connected by electronic networks.

> *"A graphical representation of data abstracted from the banks of every computer in the human system. Unthinkable complexity. Lines of light ranged in the nonspace of the mind, clusters and constellations of data. Like city lights, receding...."*
>
> *Cyberspace as defined by*
> — ***William Gibson**,*
> *Neuromancer*

# BTW, IMHO, U Need To Learn Smileys

Cyberspace lacks personal contact, and—as a result—comments that could be softened with body language in the real world can come across as more severe, more insulting, and more inappropriate on a computer screen. And the screen itself is small, encouraging brevity. Hence, the development of two cyberspeak techniques: acronyms and emoticons (or smileys).

Acronyms are just that—shorthand for commonly used phrases and expressions that would otherwise eat up valuable screen space. Among the most encountered are:

| | | |
|---|---|---|
| IMHO | = | In my humble opinion |
| BTW | = | By the way |
| FWIW | = | For what it's worth |
| LOL | = | Laughing out loud |
| PMJI | = | Pardon my jumping in (appropriate if you are joining an ongoing discussion) |
| TPTB | = | The powers that be |
| YMMV | = | Your mileage may vary (or, your experience could be different) |
| ROTF | = | Rolling on the floor (in laughter) |
| AFK | = | Away from the keyboard |
| BAK | = | Back at the keyboard |

| | | |
|---|---|---|
| BRB | = | Be right back |
| BCNU | = | Be seeing you |
| TTFN | = | Ta-ta for now |
| WB | = | Welcome back |
| GMTA | = | Great minds think alike |
| WTG | = | Way to go |

Clever acronyms are created daily, and it's likely you will run across several you may not understand.  One especially useful on-line source for other acronyms is Network Acronym and Abbreviation Serve, whose Internet address is ikind@mcimail.com.

Emoticons are combinations of characters that create a picture (if you turn your head all the way to the left when you look at them).  Some common ones include:

○ smileys :-)

○ winks ;-)

○ frowns :-(

○ astonishment :-0

You get the picture (so to speak).  When you tell someone he's all wet, you add a :-) to show that you are saying it in fun.

✚ See **emoticon** for the full list.

Domenic

## D-channel

The data channel used to carry calling information, allowing for call forwarding, call waiting, and other telephone features.

Part of the **integrated services digital network (ISDN)** interface, the D-channel carries **packet-switched** control signals. In the **basic rate interface**, D-channel operates at 16,000 bits per second; in the **primary rate interface**, D-channel operates at 64,000 bits per second.

## D/A converter

✚ See **digital-to-analog converter**.

## DAB

✚ See **digital audio broadcasting**.

## daemon

Machine or **program** that performs a task for the operator.

The name is derived from Greek mythology, where it referred to any of the secondary divinities that ranked between the gods and people.

## dark fiber

Installed **fiber-optic cable** not carrying a signal. A fiber in use is called a lit fiber.

## DARPA

✚ See **Defense Advanced Research Projects Agency**.

## DAT

✚ See **digital audiotape**.

## data

Any information—facts, concepts, sensations—represented in a formal manner, suitable for communicating, interpreting, or processing.

If, as futurist Marshall McLuhan said, "The electric light is pure information," everything perceptible is data. The word *data* is plural; the singular is *datum*. So, to be correct, you'd say, "Those data present a problem for me."

## data capture

Retaining information and putting it into a form a computer can read and display.

✚ See also **coder-decoder (CODEC)**.

## data glove

A glove with sensors on it, linked to a computer.

It translates the movements of the hand wearing it into digital coordinates so the computer can track what the hand is doing and give feedback.

Information about the glove's position in real space is fed into the computer by fiber-optic cables. This stream of positional information allows interaction with a virtual world.

Developed at VPL Industries, the data glove is a different kind of interface than a computer mouse or keyboard. Sensory feedback may be provided through the glove, rather than through a monitor. As a telepresence technology, it creates possibilities for any hand-sensitive work, such as surgery or sign language, as well as realistic video game interactions. There is a lot of development yet to go, including tactile feedback, before it can be effectively used.

✚ See also **data suit and virtual reality**.

## data link

(1) In communications, the physical interconnection between two points. (2) In computing, all the hardware, software, peripherals, and protocols needed for data transmission.

All data transmissions must take place through data links, which are collections of circuits and terminals. All of these elements operate according to standards that apply to transmission codes and modes, and controls used.

✚ See also **data link control layer**.

> "In the end, multimedia interactive won't resemble literature so much as sports."
>
> — **Douglas Coupland**, author of Microserfs
> [Microserfs, Harper Collins 1995, p.143]

## data suit

A suit with 50 or more sensors that track the body as it moves, and relays that information to a computer.

✦ See also **data glove** and **virtual reality**.

## data transfer rate

The speed at which data are read off a storage medium (such as a disk) and transferred to the controlling computer for display on a computer screen.

© Robert Neubecker/Spots on the Spot!

## database

A structured collection of information organized so you can retrieve it through a computer system.

Library collections, telephone number directories, and airline reservation systems use sophisticated databases to store and retrieve information. The proliferation of on-line information services and interactive multimedia programs have motivated developers and designers to make database access "user friendly."

## datum

✦ See **data**.

## DBS

✦ See **digital broadcast satellite**.

## DCC

✦ See **digital compact cassette**.

## DCE

✦ See **distributed computing environment**.

## decompressed file

✦ See **compression**.

## de facto

Describes an unofficial standard popularized because it either comes from a large company, has lots of users, or fills a void where no other standard is in place.

A prime example is IBM's PC operating system, Windows. Once it was released, manufacturers who make software and hardware products that work with IBM machines conformed to the operating system so their new products would be compatible.

## default editor

In a program or protocol, an attribute, value, or option that is assumed when none is actually spelled out.

For example, if you are starting a new document on your PC, and begin typing without specifying what typeface you want the text in, the computer assumes a default typeface—the one it always uses unless told otherwise.

## Defense Advanced Research Projects Agency (DARPA)

Federal agency that conducts research for the Defense Department.

It began as the Advanced Research Projects Agency, but became so dominated with defense work its name was changed. Work funded by DARPA led to creation of the Internet.

Decommissioned in 1990, it became ARPA once again.

✦ See also the sidebar The Evolution of the Net.

## de jure standards

Official standards developed by an official organization.

They often represent a consensus of computer-industry leaders. The ISO is one such standard-setting industry group.

## Department of Defense (DOD)

U.S. agency whose needs and funding have driven major developments in information systems technology, including the Internet.

✦ See also Advanced Research Projects Agency (ARPA).

## desktop

Metaphor for what PC users see on their screens.

The idea is that information is kept in files, which are organized in folders. The icons for these look like the physical files and folders in an office, organized on the top of a desk. Introduced in the early 1980s by Apple on its Macintosh computers, it was copied by IBM and Microsoft for Windows software.

## desktop publishing

Design and printing of a finished publication, using a computer and components that fit on the top of your desk.

Most systems consist of a personal computer, printer, and software for word processing, producing graphics, and laying out pages. More complex systems include a scanner, which captures photos like a copy machine and stores the image in the computer's memory. These components put the tools of the typographer, graphic designer, and printer into the hands of a single user.

When A.J. Leibling stated, "The freedom of the press belongs to those who own one," little did he know that desktop publishing would arrive in the 1980s and put a printing press on the desk of anybody who wants one. Desktop publishing has dramatically reduced the cost of printing simple documents like company newsletters, but it is no substitute for the sophisticated processes used by printers of books or magazines, which require skilled designers and printers who know the traits of papers and inks.

In recent years, desktop publishing systems are being used to prepare material that will be finished by sophisticated printers. A client who wants, say, a slick sales brochure can save considerable money by using desktop publishing to do the work printers call pre-press.

## desktop video

The editing and production of videos with a personal computer.

A PC fitted with a video capture card and A/D and D/A converters can process video signals. CODEC devices compress a video image into manageable chunks of data for storage and then decompress them for viewing. MPEG delivers full-screen full-motion video (FSFMV) and CD-quality audio even to slower computers that do not have the latest generation of microprocessor.

Desktop video has not yet become as widespread as desktop publishing because of the limitations of hardware and software. A huge amount of memory is needed to manipulate images and store enough of them to create videos of any length and acceptable resolution.

Popular programs like Quicktime allow short movies with low, rather grainy resolution and irregular motion to be viewed on a computer monitor. Before desktop video gives every aspiring director the keys to the castle, compression and decompression schemes need to become better, processors have to get faster, and memory has to get cheaper.

+ See also **video graphics**.

## device driver

+ See **driver**.

## dial-up Internet connections

Ways of connecting to the Internet that use only a personal computer, modem, and ordinary telephone lines.

Protocols that enable this to happen include point-to-point and serial line interface.

© John Clarke/Spots on the Spot!

## dial-up services

Services such as credit card verification, news retrieval, database searches, electronic bulletin boards, and educational courses that are accessed by telephone or modem.

## digital

Use of the digits 0 and 1 to represent data, and the code that instructs a computer to read, store, and operate on that data.

The first digital representations used for counting numbers were fingers and toes. In a modern computer, data are stored in millions of tiny circuits. A "0" is represented by a circuit that is off—there is no current flowing through it. A "1" is represented by a circuit that is on—current is flowing through it. By turning circuits off and on according to the code's instructions, a computer accesses data, performs operations on it, and stores the new data. The lights in each room of your house could represent data in a digital computer: They are either off or on in each room, and you can change them.

Early computers were analog: They used constantly varying physical variables, such as voltage, to represent data. In this case, the lights in your house would all be on, at varying degrees of brightness, and you could only tell the state of the data by comparing the brightnesses. That is much harder than a quick look for "off" or "on"— especially if you have got a few million rooms.

## digital audio

Sound represented by a binary system—for example, the 0's and 1's in a computer that are read by audio software, or the plateaus and pits on a compact disk that are read by a laser beam.

## digital audio broadcasting (DAB)

Broadcasting sound across the airwaves of a quality comparable to that of CD audio.

DAB is produced by compression schemes using relatively narrow bandwidth across airwaves. In combination with a digital-audio radio, digital compact cassette (DCC) or digital audiotape (DAT), the establishment of DAB would make possible mobile "record stores"—you would be able to select and download near CD-quality music directly from a central databank.

## digital audiotape (DAT)

(1) Noise-free recording and playing of sound on special cassette tape. (2) The international standard for digital audiotape recording.

Both your basic tape recorder and your fancy stereo use analog signals when playing and recording cassettes. But radio stations and recording studios uses a more sophisticated digital audiotape machine, which records sound on special tape in a digital matter. Sooner or later, DAT machines will make it down the cost curve and enter the home market.

✦ See also digital audio broadcasting.

## digital cash

Electronic currency that does not exist in the physical world, only in cyberspace.

## digital compact cassette (DCC)

Cassette that records digital sound but can be played in analog cassette players.

## digital-optical recording (DOR)

Technique for encoding and decoding digital information using laser light.

© Bryan Friel/Spots on the Spot!

# How Much Is That Doggy On The Home Page?

Cybercash is already among us. When your employer sends your paycheck by "direct deposit" to your bank, you are receiving cybercash. But a new technology—digital cash—could eventually replace paper bills and coins.

Digital cash takes two forms: A computer instruction that is transferred between buyer and seller, or a small card (like a credit card) that is purchased and inserted into a machine that can read it.

The first scheme is being tested in Holland. DigiCash BV, a Dutch company, announced it would distribute $100 in "cyberbucks" to the first 10,000 people who accessed a special Internet site the company had built. Users download a software file into their computer hard drive that represents $100 in purchasing power. The cyberbucks can buy electronic photos, song lyrics, articles, T-shirts, and bumper stickers advertised on the Internet by DigiCash. While a user is connected on-line to DigiCash, he makes a purchase using a special key number, and the DigiCash system sends a signal to his computer that deducts the cost from the "money" left in his hard drive. The purchased item is sent electronically, or via "snail mail" (the postal system).

A simple version of the second scheme is already being tested by commuters in several U.S. cities. Instead of using money or tokens to pay road tolls, commuters purchase a debit card from the local mass-transit authority, which is worth, say, $20. When they approach a toll, they use a special lane with a machine resembling an automatic teller machine. They insert the card

into the machine, it deducts the toll charge from the balance on the card, and the driver grabs his card and continues on.

The international credit card company Visa will unveil a much more complex "stored value" card in 1996. It is equipped with a tiny microprocessor and a set of gold-plated contact pads the size of a dime. You will buy the card preloaded with a certain amount of cash. When you visit a participating store, you can purchase an item by handing over your card to the shop owner, who will load it into a reader, which will subtract the correct amount from your card and add that amount into the shop's machine. At any point, the shop owner can "cash in" the balance with Visa.

The appeal of digital cash is its combination of convenience and security. It's easy; purchases can be made by computer, and with a card you can buy goods even if you don't have cash on hand. It's safer; unlike credit cards, there are no account numbers for thieves and scam artists to steal. In the DigiCash system, the only way to steal the "money" is to steal the user's hard drive. In the Visa system, if the card is stolen, it can only be used to make purchases that amount to the balance remaining on the card.

To further limit this kind of theft, First Virtual Holdings of San Diego uses a personal identification number (PIN) in conjunction with its digital cash card. When a consumer hands his card to a merchant, he must also enter his PIN on the card reader; the reader sends the PIN to First Virtual's own system for verification. The reader gets an immediate response: "Yes," "No," or "Fraud."

Developed by Philips under the name LaserVision, DOR provides long-term durability in digital and analog storage that is protected against electromagnetic damage.

## digital recording

Encoding of either audio or visual information on a digital medium such as digital audiotape (DAT) or compact disk.

To edit video on a computer or embed it in a multimedia document, you have to either create the video on a digital device or convert the video to digital.

✚ See also analog-to-digital, digital audio, and digital compact cassette (DCC).

## digital satellite system (DSS)

✚ See geostationary satellite.

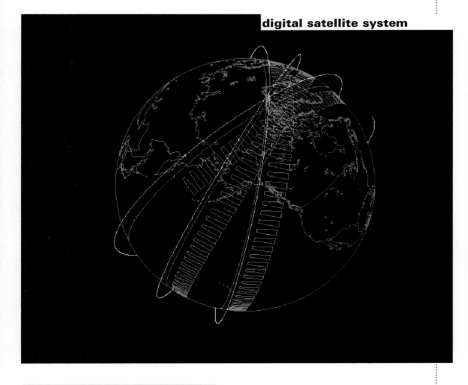

digital satellite system

## digital signal processor (DSP)

Specialized computer chip that speeds up and improves the processing of digital audio and video signals.

DSPs are everywhere—in your modem, your CD player, your VCR, your electronic piano keyboard, and, if you've got bucks (whether digital or greenbacks), your high-definition television (HDTV). They are also used in a rapidly growing array of industrial products, from fetal monitors and hearing aids to antilock brake sensors.

## Digital Telephony Act 1994

Legislation passed by Congress, in the interest of national security, that requires any future telecommunications systems to be open to wiretapping.

## digital-to-analog (D/A) converter

Device that translates digital information into analog information.

✦ See also **analog-to-digital converter**.

## digital video

Image converted from a videotape or live analog video to a digital information stream, either in **real time** or to a hard drive or other storage medium for later viewing.

A **video capture** card in a computer, usually equipped with a **compression** scheme or a software compression package like Indeo, is necessary to perform on-the-fly digitization of an analog video image.

Once digitized, video may be edited in a nonlinear fashion; that is, short clips may be assembled in a computer program using "cut and paste" commands. Images can be altered using **computer graphics** programs, and **computer animation** can be introduced. In compressed form, digital video programs can be transmitted on digital telecommunication lines. Fast hard drives or disk arrays able to display 30 frames per second of high-**resolution** video in real time are essential for ideal playback.

✦ See also **desktop video, full-screen full-motion video (FSFMV)**, and **high-definition television (HDTV)**.

## digital videodisk (DVD)

Consumer electronics product, without an agreed-on commercial standard, containing a full-length movie on one disk.

Its small format allows compact drives that can fit in Walkman-sized gear.

## digital video interactive (DVI)

Describes a powerful chip that can compress and decompress video in real time, providing full-motion video on a computer monitor.

DVI is an important landmark in the development of interactive multimedia.

## digitize

Converting an analog audio or visual signal into digital information, which can be manipulated with computer programs.

## digitizer

Colloquial term for a device that can convert analog data or instructions to digital code.

## direct broadcast satellite (DBS)

Satellite that can send television signals to a receiving dish on a residential roof, lawn, or balcony.

Unlike the big ol' satellite dishes that are up to 12 feet in diameter, dishes for DBS systems are only 18 to 24 inches across. On the down side, the reception of smaller dishes is more subject to adverse weather interference.

Then there is the matter of ideological interference. China and Iran have banned satellite usage for fear of introducing subversive ideas from the outside world—like democracy. However, the compact size of the dishes makes them hard to detect.

## disk array

System of two or more drives working together to increase the speed of input/output (I/O).

In desktop video (DTV), it is used to provide enough speed to run full-motion video on the monitor or to transfer processed video to videotape in real time.

## disk drive

Mechanism inside a computer that holds, rotates, reads from, and writes to a memory storage medium such as a floppy disk.

It's the slot in your PC where you insert your floppy disk. It is connected to the CPU.

✦ See also **hard drive**.

## diskette

+ See **floppy disk**.

## distance learning

Education occurring away from a classroom or teacher.

In computer-assisted distance learning, transmission of information is by **cable**, **satellite**, or **snail mail** (postal). The information comes on a floppy disk or CD-ROM with computer programs designed to teach and test students **interactively**.

© Randy Verougstraete/
Spots on the Spot!

## distributed computing

Allows a number of computers at separate locations to work cooperatively in gathering, storing, and processing information.

It began in the 1970s when **minicomputers** made inroads into business. Earlier, businesses and institutions had one big **mainframe** computer (the **host**) that did all the processing. "Dumb" terminals (they could not compute) at people's desks **accessed** the mainframe. Minicomputers allowed this system to be decentralized; individuals or small groups of users with different needs could handle their own computing.

Often in this configuration, the "minis" still remain linked to the mainframe, so they can call on central files. Distributed systems provide faster response, simplify system programming, and provide maximum protection against system-wide failure.

## distributed computing environment

Specifications for distributed computing.

It was developed by the Open Software Foundation —a comprehensive, integrated set of services that supports the development, use, and maintenance of distributed applications.

## Distributed Queue Dual Bus (DQDB)

A technology specification developed by the Institute of Electrical and Electronics Engineers (IEEE 802.6) for a **packet-switching** network for **metropolitan area networks (MANs)**.

The first Switched Multimegabit Data Service (SMDS) offered by local telephone companies uses it at rates as high as a seriously zippy 45 million bps.

## DOD

✦ See **Department of Defense**.

## domain

Official name of a computer, or service, on the Internet.

When you access something on the Internet, sooner or later you are dipping into data or programs stored on a physical computer somewhere. Whether it's an isolated game or database, or a huge commercial service like America Online, the information has to reside in a computer, and that computer is the domain.

Therefore, when you enter the address of the information or service you want, you specify the domain name. The last three letters of the domain name describe the kind of network the domain is part of, such as commercial (com) or military (mil).

For example, the on-line address for the President is "president@whitehouse.gov." The domain name is everything after the @ symbol, that is, "whitehouse.gov." The gov stands for government—in case you couldn't guess.

## DOR

✦ See **digital-optical recording**.

## dots per inch (dpi)

Unit of measure for printer resolution.

For example, a 300-dpi machine can print 90,000 dots in a square inch (300 across by 300 down = 90,000). The more DPI, the sharper (higher resolution) the printout.

## down

What you don't want your computer to be.

In other words, it's when a system is temporarily malfunctioning. Also, it's a favored excuse of uncooperative customer service people: "Sorry, the computer's down. I can't help you."

## downlink

(1) In satellite communications, the link from an orbiting object to one of its ground stations. (2) The act of receiving data through such a link.

© John Dykes/Spots on the Spot!

For instance, a TV newsperson reporting live from the scene of an airline crash in the wooded Denver hills uplinks her story to a satellite, and the television station downlinks it to the studio.

Uplinks and downlinks are typically purchased from different suppliers, especially in international telecommunications.

✦ See also **remote sensing**.

## download

To copy a file from a host system (such as America Online or CompuServe) onto your computer, via telephone lines and a modem.

There are different methods, or protocols, which check the file to ensure that no data are destroyed or damaged during the downloading process. Some protocols, such as Xmodem, will download only one file at a time. Others—for example, batch-Ymodem and Zmodem—allow several files to be downloaded at once.

## downstream

Flow of information from a provider to a receiver.

A cable TV company sends channels downstream to subscribers. An Internet site sends information downstream to a user.

Sending video-on-demand to a viewer requires large downstream bandwidth, while the upstream bandwidth (basically, a simple data signal from the subscriber that indicates, "Yes, I want the show") requires very little bandwidth.

## dpi

✦ See **dots per inch**.

## DRAM

✦ See **dynamic random access memory**.

## drive

(1) Device that spins computer disks or tapes, as in, "Put your floppy disk in drive a." (2) The ability to make something work, as in "The computer drives the printer."

© Peter Hoey/Spots on the Spot!

## driver

Software that, when executed, activates a peripheral device, like a printer or modem. Also called a device driver.

## DSP

✤ See **digital signal processor**.

## DVD

✤ See **digital videodisk**.

## DVI

✤ See **digital video interactive**.

## dynamic random access memory (DRAM)

Your computer's **memory**.

It is where all your stuff gets stored. A computer's memory is built with one or more DRAM (pronounced "D-ram") chips. The memory is called "random access" because the **central processing unit (CPU)** can access any item in any part of the memory, and the time it takes to get the item is independent of where it is stored.

"Dynamic" refers to the fact that when the computer is in use, the memory has to be updated (**refreshed**) constantly. Static RAMs, or SRAMs, do not have to be, but they are more expensive, take up more space, and cost more to make.

Egyptian

## Eckert, J. Presper

Developer of the concept of internal programming that he and John Mauchly used in the first large-scale digital computer, the Eniac.

Built in 1946, the Eniac weighed 30 tons, was 100 feet long, 10 feet high, and contained 18,000 vacuum tubes. Eckert also helped develop Univac, the first commercial computer, that he and Mauchly sold in 1950 to what would eventually become Unisys.

## ECPA

+ See **Electronic Communications Privacy Act**.

## EDI

+ See **electronic data interchange**.

## EDTV

+ See **extended definition TV**.

## edu

Last segment of a top-level domain name (on the Internet) for a computer that is at an educational institution.

## edutainment

Refers to interactive multimedia products that aim to teach as they entertain.

Examples are atlases, almanacs, and geography games, usually created on CD-ROM.
+ See also **infotainment**.

## EFF

+ See **Electronic Frontier Foundation**.

*"We developed a laser printer long before Canon and all these others. It used a gas laser, not a solid state. It got buried. The (IBM) sales department gets in there and says, 'Oh, it doesn't have the following 13 features.' By the time you tack the 13 features on it, it doubles the price. Now they say there is no market for it, it's too expensive. Well, you can't butter your bread on both sides and not get your fingers greasy."*

— *J. Presper Eckert*
["J. Presper Eckert", Computerworld, 22 June 1992, Section: In the Beginning...; p. 14]

Allows people to call a business or organization for free.

The institution pays a fixed monthly fee to the phone company.

The service is implemented by special private access lines connected to central office equipped to for this wide-area telecommunications service (WATS). It is provided by all major telephone companies in North America. Many other services can be added, among them time-of-day routing, call blocking, call attempt profiles, command routing, and follow-me 800.

**electromagnetic spectrum**

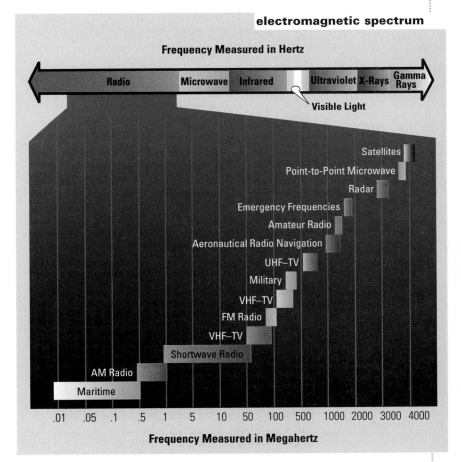

## electromagnetic spectrum

The entire range of electromagnetic radiation—energy that travels in the form of a wave.

The waves vary in length and frequency. The spectrum, in order from longest wavelength to shortest (lowest frequency to highest), includes: radio waves, microwaves, infrared radiation, visible light, ultraviolet radiation, x-rays, and gamma rays.

Visible light (colors) occupies only a narrow band in the electromagnetic spectrum. All these phenomena, if uninhibited, travel through space at the same rate—the speed of light.

Television broadcasts fall near the intersection of the radio and microwave portions of the spectrum. The Federal Communications Commission (FCC) governs the public use of the radio and television portion of the spectrum.

## electronic book

© Robert Neubecker/Spots on the Spot!

(1) Book converted into digital form to be read on a computer screen. (2) Hypermedia program, usually produced on a CD-ROM, that organizes material based on the metaphor of a book.

Not bound by printing and bookbinding constraints, electronic books offer hypertext links, perform keyword searches, provide for margin notes, and in other ways expand the notion of literacy and learning. CD-ROM books extend text with multimedia features: video, music, photographs, animation, graphics. Powerful database tools enable extensive cross-referencing links, multiple-criteria searches, and user-customized information. For example, a user who wants to compose a history of computing can search and assemble materials by subject and date simultaneously.

+ See also on-demand publishing, on-line publishing, and repurposing.

## Electronic Communications Privacy Act (ECPA)

Law placing limits on intercepting and monitoring messages transmitted mechanically.

As a result of the Watergate scandal, Congress originally passed the act to inhibit phone tapping by overly eager federal agents. Growth of the cellular phone industry prompted a revamping of the act in 1986.

The latter version did two things. First, it made intercepting messages in transit illegal, except under special narrowly defined circumstances and when a judge or magistrate finds such action absolutely necessary. Second, it prohibited access to, or monitoring of, electronic communication that is less than 180 days old, except by warrant.

The first test of E-mail privacy violation under the act was brought in 1992 against the Secret Service. Agents had seized Steve Jackson Games' entire bulletin board system containing private messages. The case was settled in favor of the company and its employees.

## electronic data interchange (EDI)

Standards that convert the format of a transmitted document into the format of the receiver's computer.

EDI enables computer-to-computer exchange of business documents between different companies.

## Electronic Frontier Foundation (EFF)

Advocacy group for preserving freedom of speech in the electronic media.

Established in 1990 by Lotus Development Corp. founder Mitch Kapor and Grateful Dead lyricist John Perry Barlow, it seeks to apply the Constitution and the Bill of Rights to computer communications. EFF works to shape laws that protect individuals' rights on-line, to focus debate on controversial initiatives such as the federal government's Clipper chip, and to lend support in legal proceedings where these liberties are violated.

## electronic mail (E-mail)

Message, typically text, sent via telephone lines and modem from one personal computer to another, or to a commercial network or E-mail service that stores the sender's message until the addressee comes to get it.

## electronic point of purchase (EPOP)

Check-out system at a store using a central computer that captures the details of each transaction.

These often use electronic cash registers (you will see a screen when you check out) and bar-code scanners.

*"I'm not using these @#$% computers, and I'm not readin' no E-mail."*

— *PJ Carlesimo, Portland Trail Blazer coach (upon receiving a laptop from team owner and Microsoft founder Paul Allen)*
[Donald Katz, "Welcome Electronic To The Arena; The Digital Age Is Upon Us, And The Sporting World Will Never Be The Same," Sports Illustrated, 3 July 1995, p. 58.]

# Walking A Tightrope

Cryptography and encryption are two topics of particular concern to the Electronic Frontier Foundation (EFF), because they are tied so intimately to privacy. In 1995, the foundation went to court to help a mathematician from the University of California, Dan Bernstein, sue the federal government for the right to publish research describing complex algorithms called hash functions that Bernstein had used to develop "snuffle," an encryption program.

Bernstein had been told by the government that such a program was considered, under federal law, a "defense article," or weapon, by the Department of Defense. Its public release, government officials warned, would be an act of treason. But EFF members have argued that good encryption is a requirement of any broad consumer use of cyberspace. Without it, credit-card numbers and other critical financial data could not travel over the Internet and in E-mail without risk of discovery.

The foundation's difficult role—how to advocate freedom without becoming a shield for cybercriminals—is highlighted in a narrative written by John Barlow, and available on the foundation's Internet site (using a gopher, type *Electronic Frontier Foundation*).

Barlow describes trying to learn the identities of two new users who'd logged on to his newsgroup. After using a finger program to try to learn their real names, he concluded they were crackers, and attempted a discourse. They asked for his address. "I had never encountered anyone so apparently unworthy of my trust as these little nihilists," Barlow wrote. "They had me questioning a basic tenet, namely the greatest security lies in vulnerability. I decided it was time to put that principle to the test." Barlow gave his address.

"Mr. Barlow," responded the one calling himself Acid Phreak, "thank you for posting all I need to get your credit information and a whole lot more! Now, who is to blame? ME for getting it or YOU for being such an idiot?" A day later, Barlow posted again, suggesting that, "with crackers like" Phreak and his partner Phiber Optik, "the issue is less intelligence than alienation. Trade their modems for skateboards and only a slight conceptual shift would occur."

"You have some pair of balls comparing my talent with that of a skateboarder," Optik quickly replied. "Hmm," he continued, "this was indeed boring, but nonetheless..." At which point, Barlow concluded, "he downloaded my credit history."

# The Snail Mail Alternative

Faster, cheaper, not likely to be folded, spindled, or mutilated when it arrives, electronic mail has turned letter writing into a far more interactive process than the U.S. Postal Service ever envisioned. The recipient (or recipients) of your message may read it, reply, forward it to another computer user, or delete it entirely (nothing personal).

The E-mail capability of the Arpanet, the Internet's predecessor, was the single most important factor in convincing U.S. government officials of its indispensability. Today, E-mail use is exploding. Microsoft CEO Bill Gates has said publicly he uses his E-mail application five times more often than any other program his own company or any other has produced.

E-mail messages are simple text. You cannot include italics, screaming headlines, or graphics. Regular E-mailers embellish their texts with capitals if they want to SHOUT; surround a word with asterisks that they'd otherwise italicize for emphasis—as in "Yes! Michael Jackson would be *perfect* as the Boy Scouts' spokesman!"; and show underlining _like this_.

There are advantages and disadvantages to E-mail. One plus is that the message stays in the recipient's system until retrieved. Another is that an E-mail will arrive in minutes—not as fast as the telephone, but considerably quicker than the postman and the hallowed FedEx guy. A minus is that the recipient has to do something—log on—to get his mail, and if he doesn't bother to do so for days, his mail sits unopened.

The Internet has grown so quickly, in part, because it provides for E-mail. It also permits messages to move outside the Internet as well, in networks such as Bitnet, commercial on-line services like America Online and CompuServe, and bulletin board systems, of which there are thousands.

A typical address will have two parts: the mailbox (which could be your name, your business or organization's name, or a group name) and the host name (the name of the Internet host computer, where the mailbox has been created). For example, the address for Internet Business Advantage, a monthly newsletter, is success@wentworth.com (pronounced "success at wentworth dot com"). The mailbox is "success," the host name is "wentworth," and the ".com" indicates the site is part of a commercial network.

E-mail messages are delivered in two parts: the header—showing the author, host of origin, and subject—and the text or message body. If you are communicating via one of the big on-line providers, you will simply follow prompts through the creation of the header and text. And you will probably be able to take advantage of other E-mail features such as aliases, attached documents, carbon copies, mailing lists, and receipt notification.

Although E-mail goes to a designated recipient, it is not really private. If someone were determined to access it, they probably could. The mind-boggling amount of mail on the Internet suggests, though, that this is as likely as your being invited to light the flame at the next Olympic Games.

But it does raise the issue of what is appropriate to include in an E-mail, and what isn't. A good rule of thumb is to eschew personal financial data, such as credit card or bank account numbers, and commentary that might be construed as libelous. To suggest, for example, in a posting on the "alt.rec.drugs" newsgroup, that your mayor was seen with a bong at the last Hootie and the Blowfish concert might be actionable...unless it was true. Office E-mail is especially incendiary: coworkers can read it at someone else's terminal, and easily forward the text to others.

Be careful about responding to messages addressed to groups of users—your reply may go to everyone listed.

✚ See also **emoticon** and **netiquette**.

## electronic publishing

Publishing on any electronic media, such as a CD or on-line, rather than in print, radio, or television.

✦ See also **electronic book**.

## electronic serial number (ESN)

Unique identification number embedded in the circuits of a **cellular telephone** by the manufacturer.

The ESN is automatically transmitted to the base station every time a cellular call is made.

## E-mail

✦ See **electronic mail**.

## emergency response system (ERS)

Commonly and generically referred to as 911 service, the ERS is designed to speed emergency personnel response.

Ambulance, police, or fire personnel who answer 911 calls can pinpoint the address of the caller. They then contact the appropriate rescue teams and services for the area being serviced. Multimedia emergency response programs include telecommunications, network, and database access. On-line video, satellite images, photographs, schematics, architectural plans, and maps enable a rescue team to locate and manage an emergency more quickly than if all these items were on paper. Systems like this are also invaluable in simulating emergencies for training.

## emoticon

Little caricatures that look like faces, made by typing keyboard characters.

For example, :-) is a smiling face. (If you bend your head well to the left, you will see it.) Senders of E-mail message use these to convey a mood or shade of meaning.

## emulation

Technique combining software and hardware that allows programs written for one computer to run on another.

## encoder

Hardware system accepting and converting a **component video** signal (professional, very high quality)

# In Lieu Of Body Language, Please Use

Some smileys are just happy faces that are a friendly "have-a-nice-day" kind of signature.  Others convey more complex emotions.  They are made by typing character combinations that form a picture when the reader looks at them sideways.  (Tip your head all the way to the left.)  Some examples:

| | |
|---|---|
| :-) | = Basic smiley face |
| :-o | = Writer is surprised |
| :-# | = Writer's lips are sealed |
| 8(:-) | = Writer is a propeller head |
| L:-) | = Writer just graduated |
| [:-) | = Writer is wearing a Walkman |
| 5:-) | = Writer is Elvis |
| ;-) | = Winking |
| :-@ | = Screaming |
| :( | = Frowning |
| >:-> | = Angry |
| :D | = Laughing |
| :/) | = Not funny |
| :-( | = Sad |
| () | = Hugging |
| ((())) | = Lots o' huggin' |
| :* | = Kiss |
| :**: | = Returning kiss |
| :-& | = Tongue-tied |
| :-J | = Tongue in cheek |
| :P | = Sticking out tongue |
| :-? | = Licking your lips |
| 8-) | = Writer wearing sunglasses |
| B:-) | = Writer wearing sunglasses on head |

into a corresponding composite video signal (standard quality, as in VCRs and TVs).

It does this by separating brightness information from discrete Red, Green, Blue (RGB) values.

## encoding

(1) Converting data to digital form, especially in full-motion video. (2) Converting data to a secondary form in such a way that it can be reconverted to its original form; used in encryption.

Encoding is the third step in the conversion of an analog signal into a digital signal. Sampling and quantizing are the first two.

## encryption

Scrambling of transmitted data so that unwelcome eyes or ears will not understand it.

There are two kinds of encryption: software, which is readily available and easy to install; and microchip, which is faster and more difficult to crack than software, but a tougher task to perform. Increased awareness of the power of crackers and cybercriminals has network users turning to cryptography (secret writings made with codes and ciphers) to protect sensitive data.

Firewalls are cryptographic protection to keep uninvited people from certain areas of a network. Although the law prohibits reading someone else's E-mail, the reality is that it is less secure than postal mail (snail mail).

Law enforcement agencies want to be able to monitor criminals and would like to see standardized encryption used nationwide. The fear is that, with the burgeoning of many cryptographic schemes, criminals will use obscure encryption to keep unlawful activities hidden.

The Data Encryption Standard (DES) and Rivest-Shamir-Adleman (RSA) are leading encryption tools used internationally. Pretty Good Privacy (PGP) is a popular encryption tool, found on networks as freeware.

## end office

Phone company's central office (nearest you) that delivers you a dial tone.

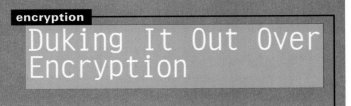

# Duking It Out Over Encryption

The struggle between the government and cybercitizens for control and distribution of encryption software shows no signs of de-escalating.

In the summer of 1995, *Wired* magazine reported that a group using a Duke University E-mail address had produced—and were selling—T-shirts emblazoned with perl/RSA encryption code. Although this code is meant to be used to protect messages, the shirt unveiled it, in both a machine-readable font and a machine-readable bar code, so it could be picked up and stored in a computer. The shirt also sported the comment that the shirt itself was a "controlled munition" (under Department of Defense guidelines), since it was giving out this information. "Want one?" queried the magazine. "Make sure your papers are in order."

A month or two earlier, three young West Coast programmers unveiled a voice-encryption program using an algorithm called triple-DES, which is believed to be unbreakable. And unlike the Clipper chip, it does not give federal agencies a "trap door" that can be exploited if the government wants to eavesdrop. The program, the three developers said, could be downloaded for nothing from their FTP site at ftp.csn.org/mpj/. By doing so, you could establish phone privacy even the government couldn't break.

✦ See also **privacy** and **Wiretap Act**.

## English

The common language used on the Internet.

Its pervasiveness has caused international concern—especially in Europe and Asia—over whether single-culture dominance will emerge in on-line knowledge exchange.

## EPOP

✦ See **electronic point of purchase**.

## erasable programmable read-only memory (EPROM)

A memory **chip** that can be filled, but not erased or altered unless exposed to a particular wavelength of light.

It can be removed from a computer for reprogramming.

✦ See also **read-only memory (ROM)**.

## equal access

It means all you have to do to initiate a long-distance phone call is to dial "1." By law, the phone company cannot require you to do anything else.

It means callers do not have to dial a long string of numbers to get to their long-distance carrier. Equal access was set forth in Federal Judge Harold Green's Modified Final Judgment (MFJ), which detailed the rules of the AT&T divestiture.

✦ See also **AT&T Consent Decree**.

## erasable storage

Memory that may be erased or written over with new data (like your computer's hard drive). Contrast with write-once read-many (WORM) memory.

✦ See also **digital optical recording** and **read-only storage**.

## erlang

International unit, which measures telephone usage (**traffic**).

One erlang is equal to one caller talking for one hour on one telephone. Erlang formulas have been used to determine the best way to predict and handle periods of heavy telephone use. (Perhaps we can coin a new term, for those phone-chatting teenagers: "erlangers.")

## error detection and correction (EDAC)

Code used to check for and correct errors in telecommunications, computing, and digital-optical recording.

## error messages

On-screen messages indicating operating system or software failure.

They can take the form of seemingly nonsensical reference numbers, or they can be a statement describing the problem, such as "The host has failed to respond" or "The file you requested is not available."

## ERS

✚ See emergency response system.

## ESN

✚ See electronic serial number.

## Ethernet

A local area network where computers communicate with each other over coaxial cable.

Jointly developed in the early 1970s by Xerox PARC, Intel, and DEC, it was subsequently adopted by the IEEE as a standard (called Ethernet/802.3 or Ethernet/IEEE). Ethernet systems will not allow two computers to send at the same time. This technique avoids the network collisions caused by simultaneous transmissions. If the bussing connections are broken at any point, the whole net comes to a halt.

✚ See also wide area network (WAN) and token ring.

## eudora

Graphical E-mail program for both Mac and Windows users.

Eudora allows users sitting at their own computer to connect to a UNIX machine, and both get and send E-mail without actually having to log in and use UNIX. Many Internet users claim this is one of the best graphical E-mail programs. A test version is available as freeware from ftp.qualcomm.com in the /quest directory.

## exchange

First three digits of a local phone number.

In the phone number (800) 555-1212, 800 is the area code and 555 is the exchange.

## expert system

+ See **artificial intelligence**.

## Extended Binary-Coded Decimal Interchange (EBCDIC)

+ See **file transfer protocol**.

## extended definition TV (EDTV)

Wide-screen television format nearly as capable as that proposed for high-definition television (HDTV), and like many 35mm movies.

To view EDTV, which has an aspect ratio of 16:9, a special wide-screen television is needed. Otherwise, the image will be displayed as a "letterbox," meaning the picture will take up the full width of the screen but not the full height (leaving black bands above and below the image). EDTV—currently being offered in Japan—is seen as an intermediate format between standard TV and HDTV, though the image resolution is no different than that of a regular TV.

## extensible

Capable of being extended, of allowing users or software manufacturers to add new features.

If a regular telephone line was able to handle simultaneous video streams, that would be a good example of being extensible. It would also be a good example of a miracle.

## eye phone

First commercially available head-mounted display (HMD).

+ See also **virtual reality**.

## eyeball tracking

Tracking the movement of a human eye by an infrared or video device.

It is one of many methods being developed to try to establish a natural interface with the computer. Eyeball tracking has been used in Air Force weapons deployment. In experimental setups, a fighter pilot can direct his guns at a target simply by looking at the object. An eye tracker calculates what the pilot is looking at, and feeds coordinates to the guiding mechanism of the weapon.

✚ See also **head-mounted display** and **virtual reality**.

**eye phone**

Courtesy of Virtual Research Systems, Inc.

# F FAQ to FSN

Futura

## FAQ
+ See **frequently asked questions**.

## fast packet
A **broadband** (high-speed, high-capacity) switching and networking approach that provides nearly error-free **transmission**.
+ See also **packet** and **packet switching**.

## fast packet multiplexing
Combination of computer processing, packeting of analog signals, and time-division multiplexing.

It has advantages over standard time-division and frequency-division multiplexing techniques, including the ability to start sending a packet before it has been completely received.
+ See also **multiplexer (MUX)**.

## fast packet switching
High-speed **wide-area network** technology to transmit data, voice, and image via short packets of information.

One form of fast packet switching, **asynchronous transfer mode**, is used for high-speed networking.
+ See also **fast packet multiplexing** and **multiplexer (MUX)**.

## facsimile transmission (fax)
Sending text and graphics on paper, or from a computer file, over phone lines to another fax machine or computer.

Faxes are good for transmitting images and other non-text artifacts, such as signatures, that are tougher to send via E-mail. They are also good for transmitting text that is already on paper, but not in a computer file. Otherwise, E-mail is faster and more reliable. In fact, E-mail aficionados think of the fax as "E-mail for wimps." The legal system doesn't think so, however; faxes are admissible in court as evidence, but E-mail records are not.

The immediate commercial future of fax technology may be as a broadcast, or publishing, medium. The National Rifle Association sends out the daily *Crime Strike News* by fax, and a Virginia entrepreneur faxes 1,000 subscribers (who pay approximately $1,000 apiece) a 14-page publication called *Sports Business Daily*.

With more than 11 million fax machines currently in operation in the United States, and another two million expected to be hooked up by 1996, fax publishing may be able to exploit a technological footbridge between the generalized daily newspapers of today and the promised future of instant computer access to any and all information. Using modems, fax publishers can "broadcast" the same material in a matter of minutes to several hundred fax machines. Some take-out restaurants in Manhattan use a fax broadcast each morning to notify regulars of daily lunch specials.

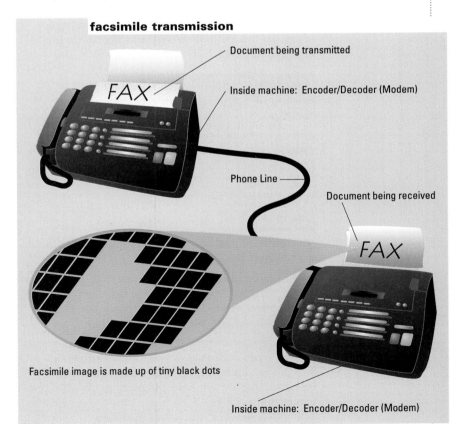

**facsimile transmission**

Document being transmitted

Inside machine: Encoder/Decoder (Modem)

Phone Line

Document being received

Facsimile image is made up of tiny black dots

Inside machine: Encoder/Decoder (Modem)

## fax

+ See **facsimile transmission**.

## FCC

+ See **Federal Communications Commission**.

## FDDI

+ See **fiber-distributed data interface**.

## FDM

+ See **multiplexing**.

## Federal Communications Commission (FCC)

U.S. government agency regulating all interstate and foreign communications in the United States.

Set up by the Communications Act of 1934, the FCC is overseen by a seven-member board appointed by the President. The FCC's authority extends to setting rates for telephone, data, and video services; determining the standards for telecommunications equipment; and acting as a gatekeeper for the telecommunications business by granting (or revoking) broadcast licenses, and allocating broadcast frequencies.

## Federal Trade Commission (FTC)

Government agency that oversees business dealings.

Among other things, the FTC is dedicated to preventing companies from becoming monopolies. It was responsible for bringing about the breakup of AT&T in 1984.

+ See also **AT&T Consent Decree**.

## feedback

(1) Return of part of a system's output to the input, which alters the system's output.

If you hold a microphone too close to a speaker and talk, the output from the speaker is picked up by the microphone and fed back into the system, causing the painful squawk we all know and hate.

(2) Process whereby a program or a system is modified as a result of user action. For example, in interactive video games, the gaming software responds in different ways depending on what the player does.

+ See also **cybernetics, input/output,** and **tracking**.

## fiber-distributed data interface (FDDI)

ANSI standard for fast, reliable data transmission through optical fiber cable, in a token ring setup.

Universities and companies that have a number of buildings at a large site, often link the computers in each building with a local area network (LAN). If they have several LANs, they can be linked with a backbone that uses FDDI. These are ten times as fast as an Ethernet link, can span a city, and can be sold as a service to other companies or institutions in the extended area.

✚ See also metropolitan area network (MAN).

## fiber-optic cable

A cable carrying laser light encoded with digital signals; capable of reliably transmitting billions of bits of data per second.

Compared with coaxial cable, fiber-optic cable delivers superior television picture quality and offers much greater bandwidth and tremendous security. Emitting no electromagnetic radiation, fiber-optic cables cannot be tapped by remote sensing equipment.

✚ See also coaxial cable, copper cable, network, and twisted pair.

## fiber optics

Technology that uses long, tiny glass or silica fibers to transport pulses of light.

Each pulse contains data or parts of a telecommunications signal. Because there is very little signal loss, the information can be securely transmitted very quickly over long distances. It is so fast that the complete *Encyclopedia Britannica* could be transmitted in about one second. Transmission by fiber optics is also less susceptible to external interference.

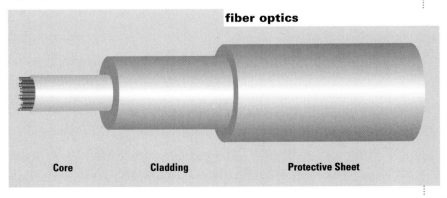

**fiber optics**

Core          Cladding                    Protective Sheet

# With The Speed Of Light

In fiber optics, fine strands no thicker than a human hair act as "guides" for single-frequency light beams generated by either a light-emitting diode (LED) or a laser. The light pulses zoom along inside the strand like cars streaking through a tunnel. A fiber-optic cable supports practically unlimited bandwidth, making it the physical medium of choice for the evolving national information infrastructure. More than 350 million conversations won't tie up a single fiber-optic phone line, and one fiber-optic TV cable will transmit 50,000 high-definition television (HDTV) signals.

A fiber-optic system such as FDDI can carry 100 Mbps of computer data over 2.5 kilometers of cable. Newer standards could improve that capacity exponentially. Fiber-optics already can carry large volumes of low-band multiplexed signals, such as telephone calls, or high-band signals for television and videoconferencing.

Additional benefits? Low cost, low power consumption, insensitivity to electromagnetic interference, and impervious to bugging. The only drawback is the power of the lasers themselves; the light signal they emit often must be amplified en route.

Given the projected growth of desktop computing, a national fiber-optic network—one to two decades down the road—is inevitable. With its arrival, supercomputing power will make high-resolution, real-time interactive and virtual reality experiences in the home a sure thing. And organizations needing clean, vast transmission capacity—including the military; factories running electronic machinery; companies with LANs, MANs, and WANs; and the telephone and broadcast industries—will experience a new era of growth.

## fiber-to-the-feeder (FTF)

+ See **hybrid fiber coax**.

## fiber-to-the-serving area

+ See **hybrid fiber coax**.

## fifth generation

Effort to perfect artificial intelligence for use in computers and telecommunications systems.

The Fifth Generation Project was a cooperative research effort between the Japanese computer industry and its government. They committed themselves in 1981 to develop "intelligent" computers for the 1990s.

## file server

Computer that stores files and programs and provides a way for other computers to access them.

File servers are like the reference departments in libraries; they house huge amounts of information, and can get it for you. In addition, they let users add to the collection. They are usually fast machines, with a very large hard disk drive. In companies, they serve various divisions. On networks, they distribute information conveniently, efficiently, and economically, and permit many people to store data on the drive and access the same files simultaneously.

+ See also **client-server** and **server**.

## file transfer protocol (FTP)

An Internet service that copies a file from one computer to another.

When you search for information on the Internet, you use a search program such as Gopher. Once it finds what you have asked for, it sends a copy to your computer. That transmission is controlled by the FTP. The transfer occurs only if the files are in ASCII or Extended Binary-Coded Decimal Interchange (EBCDIC) formats. ASCII is mostly for personal computers, whereas EBCDIC was developed by IBM for use on its mainframes.

## firewall

An electronic boundary that limits access between networks that are linked together.

Large organizations are often concerned about sensitive information leaking out. They also often have an internal network to serve employees, which is also linked to the Internet. To prevent an Internet user from accessing the information, and to stop an employee from sending it out, a firewall is built between the two networks.

Physically, it is not made of bricks; special programming on the organization's network limits the kinds of connections that can be made and who can make them.

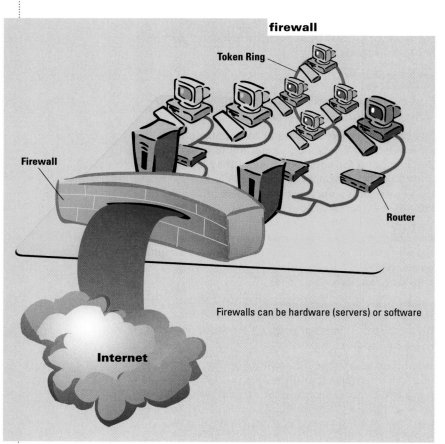

**firewall**

Token Ring

Firewall

Router

Firewalls can be hardware (servers) or software

Internet

**firmware**

Software, stored in a computer's **ROM** or **EPROM**, that is constantly in demand by the computer or communications system.

The program is permanent. It is "burned" onto the chip—that is, wired so it can never be erased, even when the system is turned off.

## 500 service

Refers to a transportable, go-anywhere telephone number.

The phone number is assigned to an individual, rather than a specific telephone or location. Wherever you go, it follows. This way, a busy businessperson or world traveler can be found by a caller, who simply dials the 500 number. The phone company routes the call to the proper destination. It works for phones, faxes, and data. It is the first personal, universal phone number system.

✚ See also **personal communication service (PCS)**.

## flame

To breathe the fire of contempt and insult on some on-line person, innocent or not.

It is a breach of on-line etiquette—or netiquette—used purposely to denigrate another user.

Unlike letter writing, E-mail is nearly instantaneous communication. It is easy to write and send, and hard to reconsider and retract. Authoring a flame, and putting it out on the system—especially if the message is profane or a personal attack—can be a regrettable act. And, if the flame is libelous or defamatory, the writer could be sued.

If you are determined to flame, and do not want to end up looking like an idiot or malcontent, follow a few protocols:

(1) *Be certain you've got your facts right.* Opponents will destroy you otherwise (and even supporters will be humiliated).

(2) *Be brief.* The idea is to elicit support for your position, not to alienate others. Several screens of text will do the latter.

(3) *Be tough.* The Marquis of Queensbury rules do not apply.

(4) *Think Netiquette.* Don't use profanity or other offensive language (such as sexual references). Quote your opponent where it supports your point. Write as clearly as you can. Spelling and grammar count.

(5) *Remember who you are.* An anonymous posting protects you, but access through a company computer gives you a semiofficial status that could

play havoc if your target decides to take your comments to a higher authority.

✦ See also **emoticon**.

## flash memory

Small printed circuit board ("card") that holds up to 64 MB of data in memory.

Flash memory is primarily used in personal digital assistants (PDAs) because of its small size and ability to hold data without using any power.

## floppy disk

Magnetically sensitive, reusable storage disk. Also called diskette.

"Floppies" used to constitute the entire memory of a personal computer. Now they are generally used to distribute software, to make backup copies of files, or as a handy way to bring a little data home or to the office. Until the late 1980s, floppies were 5" across, usually black, and were flimsy enough that if you waved them in the air they'd flop. Today, they are 3.5" across and are stiff like a cartridge, but the endearing term "floppy" endures.

Contrast with hard disks.

## FM Towns Marty

A CD-ROM–based multimedia player manufactured by Fujitsu in Japan.

It is praised for its 16.7 million colors and a graphics engine capable of supporting up to 1,024 sprites (little screen images such as a cursor or Nintendo's Mario).

## FMV

✦ See **full-motion video**.

## follow me 800

Service created by 800 number providers that allows a customer to reroute incoming 800 calls anytime.

✦ See also **800 service**.

## foo

An Internet term, used as a common placeholder for variables, functions, and persons in examples.

For example, "A given subscriber, foo, has the address 'foo@bar.com'." On a chat line, you might type, "I just inherited foo dollars. It won't buy me a new house, but that Jeep is looking good."

## FORTH

A high-level programming language created to provide a way to control the computer directly.

FORTH is used in artificial intelligence applications, process control, and video games. It was developed in the late 1960s by Charles Moore.

## fourth-generation languages (4GL)

Advanced programming languages three levels up from machine language, which aim to simplify both programming and use of the program.

A beauty of 4GL is that the commands sounds like plain English. For example, dBASE is a combination of third- and fourth-level language. Using it you can display all the records in a data file by just entering the command "LIST." Query languages, whereby you ask questions concerning a database, and report writers are written in fourth-generation languages.

## fractal compression

A technique that can squeeze digital information into memory at a whopping ratio of up to 200:1.

The technique is of special use to anyone involved with digital video.

✦ See also **motion picture experts group (MPEG)**.

## frame

Single complete picture in a moving picture sequence.

## frame grabber

Computer add-on board that enables digitizing of single video frames.

## frame relay

A protocol for transmitting small packets (pieces of data) over a network that requires less error checking than others forms of packet switching.

It efficiently handles high-speed data over wide-area networks at lower cost and with higher performance than traditional point-to-point services. Frame relay standards began superseding the X.25

protocols in the early 1990s, and are designed for digital, rather than analog, lines.

+ See also **asynchronous transfer mode (ATM)** and **cell relay**.

## freenet

A way to get on the Internet for free.

Often, local organizations such as libraries offer access to the Internet without charge. For a limited time only.

+ See also **dial-up Internet connections**.

## freeware

Copyrighted software available free of charge.

Freeware is usually downloaded from bulletin board systems or the Internet, and can be copied and given to friends. Authors who write these programs and make them available will not make any royalties; they do it to gain recognition. Sometimes, companies publish freeware that augments their other products, to woo or wow users.

+ See also **copyright, public domain software**, and **shareware**.

## frequency

How many times something happens in a given period.

The frequency of waves of energy in the electromagnetic spectrum—radio signals, broadcast TV—is measured in cycles per second, or hertz (Hz). Electric current is sent to your house at 60 Hz. An FM radio station that is "99.5 on your FM dial" broadcasts at a frequency of 99.5 megahertz (99.5 million cycles per second).

News anchor Dan Rather was beaten up one afternoon in the 1980s; his assailant calmly walked up to him on a New York City sidewalk and asked, "Kenneth, what's the frequency?" before he suddenly attacked.

## frequency-division multiplexing (FDM)

+ See **multiplexing**.

## frequently asked questions (FAQs)

Short lists of common questions—and their answers—that are provided to users of a given Internet site.

Pronounced "facks," these lists are designed to explain to a novice (or newbie) the scope of information available at the site, and the basics on how to use it. They are common on Usenet newsgroups. Because regular group members are bored silly by newbies asking the same old things, newbies are expected to familiarize themselves with a site's FAQs before joining an on-line discussion there.

## FSFMV

+ See full-screen full-motion video.

## FSN

+ See full-service network.

## FTC

+ See Federal Trade Commission.

## FTP

+ See file transfer protocol.

## full-motion video (FMV)

Video that runs at 30 frames-per-second, the same rate at which it was filmed.

Up to this point, full-motion video has been a pipe-dream. Most video on a computer screen is balky and confined to a tiny section of the screen. But with faster hard drives and efficient compression techniques, full-motion video is on the verge of a new era.

For example, fractal compression, adopted as a standard by the Motion Picture Experts Group (MPEG), achieves compression ratios of up to 200:1. So FMV video will play at higher resolutions and in larger areas of a monitor's screen. Full-time video on a computer monitor is the key to making interactive multimedia a commercial and artistic success. Games and edutainment become captivating with the believable illusion of full-motion video.

+ See also digital video interactive (DVI).

## full-screen full-motion video (FSFMV)

Advanced full-motion video, delivering 30 frames-per-second at a resolution close to VHS videotape and at the size of a full computer screen image— 640 x 480 pixels.

It was first accomplished by digital video interactive (DVI) and then by the Motion Picture Experts Group (MPEG), now the sought-after goal of any worthy compression scheme.

✦ See also **compact disk-interactive (CD-I)** and **interactive movies**.

## full-service network (FSN)

A video network using a special set-top box allowing the television to behave like a computer, and the remote control like a keyboard.

FSNs make it possible for a cable TV company to provide video-on-demand, news-on-demand, home shopping, and interactive video games played with other people on the network. As of the mid-1990s, testing has produced only mixed success.

# games to guide

## games

Software based on traditional game categories, such as adventure, role-playing, or strategy.

From Pong to Mortal Kombat, arcade games, video games, on-line games, PC games, and interactive multimedia and CD-ROM games all depend on controllable, programmable computing machines. Though the sometimes violent and sexist content may be controversial, these games have taught "computer literacy" to millions of children. New conceptual developments include hybrids combining education with entertainment; sports and machine simulation; and the use of hypertext, hypermedia, and digital video to create interactive multiple-narrative games.

© M. E. Cohen/Spots on the Spot!

> "Flight simulation games are actually out-of-body experience emulators. There must be all of these people everywhere on earth right now, waiting for a miracle, waiting to be pulled out of themselves, eager for just the smallest sign that there is something finer or larger or more miraculous about our existence than we had supposed."
>
> —**Douglas Coupland**, author, Microserfs
> [Microserfs, Harper Collins, 1995, p. 142-143.]

## games network

A network of many personal computers linked together through a games server.

It permits one-on-one cross-country competition, or many players to participate in the same game simultaneously. Sometimes offered at arcades, over the Internet, and on special cable or satellite TV channels.

## garbage in, garbage out (GIGO)

The notion that if you put lousy data into a computer you'll get lousy results back out.

The idea can also be applied to work ethic: If you don't give it your best, you won't get the best results.

## Gates, Bill

Cofounder and chief executive of software mega-giant Microsoft.

He is No. 2 on the Forbes "rich list" of billionaires. And he is barely 40.

✚ See also **Microsoft Windows**.

## gateway

(1) A system allowing authorized material such as E-mail to pass between dissimilar networks, by dovetailing one network's protocol with the other's. (2) A site on one on-line service that lets you operate on another on-line service. For example, America Online and CompuServe offer gateways to airline reservation systems and to the Internet.

✚ See also **bridge**.

## geographical information system (GIS)

A computerized information system that lets you look at and search maps.

It ranges from a simple database to a sophisticated hypermedia production, and is used for tourist information services, educational multimedia, and car navigation systems.

✚ See also **hypermap**.

## geostationary satellite (GEOS)

A satellite that remains stationary over a fixed point on the earth's surface.

It is positioned 22,300 miles above the equator, and moves through space in sync with the earth's orbit. Three GEOS can transmit a signal over the entire earth's surface. To receive clear transmission, a satellite dish is pointed at an exact spot in the sky. GEOS function effectively in orbit for 10 to 12 years and consume a lot of solar power.

## GIF

✚ See **graphic interchange format**.

## giga

Prefix indicating one billion; five gigahertz is five billion hertz.

*"(In 25 years), you'll have computers seeking out information and fiber-optic communications to the home. Whether it's calling up pictures that you've taken or sending pictures to your relatives or calling up movies or using interactive materials to learn."*

*—Bill Gates,*

Bill Gates interviewed by Paul Gillin, *Computerworld,* 22 June 1992, Sec. World At His Fingertips, p. 32

## GIGO

+ See **garbage in, garbage out**.

## GII

+ See **global information infrastructure**.

## GIS

+ See **geographical information system**.

## glitch

A screwup, mistake. Often refers to hardware.

+ See also **aliasing, artifact,** and **bug**.

## global information infrastructure (GII)

Term coined by the Clinton Administration to describe the hardware and networks of the global information superhighway.

Chief among the components are the Internet and on-line services, the host computers that direct them, and the physical fiber-optic and coaxial cable networks that connect them.

+ See also **national information infrastructure**.

## global kill file

Allows a user to program a computer to automatically wipe out certain entries in newsgroups on the Internet.

To do so, a user types the word, phrase, or name she does not want to see on the text editor's first line. The technique is used to avoid cascades— responses to a posting the user made in an on-line debate. In plain English, if you make a controversial comment on-line, you may get a ton of responses; a kill file will wipe them out of your way.

Note that complaining about a cascade on-line generally results in more cascading, along with flames on your apparent ignorance of First Amendment rights—which some people interpret to mean that you should have to sit there and listen to all their claptrap. A terrific source of kill-file information on the Internet can be found at the frequently asked questions file of the Usenet newsgroups, *news.newusers.questions* and *news.answers*.

## global positioning system (GPS)

A navigational satellite system that tells users on land or sea exactly where they are on the earth's surface.

GPS sends you your longitude and latitude coordinates. For example, navigators on ocean freighters who have GPS receivers communicate with the GPS to be sure they are staying on course. GPS has become so fine-tuned that surveyors can use the system to plot property lines.

## GMT

✚ See **Greenwich Mean Time**.

## Gopher

A program made for browsing the Internet in which one finds information by using menus.

With Gopher, you can look for files by subject, even if you do not have an exact file name. Developed at the University of Minnesota (whose sports team is the Golden Gophers), Gopher was created as a campus-wide information system providing E-mail connections to faculty and staff, news announcements, general information, and other databases. It also provided access to the Internet.

An on-screen menu made Gopher simple to use— no need to memorize domain names, directories, or computer commands. It worked so well that the university distributed it free throughout the Internet. It is still common on campuses, but now thousands of other sites run the Gopher server software.

## gov

The Internet domain name assigned to a federal, state, or local government organization.

## GPS

✚ See **global positioning system**.

## graphic interchange format (GIF)

Format for displaying and exchanging images on bulletin board systems and the Internet.

When you see a file that has ".gif" as part of its name, the file contains compressed graphics, not text. The GIF standard uses lossless compression, and is giving way to lossy compression standards such as JPEG, which makes the file smaller with no perceptible loss of detail. A large number of commercial programs, as well as **shareware**, read and write .gif files, which require a high-**resolution** monitor for viewing.

## graphical user interface (GUI)

Pronounced "gooey," this is the part of the computer that creates **icons** and puts them on the screen for you to work with.

You activate an icon by clicking on it with a mouse.

## graphics tablets

A pressure-sensitive drawing board connected to a computer.

As someone draws or writes on the tablet, the movements of the pen appear on a monitor. This allows the creation of computer images that look like actual pencil drawings or handwriting. The United Parcel Service and other deliverers also use the tablets to capture a signature of a customer who receives a shipment.

✚ See also **computer graphics**.

## grayscale

Display on a monitor, or a printed page from a printer, that has shades of gray, not just black and white.

## Great Renaming

The 1986 reorganization of **Usenet**, the UNIX User Network created in 1979 to exchange information and research in the scientific community.

Prior to the Great Renaming, all Usenet **newsgroups** were hierarchically labeled either *net* (for unmoderated group) or *mod* (for moderated). By 1987, the current *comp, misc, news, rec, sci, soc,* and *talk* had been formed, giving system administrators greater ability to exclude undesirable groups. The **alt** group was the last, with two of its first four newsgroups becoming *alt.drugs* and *alt.gourmand*.

## Greenwich Mean Time (GMT)

Time at 0 degrees longitude, or the meridian that passes through Greenwich, England. Also known as **Zulu Time**.

Universal time—that is, "planet earth time"—became tied to GMT as a global standard in 1884, although 0 degrees longitude has no special geophysical significance.

> "[After I created alt.sex on April 3, 1988], that meant that the alt. network now carried alt.sex and alt.drugs. It was therefore artistically necessary to create alt.rock-n-roll, which I have also done. I have no idea what sort of traffic it will carry. If the bizzaroids take it over I will regroup it or moderate it; otherwise I will let it be."
>
> — **Brian Reid**, creator of the alt. hierarchy of newsgroups
> [From a note Brian Reid sent to the Backbone Cabal (a small group of computer expers), 3 April 1988]

# The Secret Of Apple's Success

One of the principal reasons Apple Computer met with such fast success in the personal computer industry was its revolutionary GUI. It gave users simple windows, pull-down menus, icons, and on-screen fonts. IBM and UNIX operating systems, by contrast, used menu-driven interfaces or command line interfaces; basically, you had to enter arcane codes every time you wanted to do anything. Apple users could move a mouse to point to windows and click on icons that opened applications or files.

Apple's GUI was so intuitive that you could begin to use the computer without reading a manual. By pointing at a choice in a pull-down menu and by clicking on icons, you could teach yourself a simple program and actually get work done. Many other operating systems have since copied the approach, most notably Microsoft's Windows for the IBM PC and compatibles.

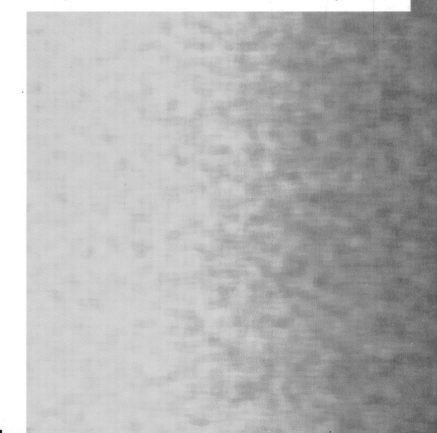

## groupware

Software applications that enable several computer users in different locations to work together on the same project.

Groupware is coordinated by a central computer, database, or expert system. Lotus Notes is an example, though Lotus Development Corporation categorizes it as *Computer Supported Cooperative Work*.

✦ See also **workgroup computing**.

## Groupe Speciale Mobile (GSM)

Primary digital telecommunication standard for cellular networks throughout Europe and in some parts of Asia.

The standard covers mobile communications between remote terminals such as personal digital assistants (PDAs) and laptop computers, and enables a European traveler to use a cellular telephone in more than 20 countries, with each call billed to one account.

## Grove, Andrew

Founder of Intel, the developer of state-of-the-art microprocessor chips, which many consider the industry's best.

He has also made himself into a corporate management guru. Author of *High Output Management*.

## GSM

✦ See **Groupe Speciale Mobile**.

## guardbands

✦ See **broadband channel**.

## GUI

✦ See **graphical user interface**.

## guide

In hypermedia, a device that helps you go through specific routes, viewing from predetermined perspectives and levels.

For example, you might be given the option in a hypermedia encyclopedia of following various guides such as a space pioneer, a soldier, a slave, and so on.

> *"The computer industry is a kind of laboratory for the (general business models) of the '90s. You can see the patterns of the computer industry in completely unrelated fields — very standards-oriented, very deregulated, very time-oriented. The competitive differentiator is who gets there first."*
>
> **— Andrew Grove**
> [Andrew Grove, interviewed by Michael Fitzgerald, *Computerworld*, 22 June 1992, p. 40]

Harem

## hack

(1) Job or assignment done quickly; may or may not be done well. (2) To work on a specific computer program or in a specific area. "I hack calculus" means it's a major focus of your life. (3) To interact with a computer in an exploratory, casual way.

*Hack* has also been used to describe Dungeons and Dragons–like behavior on campus: illegal exploration of tunnels, basements, and rooftops, to the dismay of the campus police.

## hacker

Person with computer expertise who delights in attacking computer problems and navigating through systems.

Often, it is a person who gains unauthorized **access** to a **network** or **mainframe** computer, and once inside, looks around, gets information for hacking further forbidden areas, and leaves without a trace. Hackers, in the culture of **cyberspace**, are perceived as more benevolent than **crackers** and computer **virus** creators—criminals using their skills maliciously.

One member of the Masters of Deception, a ring of hackers who were caught and prosecuted for illegal entry, reiterated that the one rule during their reign was "Thou shalt not destroy." The term *hacker*, recently, has evolved to the rather benign meaning of a skilled **code** writer or capable **program** manipulator, or simply somebody who feels at home in the digital domain. Unfortunately, the media interprets *hacker* as only one thing: the bad guy.

Dream job? The Defense Department employs a small number of hackers to try to uncover security weaknesses in their systems.

## hacker ethic

The conviction that information-sharing is a powerful and worthy tool, and that system-cracking for fun and exploration is ethically acceptable as long as no theft, damage, breach of confidentiality, or vandalism is committed.

In this way of thinking, hackers should share their expertise. They can do so by writing free software and facilitating access to information and computing resources. But many consider any cracking to be criminal. Hackers who don't believe that often use the cracking exercise to explain to a systems operator that there is a weakness in the system's security.

Sharing is a common characteristic of the hacker ethic: Technical shortcuts, software, even hardware resources can be found on Usenet and the Internet.

## hard disk

Your computer's main memory.

The data on a hard disk are erasable, meaning you can add to and delete from them. It is either installed internally in the computer or housed externally and connected to the computer with a SCSI cable.

The question, "How much memory does your hard drive have?" is getting to be as common as "What kind of car do you drive?" Most PCs have anywhere from 80 megabytes to 1 gigabyte. Just five years ago, 20 megabytes was considered pretty hefty.

## hard drive

✚ See **hard disk**.

## hardware

Physical components that comprise a computer system.

For example, the hardware necessary for multimedia production includes a computer, a scanner, a storage medium, an audio digitizer, and a video frame grabber. A hardware system requires software for operation; without it the hardware makes a good doorstop.

✚ See also **workstation**.

## HDTV

✚ See **high-definition television**.

## head-end

The point from which a cable television signal is sent on its journey through the coaxial cable to subscribers.

✦ See also **addressable programming**.

### head-mounted display

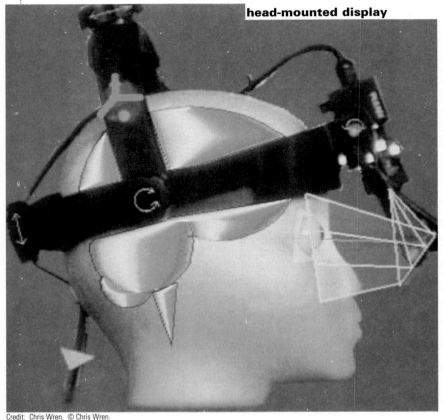

Credit: Chris Wren. © Chris Wren.
Courtesy of the M.I.T. Media Laboratory

### head-mounted display

Helmet with stereo video screens mounted right in front of the wearer's eyes, and stereo headphones over the ears.

The head-mounted display can show an overlay of a video or computer graphics. Derived from military research on new methods for controlling fighter planes, HUD images can be presented to the retina in a wide variety of ways. Sensors track the motion of the head and/or eyes and tell the computer what the wearer is looking at so the system can render in real time the appropriate right and left images for stereoscopic display.

A head-mounted display is the key device in a **virtual reality** construct, the primary interface through which someone experiences a virtual world. As the technology advances, head-mounted displays will get more comfortable, using lighter display technology and providing higher **resolution**. However, discomfort from long-term viewing of close-up stereo screens will remain a significant hurdle to acceptance.

✚ See also **eyeball tracking**.

## header

Portion of a **packet** or an **E-mail** message that comes before the content. Like the heading or greeting on a letter.

It contains the addresses of the sender and the recipient, and error correction information that is used to put the data back together at its destination. It can also contain information on data origination, copyright holder, and associated cost of use.

## hertz (Hz)

Number of complete cycles per second of an electromagnetic wave.

One hertz equals one cycle per second.

✚ See also **digital audio, electromagnetic spectrum,** and **frequency**.

## hexadecimal notation (HEX)

Shorthand machine language of numbers (0 to 9) and letters (A to F) used to represent a more lengthy **binary** code.

It uses 16 characters instead of two, so a statement can be expressed in a smaller information package.

## HFC

✚ See **hybrid fiber coax**.

## Hi-8

**Video format** that improves the **resolution** and image quality of regular 8mm videotape.

It does this by separating the luminance (brightness) and the chrominance (color) of the video signal.

✚ See also **composite video**.

## hierarchy

Pyramid method of organizing general groups of information, processes, and systems.

The folders on Macintosh computers and directories on IBM PCs are organized hierarchically. At the top level are a small number of folders or root directories of major consequence; at the bottom level there are a large number of smaller files.

## high-definition television (HDTV)

A video system with higher resolution (1,150 scan lines), better color, and better audio (4-channel digital sound) than any existing TV standard.

The promise of HDTV is great, but its adoption is lagging because participants in international standards-setting activities cannot seem to reach consensus. Because manufacturers realize that existing television equipment could become obsolete rapidly once an HDTV standard is adopted, HDTV is currently being used only as a production tool in a few studios, and is in limited commercial distribution in Japan.

Once an infrastructure of fiber-optic cable and digital satellite broadcasting is in place, which will make distribution of HDTV transmission more widespread, pressure will increase to settle on a standard. Present HDTV standards have a wide-screen aspect ratio of 16:9, so that a set would be wider and larger than a standard set (similar in shape to a cinema screen). More advanced HDTV standards will allow any aspect ratio. A complete HDTV home system, able to store and play digital video, would be more like a "teleputer" than a television.

## high-level

In describing a computer language, it means closer in form and structure to a spoken language like English than a machine language consisting of arcane sets of numbers, letters, and/or symbols.

## high-sierra format

ISO standard (ISO 9660) for CD-ROMs that permits them to be used in different operating systems.

## HMD

✦ See head-mounted display.

## home page

The first page of a site on the World Wide Web.

It appears by default when you access a World Wide Web client. It can display text, graphics, video, or audio. The term is also used to indicate that someone has a site on the Web. If your daughter tells you she's "got her own home page," it means she has designed a Web site. Send the kid to MIT.

## home shopping

A way to view merchandise and order it from home.

There are several home shopping channels on cable TV, where you can see products on display, hear (somewhat incessant) descriptions of the goods, and order by calling an 800 number. On-line, you view products on a monitor and enter credit card information to order. The convergence of computers, telephones, and television promises a day when anyone can enter a PIN and choice of product with a smart card into a set-top box, and the item will be delivered to the home. Already, large companies

**home shopping**

# Home, Sweet Home

The White House has one. Rush Limbaugh, too. Off-shore gambling operations in the Caribbean have them. So do the Rolling Stones. MTV has one. So do network affiliates in every major U.S. market. And, it's entirely possible your neighbor or relative does, too.

The home page is the multimedia entry point for a World Wide Web site, and the fastest-growing phenomenon on the Internet. Home pages are designed using the "hypertext markup language" (known as html). All you need to activate your page is to place it on a server. Commercial firms all over the country can provide you with a server site for a relatively cheap monthly fee.

This has already led to some curious sites. At one Midwest site, a couple announces the smallest details of an upcoming wedding, including a line-item budget. Another home page features current water temperature readings of the site owner's backyard hot tub. A Massachusetts family has posted the sonogram of their unborn child on their page.

This is empowerment of the people—anyone, anywhere can become a broadcaster with a potential global audience of millions. And it's the truly revolutionary aspect of the Internet. For the moment, it has led to a preponderance of autobiographical data—pets, favorite movies, links to other "cool" pages—that stands as an ironic counterpoint to the original intention of the Net: to share scientific data within the academic and military communities.

"I'm not totally sure I understand why it's evolved that way," Net celebrity David Mirsky told a newspaper reporter in June 1995. Mirsky's self-published "Worst of the Web Page" chronicles the most egregious excesses of ego-driven Web sites. "I think part of it is the fact that it's just exciting to have something that hundreds of other people conceivably could read...In any case, a lot of people see the Web not as providing something for other people, but as an opportunity to talk about themselves."

offer CD-ROMs that display catalogs complete with sound and video clips.

But the brave new world of home shopping is the virtual mall. As lampooned in *Doonesbury* in the summer of 1995, people can walk through a mall via interactive television or a head-mounted display. This personalized virtual mall will be open 24 hours a day, constantly update the range of products available, and provide sales assistance at the ready. A dream, or nightmare, not so far away.

✚ See also **remote services**.

## Hopper, Rear Admiral Grace Murray

Developer of the first computer programming language for business applications. Died in 1992.

## Hopper, Max

Inventor of the Sabre reservation system for American Airlines; Hopper is considered the technologist who changed the airline industry.

The Sabre system transformed the way airlines interact with each other, with travel agents, and ultimately with the traveler.

> *"If you think of this being the information revolution, we're gradually creating the information around 'What is information? What does it consist of? How do we take data, group it, put it together, formulate it, process it, and really understand the processes in such a way that it can be utilized?'"*
>
> —*Max Hopper*
> [Max Hopper, interview by Glenn Rifkin, *Computerworld*, 22 June 1992, p.21]

*"If it's a good idea, go ahead and do it. It's much easier to apologize than it is to get permission."*

—*Rear Admiral Grace Murray Hopper*
[Mitch Betts and Paul Gillin, "Breaking molds," *Computerworld*, 22 June 1992, p.1]

© Peter Alsberg/Spots on the Spot!

## host

Originally, the central computer in a time-sharing system; currently, a computer that is at either end of a data transfer on the Internet.

The host can be either a PC, workstation, minicomputer, or mainframe. The term is a bit confusing. Anyone can become a host with a direct (as opposed to dial-up) connection to the Internet. Indeed some networks—such as the Internet, or those at large universities and multinational corporations—have thousands of hosts.

## host name

(1)  Name of a primary or controlling computer in a multicomputer installation; the computer system to which a network is connected.  (2)  Address assigned to the computer that is used to compile, link, edit, or test programs for use on another computer or system.

## HTML

+ See hypertext markup language.

## HTTP

+ See hypertext transport protocol.

## hub

A central switchbox that permits multiple network devices to connect to a local area network through a single point.

It may also serve as a spoke—a configuration that improves the reliability of Ethernet systems that were previously connected in a chain and failed every time there was a break in the chain.

## hybrid

A technology resulting from the convergence of two systems or technologies.

Examples are the set-top box, which involves television circuitry and a computer; a platform that can run multiple operating systems, like Macintosh and Windows; and a network that uses fiber-optic cable for its main arteries and existing copper and coaxial cable to branch off to individual systems or homes.
+ See also cross platform.

## hybrid fiber coax (HFC)

Telephone industry term for broadband network combining standard cable television transmission components (like coaxial cable, amplifiers, and power supplies) with optical transmitters and receivers.  In the cable industry, HFC is also referred to as FTF (fiber-to-the-feeder) or FSA (fiber-to-the-serving area).

HFC defines a network featuring optical fiber from a central office or head-end location to a neighborhood of 500 homes or fewer.  Thereafter, the signal is delivered by coaxial cable.  The HFC is sometimes a parallel network to a separate telephone network.

In other cases, the HFC replaces the existing **twisted-pair** telephone network, offering services over a single physical infrastructure.

## HyperCard

A software program, developed by Apple, allowing fairly easy **programming** using the organizing structure of a stack of cards; based on **hypertext**.

In simple HyperCard programming, you either flip through the cards (each can have sound, pictures, text, and/or choice buttons) in sequence, or jump from one card to another. To program a more sophisticated interface or greater interaction with the cards, another programming language is necessary. HyperCard was part of Apple's campaign to demystify programming, and in the early days of the Macintosh computer, it was distributed free as a programming "starter kit."

✚ See also **authoring**.

## hyperlink

Programming that lets you jump from one site or source of information to another on a network, notably the **World Wide Web**.

For example, say you're in a Web site about California, and the term *San Diego* is highlighted. If you click on it, it will bring up a different home page with detailed information about San Diego. There is almost always a hyperlink to click you back to the original home page.

✚ See also **code**.

## hypermap

An **interactive multimedia** map with hyperlinks that allow exploration of a place in depth.

It may include a **geographical information system (GIS)** or function as a guide book, with expert **agents** leading your **virtual** journey across a city, around the globe, or through the Milky Way.

## hypermedia

A **hypertext** system that can display multimedia in addition to text; often used interchangeably with **interactive multimedia**.

## hyper-movies

✚ See **interactive movies**.

### Hypertalk

Scripting language used by HyperCard.

### hypertext

A method of organizing information retrieval that brings together related material.

Hypertext lets a user access words and sections in various, scattered documents or files without having to shut the file the user is in. For example, World Wide Web, as a hypertext program, connects all the bits and pieces of related information from files all over the world and brings them together in a "web" of links. Hypertext was conceived in 1965 by Ted Nelson, the visionary who spent the next three decades trying to design Xanadu, a worldwide hypertext system abandoned in 1992 by Autodesk Systems. That same year, CERN's Web software was distributed over the Internet, effectively realizing the first incarnation of Nelson's dream.

In a hypertext environment, for instance, if you want to study palm trees, you also could go to other files to see how they evolved, what other animals evolved alongside them, what roles coconuts have played in world history, the architecture of palm-thatched houses, their use as an icon of Los Angeles, and where you can find palms growing in an oasis—all without ever closing any of the files you opened.

### hypertext markup language (html)

Language used to create hypertext links in World Wide Web documents; a necessity for any document display on the Web.

### hypertext transport protocol (http)

The connection protocol and its software for the World Wide Web.

Distributed as freeware, it allows a user, through links in a hypertext document, to shift to another document that could be located in a host thousands of miles away.

 See also **secure HTTP**.

### Hz

 See **hertz**.

# IC to iway

## IC

+ See **integrated circuit**.

## ICMP

+ See **Internet control message protocol**.

## icon

A small picture or symbol representing a computer program, file, or feature.

As the foundation of a **graphical user interface (GUI)** system, icons let you to point and click on the screen and call up whatever program or file available. In the go-go world of electronics, the once-simple icon already has a number of brethren:

Ink Pad

Images courtesy of Apple Computer, Inc.

- micon—a motion icon or an animated icon, used to signify that a process is under way, such as Macintosh's moving clock face.

- picon—elaborate icon, more like a small illustration than a symbol.

- tricon—an animated, three-dimensional icon, such as Macintosh's rotating globe.

- cuecon—a more simplistic form of icon, such as an arrow, that prompts you to follow a path to a particular part of the screen.

+ See also **interface**.

## IEEE

+ See **Institute of Electrical and Electronics Engineers**.

## IEEE 802

A **standard** for managing a network that provides for compatibility between network components made by different manufacturers.

Written by the **Institute of Electrical and Electronics Engineers**, Standard 802.1 covers network management and related items, and standard 802.2 specifies the data link layer for various access methods. IBM uses this standard with its token ring products.

## image processing

Alteration of a computer image, using techniques to highlight or filter out certain attributes.

It is required for providing satellite images that can be appreciated by most people.

## imaging

Capturing and displaying a nonmoving picture (image), in digital form, on film or an electronic file.

The term *imaging system* refers to the software and equipment used to put images into digital format, or to compress, store, or retrieve an image. Examples of imaging equipment are scanners, digital optical recorders, and digital still video cameras.

## immersive display VR

Virtual reality technology that uses head-mounted displays and sensors attached to the body to "immerse" a user totally into a virtual world.

## independent telephone company (ITC)

One of the approximately 1,400 private telephone companies not affiliated with any Bell telephone company.

ITCs are small, local operations. Some cover a lot of real estate, but most of it is sparsely populated. ITCs serve more than half of the United States' geographic area, yet only 15 percent of the country's telephones. Still, that is a significant share, and many Americans don't even know ITCs exist. Did you?

✦ See also **Bell operating company (BOC)** and **regional Bell operating company (RBOC)**.

## industrial revolution

The 100-year social and technological upheaval begun in England with the harnessing of hydroelectric and coal-fired power, and the automation of mechanical tasks such as weaving cloth and moving heavy objects.

## infobahn

Colloquial (and trendy) synonym for the information superhighway; derived from *autobahn*, German for expressway.

# Nearing The End Of The Industrial Era

In the second half of the 1700s, machines began to augment human labor. The crucial technical development was the invention of the steam engine by James Watt in Britain in 1769. For the next 100 years, mechanization would change the nature of labor. Although the historical period known as the Industrial Revolution came to a close by the late 1800s, the forces it set in motion continued to drive an ever-faster, bigger, and more complex industrial era.

The scheduling of manufacturing became highly defined and critical to success. The concentration of workers and manufacturing processes brought millions to the cities. Railroads tied resources, workers, cities, and markets ever more tightly together.

Eventually, internal combustion engines would lead to a flying machine. New industries developed, based on electric generation. And the availability of light gasoline engines and inexpensive steel brought about interlocking industries such as autos and aircraft.

Motor vehicle manufacture transformed the lives of people, the economy of industrialized nations, and the habits of industry through mass production. As business became all-powerful in the early 1900s, it permanently altered social and political alignments.

The invention of the telephone and the use of radio waves for broadcasting brought culmination to the Industrial Revolution. With the invention of the computer and electronics, manufacturing became less of a focus, and information became the most highly prized commodity in the economy. The Information Age was born late in the twentieth century. The interplay between technical invention, economic exploitation, and social transformation that informed the Industrial Revolution continues in the Information Age.

## Information Age

Term describing the close of the twentieth century, when telecommunications, computers, and the exchange of information have become the life-blood of the economy and leading drivers of social change.

## information provider

A business that provides information for a fee. Also known as an *information vendor*.

It's a service, such as a 900 telephone number, whereby you select information such as weather reports, sports scores, stock prices, and psychic pre-dictions by using a key pad. You receive an answer and pay by the minute. Information providers use on-line services to supply myriad products and ser-vices including music, news, video clips, encyclope-dias, research data, hardware and software support, and airline reservations. The subscriber receives the information either as part of a monthly fee paid to the on-line service or for an additional charge paid via credit card to the information provider.

## information superhighway

Vision of a worldwide telecommunications network linking all personal, public, and commercial comput-ers and their peripherals.

It was first promulgated by United States Vice President Al Gore, and later by his boss, Bill Clinton. And has been designated cyberspace as the place where the transactions of modern life take place—business, education, politics, health care, research, entertainment, even social interaction. The concept gained popularity in Bill Clinton's first days as presi-dent, when he and his VP acknowledged the impor-tance of the Internet.

By comparing this electronic network to the road system built in the United States after World War II, the government indicated its unique ability to link together the entire country and open up new areas for development. The telecommunica-tions, cable television, and computer industries are eagerly merging and converging in order to provide the infrastructure.

Can you imagine life now without telephones, tele-visions, or computers? In the future you may find it hard to imagine what life was like without the

*"The semiconductor is the V-8 engine of the information superhigh-way."*

—**Vice President Al Gore**

[Stephan Ohr, "Somebody up there likes us…I think; Mixed-Signal Design; Column" *Computer Design*, May, 1994, Sec: Vol. 33; No. 6; p. 118]

*"Ronald Reagan used Star Wars to bring down Communism. Now Al Gore is using the same tactics with the information super-highway to gain con-trol of our culture."*

—*French film (Diva) director* **Jean Jacques Beineix**

[Mavis Clarence, "Warning lights on infobahn," *The Hollywood Reporter*, Friday, 24 February 1995.]

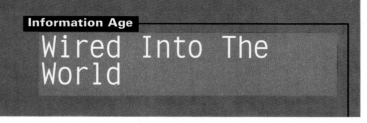

# Wired Into The World

Once upon a time, when you wanted information, you went to a library or looked in the Yellow Pages. Now, a cornucopia of information is available at your fingertips, and a plethora of work and leisure activities are *defined* in terms of information.

The capture, manipulation, and transmission of information— whatever the business, art, or science to which it relates—has assumed center stage in the U.S. and world economy. The technology of the Information Age has touched us all.

In the late twentieth century, the digitization and networking of information that has been made possible by the computer promises to radically transform all aspects of our lives. Reading, watching movies, making telephone calls, and listening to music will no longer be done with individual technologies. They will converge into a single, continuous form of media. And virtual re-creations will be instantly available whenever and wherever we want.

Business is rapidly becoming virtual, too. Whole layers of middle management are gone. More and more, the exchange of products and services takes place electronically, and ever-faster. In the industrial economy, people worked at producing goods. In the information economy, people work at producing and processing information.

A digitized world will involve the majority of the work force in the production of information. Goods will no longer be mass-produced but created as, and where, required. As the Information Age matures, low-cost, high-speed transmission capacity—wired and wireless—will also change the communications industries beyond recognition.

The computer's infinite malleability is making it invisible, embedded throughout the environment—in appliances, walls, telephones, cars, video games, theme parks, even clothing. And the self-contained computer is rapidly metamorphosing into the network.

In the postindustrial world, the universal language of machines is 1s and 0s. For business, mastery of digital information will determine success or failure. For ordinary citizens, low-cost, high-speed communications will make contact instant all around planet earth—the saving grace and destiny of citizenship in the global village.

immediacy of the information superhighway that connects you to the rest of the world.

## information theory

Mathematical model of information leading to applications such as data compression.

Developed in 1948 by Bell Labs' mathematician Claude Shannon, the "Mathematical Theory of Communication" provides a philosophy of information from the point of view of communications. It also offers a mathematical model of information and a mathematical measure of the information capacity of a communications channel.

His breakthrough definition of *information* was "the resolution of uncertainty." Shannon saw that the key to measuring information was in the answer to the question, "How much do we need to know to resolve uncertainty?" Or, put another way: "What is the minimum number of yes/no questions required on average to obtain the given data?"

Many practical applications have arisen from information theory, including new ways to compress data. Information sent over telephone, computer, and cable television channels has a high degree of predictability. By assigning codes to letters, colors, and sounds that accommodate certainty and uncertainty factors, a message can be compressed to facilitate transport and decompressed by computers at the destination.

## information vendor

✦ See **information provider**.

## infotainment

"Informative entertainment"—a genre of multimedia that presents educational information in an entertaining interactive format, usually CD-ROM.

## INMARSAT

✦ See **International Maritime Satellite Organization**.

## input/output (I/O)

(1) The entry or extraction of data into a computer or device. (2) The circuitry in a computer that receives data or instructions and transfers them in the proper form to the CPU.

Once processing is done, the I/O transfers the results back out of the system to the user.

## Institute of Electrical and Electronics Engineers (IEEE)

Referred to as "I-triple-E," the global professional association of electrical and electronics engineers.

These are the designers and fabricators of all the hardware and much of the software that bounds and underpins cyberspace. IEEE is the publisher of standards for many telecommunications and computing applications.

Logo courtesy of IEEE

## integrated circuit (IC)

Complete electronic circuit— including transistors, capacitors, resistors, and all the connections between them—miniaturized and integrated on a single semiconductor base, usually silicon. Lovingly called the computer chip.

Invented in 1958 and a precursor of the modern computer, it can store millions of bits of information in a space smaller than your fingernail.

✚ See also **microprocessor and transputer.**

## integrated services digital network (ISDN)

High-speed transmission of any digitized signal— whether voice, video or data—directly over telephone lines at four times the currently highest modem speeds.

ISDN offers efficient use of bandwidth and end-to-end digital transmission of two channels of 64 kbps each, using existing telephone lines. It also combines voice and digital network services in a single medium, making it possible to offer digital data services, as well as voice connections, through a single connection.

Though video may be transmitted by ISDN, high-resolution video cannot be transmitted without a fiber-optic infrastructure. Although about half the cities in the U.S. have ISDN capability already, the major impediment to widespread acceptance of ISDN is that the cost of ISDN terminal equipment, and of upgrading central office equipment, is high.

ISDN is also a set of standards that describe how all this wonderful transmission takes place.

✚ See also **Broadband Integrated Services Digital Network (B-ISDN).**

## intellectual property

Data, information, or ideas that can be used to create, design, or build an item that has economic value.

Examples: Software, patents, texts, manuals, blueprints, databases, formulas, manufacturing specifications. Intellectual property, despite copyright and patents, is easy to steal. In cyberspace, data can be moved around the world on telephone lines without the owner ever knowing—or receiving royalties for its use.

The challenge of protecting intellectual property—and defining its proper boundaries in patent law—is crucial to the future of the information industries and international trade.

## intelligent

Describes devices such as printers and computers that are able to process data.

The term does not necessarily imply artificial intelligence.

## interactive

Computers, games, multimedia systems, and other hardware that responds in different ways depending on the actions of you, the user.

The system's response is directly communicated to the user.

## interactive advertising

Promotion of products over networks, where the user selects product descriptions and orders what he or she desires.

Television home shopping channels and point-of-sale kiosks are early examples. Payment usually requires a telephone and credit card. Through the use of hypermedia, virtual reality, three-dimensional graphics, and simulation techniques consumers may soon shop at personal virtual shopping malls, tailored to a users' specific desires. A wider range of goods—and therefore choices—will be available.

The downside in this consumer-topia is electronic junk mail and potential privacy violations. For the advertiser, the virtual mall provides an innovative way to present products, target customers more precisely, and get immediate feedback on consumer preferences.

## interactive broadcast TV

Two-way real-time dialogue with a television program, combining broadcast television with another communication component—usually the telephone.

Viewers participate by feeding their answers via modem to a central computer. Most programming of this sort has been limited to game shows. Future developments may include electronic opinion polls, interactive advertising, and interactive movies. Nevertheless, interactive broadcast television may be an interim phenomenon. Future high-definition systems and the teleputer linked to a fiber-optic distribution channel will likely supersede it.

## interactive cable TV

Two-way cable television network that allows viewers to participate in quiz shows, game shows, and sports events, among others.

For example, in live coverage of a baseball game, viewers could choose one of four different camera views, each narrowcast simultaneously in a window on the main screen. They could also send in their vote for the MVP of the game.

Already being tested in certain communities by industry giants such as Time Warner, Microsoft, Bell Atlantic, and GTE, interactive television currently requires fiber-optic cabling to individual homes. For this to be nationwide, an estimated $120 billion investment in infrastructure would be needed.

✦ See also **branching** and **interactive broadcast TV**.

## interactive movie

A movie in which the viewers determine the course of action.

They do this by making decisions at key points or by choosing the point of view of a particular character in a fixed narrative.

Several factors will determine the fate of interactive movies, including hardware systems, distribution media, and the culture of television and movie viewing. First, double- and quad-density CD-ROMs will increase storage capacity. Later, fiber-optic networks will deliver both linear and interactive movies directly to a teleputer.

This technology will eventually support hypermovies that combine virtual reality, expert systems, and real-time computer graphics to provide an environment where the viewer wanders through the movie at will interacting with the characters. However, the movie viewing experience may, for some time, remain resistant to technological tinkering with the ritual of linear story-telling. The absence of stars other than B-movie regulars in current interactive fare suggests a resistance among the members of the Hollywood establishment as well.

## interactive multimedia

Computer-based programs that incorporate audio, video, animation, still images, photographs, and text—all controlled by the user.

Directory-style databases—information and reference works—lend themselves to the interactive multimedia format. Training and educational programs, remote catalog shopping, and many entertainment programs are available on CD-ROM and videodisk, the most common distribution channels for interactive multimedia now.

In the future, telecommunications and computer services, such as the telephone, videophone, videoconferencing, expert systems, and virtual reality will combine to create interactive entertainment.

## interactive video (IV)

User-controlled video; video whose program path can be affected by viewer choice.

+ See also interactive multimedia.

## interactive visualization

A program in which you interact directly with a computer.

When you play chess against a computer, you are engaging in interactive visualization. You enter a command and the display indicates the result. The computer responds, and you make your next move based on the response.

## interface

(1) Where man and machine meet; the interface for a computer is its screen. (2) The hardware that connects different devices, such as a computer and its printer.

## interlace

Pattern of interlocking scan lines of two separate video fields that join to form a complete video frame. (For details, see cathode ray tube.)

## INTER-LATA

✦ See Inter-Local Access and Transport Area.

## interleaving

Alternating parts of one sequence of data with parts of another sequence of the same type of data.

Some systems store audio, image, or text data by sending alternating segments of items to different parts of the storage medium. When a particular item is retrieved, the system puts the right segments back together again. It makes for more efficient storage.

✦ See also compact disk-interactive (CD-I) and compact disk read-only memory extended architecture (CD-ROM XA).

## Inter-Local Access and Transport Area (INTER-LATA)

Mind-boggling term of the phone industry that basically means the phone traffic controlled by a long-distance carrier.

✦ See also local access and transport area (LATA) (if you really want to).

## International Maritime Satellite Organization (INMARSAT)

British company that provides international satellite telecommunications for ships, airplanes, and people in remote places on the globe.

It uses geostationary satellites for transmitting voice and fax signals.

## International Standards Organization (ISO)

Nonprofit organization founded in 1946 to develop international standards.

Among them is the open systems interconnection protocol suite, which competes successfully with the Internet protocols in Europe. ANSI is the U.S. representative of ISO.

## International Telecommunications Union, Telecommunication Sector (ITU-TS)

The body that recommends specs for telecommunications devices and systems. ITU-TS is based in Geneva.

These devices and systems, from modems to ISDN, are the ones most often adopted by manufacturers. Until recently, it was known as the Comite Consultatif Internationale de Telegraphique et Telephonique (CCITT).

## internet

The linkage of two or more computer networks, connected by a common communications protocol.

## Internet

Nirvana of the Nineties.

The largest worldwide electronic network, interconnecting thousands of smaller networks and millions of computer users.

## Internet control message protocol (ICMP)

A protocol used to manage errors and control messages at the Internet protocol layer.

## Internet protocol (IP)

Type of numeric address the Internet needs to send the streams of packets that carry E-mail and other data between computers.

## internet relay chat (IRC)

Chat service on the Internet, available by telnetting to an IRC server.

IRC allows many people to talk electronically with each other in real time. It's like CB radio via a keyboard. When connected to an IRC, the user decides what channel to tune in to. There are scores of special discussion groups, ranging from Rush Limbaugh's latest rantings and ravings to "cybergrouping" in the hot tub.

Though these chat lines tend to veer far from scholarly discussion, "cybervets" point with pride to the IRC use during the Moscow uprising in 1993 against the Boris Yeltsin regime, and the timely, up-to-the-minute reports those Russian commentators were able to broadcast thanks to the IRC.

# How The Internet Works

The Internet has emerged as a massive, rapidly growing global universe of computer space in a relatively short time. In 1969, an obscure Department of Defense agency—the Advanced Research Projects Agency—realized the need for a simple-to-use means of exchanging military-supported information between scientists and researchers at facilities far from each other. Arpanet, a simple network of four computers, was their solution. The rest, as they say, is history. (If you want to know that history, see *The Evolution of the Net*.)

The Internet's growth challenges the imagination. The number of sites on its interconnected worldwide networks jumped from two million in 1994 to five million in 1995. Users numbered roughly 40 million, as of the summer of 1995. Argentina went from a single site in 1994 to 1,415 in 1995. And Japan leapt from 38,267 to 99,034.

The transparency and speed by which these networks and sites can exchange information results from the Internet's technical means: TCP/IP protocols that can be used on different kinds of nets, from local area networks such as Ethernet to metropolitan area networks to the backbones that carry Internet data across the continent and overseas. The data travel on a variety of media: telephone wires, fiber-optic cable, communications satel-lites, and microwave relay systems. Before long, it may also use the gigabyte networks proposed by the Clinton Administration and others for the National Information Infrastructure. So the Internet is not a single thing; it's a collection of other nets and the tons of information on them.

To be on the Internet, you can pay a local provider who man-ages a server that connects you. Many freenets and on-line ser-vices can put you onto the Net, too. The cost of all these options is reasonable. Organizations can lease their own direct line for a few thousand dollars. With an internal local area net-work, every employee or member then gets access through that leased line. For schools, colleges, and others wanting to get more out of their own computer systems, the Internet is a pow-erful tool.

The concept of the information superhighway is founded on the viability of the Internet. Though the terms *information superhighway* and *Internet* are often used interchangeably, the two are not the same. The information superhighway does not yet exist.

## Internet Society (ISOC)

Nonprofit group for the voluntary connection of computer networks into a global communications and information infrastructure.

It was founded in 1992 and is based in Reston, Virginia.

## interpretability

(1) In telecommunications, the ability to inter-operate between networks of different kinds.

(2) Capacity of an application or other program to work on many different platforms.

## Intra-Local Access and Transport Area (INTRA-LATA)

Telecommunications services, revenues, and functions that originate and terminate within a local or regional area.

In short, the local phone company.

+ See also Inter-Local Access and Transport Area (Inter-LATA) and local access and transport area (LATA).

## intranet

An internal communications network that allows all the people within a company or organization to access information and transmit documents in the same way that these tasks are done on the Internet and the World Wide Web.

The purpose is to let company employees, for example, work with each other using the same familiar protocols they use when on the Internet or the Web. Also, an intranet can easily be linked to the Internet and the Web, so that outsiders can access the company's network with their standard Internet or Web software.

## I/O

+ See input/output.

## IP

+ See Internet protocol.

## IRC

+ See internet relay chat.

## Iridium

A satellite network planned by Motorola.

Plans for the network, named after the 77-proton element, have has been reduced to a still-impressive array of 66 satellites. Iridium will allow a user to make a telephone call from the top of Mount Everest, or receive a fax at the South Pole, feats not presently possible except via the rarest and most expensive military communications equipment.

Its financing is secured, and launch contracts with the Russians and Americans have been signed. When Iridium is activated in 1998, users will carry global communicators that are smaller than today's cellular telephones. The cost of service will be high—possibly $3 per minute—but the capability will be unprecedented.

✚ See also **LEOS**.

## ISDN

✚ See **Integrated Services Digital Network**.

## ISO

✚ See **International Standards Organization**.

## ISOC

✚ See **Internet Society**.

## ITC

✚ See **Independent Telephone Company**.

## ITU-TS

✚ See **International Telecommunications Union, Telecommunication Sector**.

## IV

✚ See **interactive video**.

## iway

Shorthand for the information superhighway.

Could also be part of Australian movie character Crocodile Dundee's plea to get home from his favorite bar in the Outback. "Ay, mates, I'd like to catch a ride down the iway ta town. C'mon, I'll throw some shrimp on the bar-b."

# ISDN

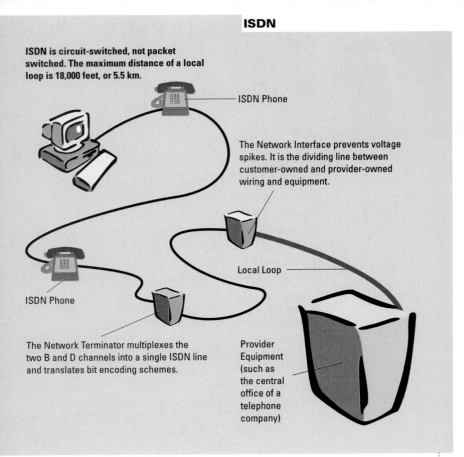

ISDN is circuit-switched, not packet switched. The maximum distance of a local loop is 18,000 feet, or 5.5 km.

ISDN Phone

The Network Interface prevents voltage spikes. It is the dividing line between customer-owned and provider-owned wiring and equipment.

Local Loop

ISDN Phone

The Network Terminator multiplexes the two B and D channels into a single ISDN line and translates bit encoding schemes.

Provider Equipment (such as the central office of a telephone company)

# ℐ jaggies to jukebox

Janson

## jaggies

Slang to describe the unwanted visual effect of jagged edges along what's supposed to be a smooth surface.

Jaggies show up on curved lines, say along the letters O or S. On diagonal lines, they look like saw blades or stair steps.

✦ See also **aliasing, anti-aliasing,** and **vector graphics.**

## Java

A programming language developed by Sun Microsystems that enables you to create animations and interactive features on your own World Wide Web home page.

Java is akin to the popular C and C++ programming languages, but without many of the complexities. To use Java, you log on to the Internet, find a Java application server, and download a Java application onto your computer. You use the specific application on your computer while the main Java program remains on the server. As of 1996, Sun also began selling full-blown, stand-alone software applications written in Java. One of them is HotJava, a browser for the Web.

✦ See also **applet**.

## Jobs, Steve

Cofounder of Apple Computer (with Steve Wozniak) in 1975.

He introduced the Macintosh in 1984, which many believe was a pivotal moment in the acceptance of the personal computer by the masses. He left Apple shortly thereafter—in fact, was forced out by the chairman, John Sculley, whom he had recruited in 1983. In 1985 Jobs founded NeXT Inc., the builder of unusual black cube workstations.

Steve Wozniak and Steve Jobs.
Photo courtesy of Apple Computers, Inc.

## Joe

Name given by crackers to a UNIX system account where people's own first names serve as passwords.

Computer criminals love Joe accounts because they are so easy to break in to.

## joint photographic experts group (JPEG)

Image compression standard for still photographs (pronounced "jay peg").

To represent a photo using less data, compression software segments the picture into blocks and computes an average value for each block. To retrieve the photograph, the process is reversed. When creating a JPEG file, you can choose different levels of compression in order to display more or less of the original quality of the photograph. JPEG compression ratios vary between 7:1 and 50:1.

## joystick

Small hand grip, like the stick shift in a car, widely used to play arcade games and video games.

The joystick moves a car, plane, basketball player, and many other objects on the screen. Often has a button on top to instruct the object to shoot, fire, jump, and so on.

## JPEG

✦ See **joint photographic experts group**.

## Jughead

A program that helps you find directories when operating in the Gopher mode on the Internet.

Stands for: Jonzy's Universal Gopher Hierarchy Excavation And Display software. Word has it there is no Jonzy—it just makes for a convenient acronym.

## jukebox

Machine that holds and plays many disks—vinyl records, videodisks, or compact disks.

For the conventional kind, pop in a quarter, pick your song, and it plays. A fixture of the '50s, it made a comeback in 1994 with Joe Diffie's hit country single, "Prop Me Up (beside the juke box when I die)."

*"What's going to happen in the next 10 to 20 years? I don't know. I know that computers are getting dramatically faster and a lot of that speed is going to be put into intensive graphics and communication. Whereas the '80s was the decade that personal computing became pervasive, the '90s will be the decade everybody gets connected."*

**— Steve Jobs**

[Steve Jobs, interviewed by James Daly, *Computerworld*, 22 June 1992, p.8]

# Kapor to knowledge-based system

## Kapor, Mitch

Founder of Lotus Development Corporation.

Kapor was co-designer of Lotus 1-2-3, the most successful computer application of all time. It set the standard for all spreadsheet programs. He retired from Lotus in 1986 and became chairman of On Technology Inc. Also in 1990 he cofounded the **Electronic Frontier Foundation**.

> "There's one area I think technology can have a big impact in: helping people form communities. It might be disabled people finding out they are not alone. Or it might be Star Trek fans /or disabled Star Trek fans. Name a human attribute, characteristic, interest, avocation, and there's probably already a bulletin board devoted to it. Coin collectors. Left-handed libertarians. Greenpeace. Neo-Nazis. Technology doesn't discriminate."
>
> — *Mitch Kapor*
> [Mitch Kapor, interview by Joseph Maglitta, *Computerworld*, 22 June 1992, p. 46].

## Kay, Alan

Head of the research team at **Xerox PARC** in the 1960s, where a great deal of the innovation that led to the personal computer took place.

Among other successes, the team developed the user-interface concepts that were adopted for the Apple Macintosh. Kay also designed the Dynabook, a precursor of **notebook computers**, and invented Smalltalk, a groundbreaking **object-oriented programming** language.

> "Aldus Manutius was the one who decided that books should be the size they are today—not big things like the Gutenberg Bible—because they could fit into a saddlebag. Making a small book did not seem that significant to me in 1965, but it became significant later when I saw Seymour Papert's work (with LOGO programming language for children). That's when I was struck by the idea that the computer isn't a vehicle...

## Kbps

Abbreviation for kilobits (one thousand bits) per second.

✚ See also **bits per second**.

## KBS

✚ See **knowledge-based system**.

## key

A computer code needed to unscramble an encrypted message.

When someone encrypts a message, they design a short bit of data that must be unlocked before the message can be read. The recipient of the message has to enter the right key, or the message remains as comprehensible as a United Nations' peace plan for Bosnia.

✚ See also **encryption** and **privacy**.

## key escrow

Placing the key for an encrypted communication or software program in safekeeping so only the government can get it, and then only if a court agrees it is necessary.

The idea is to allow the private development, sales, and export of advanced encryption (secret code) programs while still ensuring that the government can decipher any coded communications if there is just cause to suspect illegal activity. In September 1995 the Clinton Administration proposed this policy to the National Institute of Standards and Technology. Some privacy advocates oppose any such proposals that would aid the government in network wiretapping.

✚ See also **Clipper chip**.

## key frame

(1) In computer animation, the first frame of each scene change. (2) In hypermedia, indicator of branches in the user's path. (3) In video compression schemes, the only frame that holds complete video information.

✚ See also **full-screen full-motion video (FSFMV)** and **interactive multimedia**.

## keyboard

If you are reading this book, you probably have one. These days, computer keyboards have the standard typewriter keys plus programmable ones that enable you to carry out a sequence of steps with just one keystroke. The standard English language keyboard is known as a QWERTY—which stands for the first six letter keys at the top left. There are other keyboards for languages using other characters, and even some that are broken into two or three pieces that can be moved around your desk for more comfortable typing. From time to time some tinkerer designs a keyboard with a different layout of letters that supposedly makes more sense, but people are so ingrained with the standard layout that the renegades never make it commercially.

## keyword searching

Hunting for information in a database, using the most prominent words in a subject being researched or accessed.

Keyword searching is the easiest way of finding information in large databases; if you want information on OJ, enter "orange juice" and the database will find all references with it. Most keyword search functions allow the use of Boolean logic terms to narrow the search. So if you get 650 articles that contain the words "orange juice," you can try again by entering "orange juice and milk," or "orange juice and milk not Simpson." Subjects that are not word-based—such as large video libraries or collections of sounds—defy keyword searches.

## kill

To program your computer to exclude certain subjects, words, phrases, or individuals from the list of articles that are automatically collected and displayed on your screen when in Usenet.

Killing certain newsgroup writers or topics is a frustration-saver. You won't be tempted to respond with a flame to statements you think are absurd or moronic, and—as a result—won't open yourself to a mail bombing that suggests you have no more respect for free speech than George Steinbrenner. You can keep a list of kill terms or names in a kill file.

## killer app

Abbreviation for "killer application"—a creative, breakthrough software program that is so awesome it drives demand for the hardware that runs it.

Over the years, killer apps have set off major market changes. Examples are VisiCalc and Lotus 1-2-3, which bolstered development of better mathematical capabilities of PCs, and Pong and Pac-Man, which created the video game craze.

After the initial killer app helps create the market, subsequent apps often make a killing that most marketers would kill to get their hands on. The CD-ROM game "Myst" and Internet browsers such as Mosaic and Netscape are success stories that every software company dreams of emulating.

## kill file

✦ See kill.

## kilo

Prefix indicating one thousand; five kilohertz is five thousand hertz.

## kiosk

Self-contained, free-standing system used in public areas such as shopping malls and airports to provide product information.

Marketers call this a point-of-purchase or point-of-information program because it is placed in a strategic location to influence a customer to buy goods available right there. Originally, a kiosk referred to a small, enclosed vending station from which newspapers, magazines, cigarettes, and candy were sold, but the term now also has a "cyber" meaning.

**kiosk**

A wall-mounted kiosk

## kludge

A method used to repair bugs that do not follow standard engineering approaches.

Pronounced "kloodj," it is an ironic use of the German word for *clever*. It relates to software or hardware fixes that solve the problem, but in a Rube Goldberg manner or for the wrong reason.

## knowbot

Computer program sent to retrieve specific information. Also known as a softbot.

Knowbot is an independent program, described in cyberspeak as an intelligent agent, that self-destructs when the job's done. The Knowbot Information Service acts as a directory retrieval service for addresses on the Internet.

✚ See also **artificial intelligence** and **telescript**.

## knowledge-based system (KBS)

A software system used in various computing environments that stores, retrieves, and analyzes large amounts of data.

KBS uses "If...then..." rules to increase the intelligence (sophistication) of information processing. It both simplifies and enhances processes such as production scheduling, product design, forecasting, database management, and training and education programs.

✦ See also **artificial intelligence**.

Lemiesz

## LAN

+ See **local area network**.

## language

The nomenclature and system of commands used to write computer software and other programs.

The most fundamental language is machine code: a series of binary digits (1s and 0s) that are combined to spell out instructions and data—not unlike the dots and dashes of Morse code. Machine code is the language that actually instructs the switching of circuits in the computer.

One step up from machine code is assembly language, a low-level symbolic language that must be translated—or "assembled"—into machine code. Assembly language has some bearing to spoken language, executes quickly, and takes up the least storage space. However, it is difficult and time-consuming to write. A higher-level language such as C++—closer to the languages humans speak—is preferred. When using a high-level language, a compiler program translates the instructions into machine code.

> "The day is coming very fast when every cop will be issued a badge, a gun, and a laptop."
>
> — **Charles Rinkevich**, director, Federal Law Enforcement Training Center
> [Vic Sussman, "Policing cyberspace," *U.S. News & World Report*, 23 January 1995, Vol. 118, No. 3, p. 54.]

## laptop

Computer that is portable enough to be used (surprise!) on your lap.

+ See also **personal computer**.

## laser

+ See **light amplification through stimulated emissions of radiation**.

## laser disk

Platter like a compact disk that stores information optically to be read by a laser beam.

The distinction is that laser discs are usually larger than CDs, and they are mostly used for storage and playback of video and audio together, such as movies. They are also used in special applications to store computer data.

## LaserDisk

Trademark of Pioneer Electronics USA, for its optical videodisk products, many of which are available in the remainder bins at local video stores.

## LaserVision

Reflective optical videodisk format developed by NV Philips.

## last mile problem

Phrase used to describe the roadblock to delivering high-bandwidth digital networking to homes, schools, and offices.

The real limiting factors to the information super-highway are the final off-ramps. A high-bandwidth backbone of fiber-optic and coaxial cable already exists nationwide. But at some point this great infrastructure has to be connected to each house and building.

About two-thirds of American homes have two last-mile delivery systems: a twisted-pair telephone line and an analog coaxial cable for cable television. Twisted-pair cannot carry enough bandwidth to support an integrated services digital network (ISDN) capable of delivering multimedia, and coaxial cable has its own limitations. To exchange these for fiber-optic cable—the ideal solution—would cost well over $100 billion nationally.

Coaxial cable coupled with analog-to-digital signaling (which the phone companies are expected to adopt early in the next century) are the most likely solutions to the last mile problem, and will probably accompany mergers of regional phone companies and cable television providers.

## LATA

✚ See **local access** and **transport area**.

## layer

(1) In communications, a protocol working together with other protocols to provide transmission services. (2) In computer graphics, a drawing board on the screen that you use to create a picture. (3) In desserts, seven layers creates a nice cake.

## LBE

+ See **location-based entertainment**.

## LCD

+ See **liquid crystal display**.

## LEOS

+ See **low earth orbit satellite**.

## light amplification through stimulated emissions of radiation (laser)

Narrow, finely focused beam of coherent light, generated at a single frequency.

Strictly speaking, a laser is the mechanical device that actually generates the light. The light itself is the laser beam, which can traverse great distances with little loss of power.

From bar code readers at supermarket checkout counters to **compact disk** players and surgical tools, lasers are part of everyday life. They have been functionally integrated into computers in optical devices such as laser printers and hand **scanners** for importing graphic images, and lie at the heart of every **fiber-optic** telephone line and network **backbone**.

+ See also **compact disk read-only memory (CD-ROM)**, **digital optical recording**, and **LaserVision**.

## linear video

A video that you view and move forward in a linear way—your basic rented movie.

Nonlinear video enables you to jump around from one clip to another while editing or interacting, as in a **CD-ROM**– or **videodisk**-based game.

+ See also **full-motion video**.

## link

(1) In communications, a line or channel that you transmit data over. (2) In data management, a connection made in **hypertext** between documents. (3) In programming, the calling up of another program or subroutine.

If you open the Martha's Vineyard home page on the **World Wide Web**, for example, you can click on a link to reserve a room at an Edgartown bed-and-breakfast, and another to view the ferry schedule from the Massachusetts mainland. (There is no link that will get Carly Simon to join you for a sunset cruise, however.)

## liquid crystal display (LCD)

Display screen made from liquid crystals, used in calculators, digital clocks, and laptop computers.

For decades after the first radars and TVs, the "screen" was always one thing—a cathode ray tube. But work in the 1970s led to the LCD. It used much less power, and had much less bulk and weight than a CRT. But because it did not have fine resolution or full-color capability, it was limited to small displays such as those in clocks or digital watches. By the 1980s, higher resolution, greater brightness, and full-color capabilities were perfected. It made possible a small, light computer—the laptop. It can now be scaled up further, and may

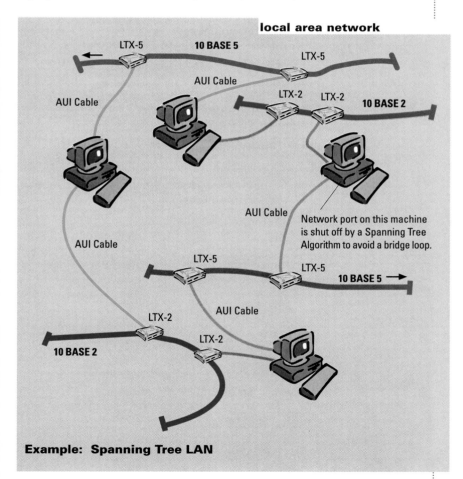

**local area network**

Network port on this machine is shut off by a Spanning Tree Algorithm to avoid a bridge loop.

**Example: Spanning Tree LAN**

become the technology of choice for large, flat-panel TVs used for HDTV.

## lit fiber

✦ See **dark fiber**.

## local access and transport area (LATA)

One of 200 geographic local telephone calling areas in the United States.

It's a consequence of the AT&T Consent Decree, which separated local and long-distance service.

✦ See also **Inter-Local Access and Transport Area (Inter-LATA)** and **Intra-Local Access and Transport Area (Intra-LATA)**.

## local area network (LAN)

A network, such as an Ethernet, connecting computers in a close area, such as a skyscraper, office building, or college library.

The computers share information through a cable that links them together.

✦ See also **integrated services digital network (ISDN)** and **wide area network (WAN)**.

## local loop

Wires that run from a subscriber's telephones to the telephone company's central office.

## location-based entertainment (LBE)

Dedicated rooms or environments featuring devices such as special wrap-around movie displays, motion platform rides, and immersive interactive games.

An outgrowth of experimentation in simulation rides and immersive display VR technologies, LBEs range in size from small virtual reality installations in shopping malls to the arena-sized ShowScan immersive movie displays at the new Luxor in Las Vegas.

✦ See also **cafe**.

## log on

The act of connecting to a host computer or network, or public access site.  Also called *log in*.

When you *log off*, you're out of there.

## long distance

Telephone call to a location outside the local service area.

> "The most exciting phrase to hear in science, the one that heralds new discoveries, is not 'Eureka!' but 'That's funny!' "
>
> — *Isaac Asimov*, science fiction writer

# How A LAN Works

Computers connected to a local area network operate as peers. Unlike terminals, which are tied to a mainframe and cannot perform any functions on their own, each computer on a network has its own storage and processing capabilities. Each user controls who can assess the files on her machine, and how. This decentralization may be mitigated by a file server, which will hold resources such as applications and a shared database. Otherwise all users are on their own.

The phenomenon of two workstations trying to access the LAN at the same time is called, aptly enough, *contention*. But the potential traffic jams this structure could create are redirected by a medium access control (MAC) protocol. The first successful MAC protocol was the Ethernet, developed from research conducted in the 1970s at Xerox PARC (Palo Alto Research Center). The Ethernet's contention control protocol is called CSMA/CD, for *carrier sense multiple access with collision detection*, which became the standard IEEE 802.3. Newer MAC protocols include token bus and token ring designs.

The Ethernet design evolved from the Arpanet's packet switching architecture, which gave the Xerox PARC engineers the inspiration to figure out how their own workstations could be connected.

Today, Ethernet packets are given specific addresses, which enables them to be translated into the Internet protocol format and transmitted to computers outside the boundaries of the LAN. As the Internet has grown, so have local area networks. And the prices of the equipment to run them—routers, network cards, file servers, and cable—has dropped. Physically separate LANs may be joined by bridges, devices that can extend a LAN through a corporation's or university's various offices and buildings. And using wide-area network (WAN) connections breaks all geographic barriers, extending a LAN coast-to-coast within an organization.

Long-distance service is offered by long-distance carriers such as AT&T, MCI, and Sprint. With deregulation, long-distance companies can now offer local service, but the AT&T Consent Decree still prohibits the local companies—the regional Bell operating companies—from providing long-distance service in most cases.

## loop transmission facilities

Equipment that connects telephone switching systems to customer phones throughout a local serving area.

## low earth orbit satellites (LEOS)

Global communications satellites in orbit 420 miles above the earth designed to provide global availability of wireless telephone, fax, and paging.

LEOS enable pocket-sized telephones to act as receiving earth stations. Whereas long distance telephone calls made with geostationary satellites are plagued with echo, LEOS conversations have little voice delay.

Motorola's Iridium and Loral and Qualcomm's Globalstar projects will be launching fleets of LEOS beginning in 1997. For worldwide coverage, "constellations" of 48 to 66 LEOS will orbit the earth. LEOS and MEOS—medium earth orbit satellites—are competing with each other to be the first to provide service to PDAs for business travelers as well as to bring telephone service to villages in undeveloped countries.

## machine code

+ See **language**.

## Macintosh

Family of Apple personal computers that first used icons, windows, the mouse, and a user-friendly interface.

Macintosh also referred to the computers' operating system. "The Mac" was introduced in January1984 and touted as "insanely great" by Steven Jobs— the cofounder, along with Steve Wozniak, of Apple Computer. Marketed as "the computer for the rest of us," the Macintosh created the desktop publishing market and awoke the computer world to the value of the graphical user interface. Although the Mac was more expensive than IBM's PC, it set a new standard for ease of use, and enjoyed rapid popularity. Unfortunately for Apple, there were not as many applications developed for the Mac, so a large portion of users stuck with the PC and compatibles. Microsoft subsequently copied the approach a half-dozen years later and released its Windows operating system for the PC and compatibles.

Motion

Photo courtesy of Apple Computers, Inc.

## magnetic storage

Thin, nonelastic plastic tape coated with ferromagnetic emulsion, which can record, store, and play back information on multiple tracks.

An audiocassette tape is the most common form of magnetic storage. It can hold multiple tracks of sound. A VCR videotape holds image information on the primary track and audio and time code on separate tracks. Other magnetic storage media include computer floppy disks and hard disks, credit cards with the black magstripe on the back, and the big, old computer "tapes" that whirred around in jerking, clockwise and counterclockwise motions.

Oh yes, there were those things called 8-track tapes, once, too.

+ See also **flash memory and smart card**.

## magstripe card

Credit card or smart card embedded with a magnetic stripe in which data are encoded.

A magstripe card encoded with your bank account information allows you to retrieve money from an automatic teller machine (ATM) by using a valid personal identification number (PIN).

+ See also **Personal Computer Memory Card International Association (PCMCIA)**.

## mail bombing

Act of flooding a person's E-mail mail box with huge, lengthy files that have nothing to do with each other.

Bombing is a form of electronic harassment that is one (large) step beyond flaming and can, on many systems, result in the cancellation of the bomber's account. Yet another stupid ploy for Net surfers who don't have a life.

© John Dykes/Spots on the Spot!

## mail box

On a network, a storage spot residing in a host computer or server that holds E-mail until it is retrieved by the recipient.

## mailing list

Electronic list analogous to those in the paper world.

It costs almost nothing to send lengthy items to many people. Subscribers to Usenet newsgroups receive postings that are periodically sent to everyone on the newsgroup mailing lists.

## mainframe

Central computer that handles multiple jobs and heavy-duty processing.

Mainframes are linked to terminals that serve individual users. Nickname: big iron.

The term *mainframe* derives from the strong metal racks required in the early days of computing to hold the big, heavy computer components, memory, and cabinets. Mainframe computers are characterized by enormous amounts of RAM and are linked to a large set of peripherals including printers and memory **storage** devices.

In the past, at the corporate level, reliance on mainframes was imperative for any serious processing job. The increase in power of **workstations** and the use of networked personal computers to distribute workloads has relegated mainframes to more specialized applications, such as airline ticket reservation systems and other large-scale transaction processing. One trillion dollars in mainframe hardware–software systems are still operating today, persisting as the heart of many of the largest corporations and government agencies.

## MAN

✚ See **metropolitan area network**.

## markup language

**Codes** embedded in an electronic text to specify format information such as fonts and paragraph indents for printers and displays.

Markup language enables a computer or printer to show or print formatting, fonts, and other typographic features on a document from another computer. On the Internet, where many incompatible systems are linked, markup languages communicate by using the codes of their common denominator, **ASCII** text.

There are two types of markup language: declarative (e.g., SGML for *standard general markup language* and **HTML** for *hypertext markup language*) and procedural (e.g., PostScript). Declarative merely tells what each part is (a question, for example, will be indicated by <Q>), while procedural includes the instructions the computer uses to know how to display or print the document. Within the Internet, SGML is used for electronic texts, and HTML is the standard for **hypertext** documents on the **World Wide Web**.

## martian

A **packet** of information that appears unexpectedly on the wrong network because of a confused address or a mistake in routing.

## Mb

Abbreviation for megabit.

### MB

Abbreviation for megabyte.

### M-Bone

+ See **multi-cast backbone**.

### Mbps

Abbreviation for megabits per second; roughly one million bits per second.

**Media Lab (at MIT)**

Media Lab (at MIT). Wiesner Building. Credit Bea Bailey. © MIT Media Lab.

Media Lab (at MIT). David Koons, Advanced Human Interface Group. Credit: Hiroshi Nishikawa. © Hiroshi Nishikawa. Courtesy of the MIT Media Laboratory.

### Media Lab (at MIT)

Department of the Massachusetts Institute of Technology (MIT) devoted to investigating the full spectrum of possibilities for digital media.

The Media Lab is exploring virtual reality, artificial intelligence, news-on-demand, holography, and the commercial applications of these and other fields. The influential group of scientists and engineers that work at the lab have been at the forefront of the digital revolution for years, and often lead the world in assessing the next wrinkle in electronic media. Nicholas Negroponte, cofounder of the Media Lab, is known for his outspoken opinions on the ways digital media impact society.

*"The basic difference between today's TVs and PCs has nothing to do with location, social habits, or our need to relax. It has to do with how the bits arrive. The TV takes in bits radiated by*

## medium

(1)  A substance or object on which information is stored (a hard disk is your PC's storage medium). (2)  Means for communicating, such as radio, television, hypermedia, and personal digital assistants (PDAs). (3)  Technology for distributing communications, such as fiber optics or local area networks.

✤ See also **information superhighway**.

## medium access control layer (MAC)

A protocol sublayer for controlling access to the physical transmission mediums (the wires) on a local area network.

## medium earth orbit satellites (MEOS)

Global communications satellites to be launched into an orbit 6,400 miles above the earth in 1998 as TRW's Odyssey project.

They are similar in purpose to low earth orbit satellites.  LEOS require 48 to 77 satellites for worldwide coverage.  MEOS, because of their relatively high orbit, require only 9 to 12 satellites.

## mega

Prefix indicating one million; five megahertz is five million Hertz.

## mega-CD

Compact disc that plugs into a video game console connected to a television set, to provide very high-quality multimedia.

Based on the technology of CD-ROM, a mega-CD multimedia ensemble delivers longer-playing interactive games with higher quality sound, graphics, and video than previously available on game cartridges.

✤ See also **Nintendo** and **Sega**.

## memory

Major component of all computers, storing all the data and instructions that tell the computer the operations to perform.

Internal memory is located within the computer, along with the **central processing unit (CPU)**. External memory is separately housed and connected to the CPU via a **SCSI** port.

✛ See also **dynamic random access memory (DRAM), erasable programmable read-only memory (EPROM),** and **programmable read-only memory (PROM).**

## Memory Array Redcode Simulator (MARS)

✛ See **core.**

## memory card

Small board (card) inserted into the inside of a computer to increase its memory capacity.

## menu

List of options displayed on a computer screen, or announced over the telephone line as part of **audiotex.**

For years, computer users had to know (or find) specific codes—strings of characters—to tell the computer what to do. Today, menus are everywhere. Most often they are "pulled down" from a bar across the top of the screen; all you do is highlight an item from the menu and click on it to activate it. Examples of menu choices are "save file," "print file," "check spelling," and so on. Menus also come up when you access a site on the Internet.

Menu-driven computer programs are easier to use but not as flexible, say, as a **UNIX operating system.** However, when you are faced with an unfamiliar blank screen waiting for cryptic UNIX entries, a menu can be a blessing. On the other hand, few frustrations match listening to a telephone recording enumerate every department and service of the company you just called, when all you want is to reach a particular person.

## MEOS

✛ See **medium earth orbit satellite.**

## merger

Two or more companies fusing into one.

Usually, one company buys another, and the acquired company gives up its independent existence. Companies merge when they see their paths crossing, and they want to have more power in the marketplace.

In the rush to service the interactive home and office of the future and take advantage of all that the convergence of technology has to offer, many cable television, telephone, and entertainment companies are merging and becoming indistinguishable from each other. Cable, computer, and telephone companies—such as IBM, TCI, Time Warner, Viacom, and many of the regional Bell operating companies—are assembling ever-larger unified enterprises.

Other companies—with AT&T the prime example— are competing by breaking themselves into different, more specialized companies.

✦ See also **regulation**.

## message handling system (MHS)

Basic E-mail standard. Also known as X.400.

MHS is the internationally recognized standard that enables both text and graphics to be transmitted between dissimilar computers.

## message

Communication from your computer or on-line service telling you that you are out of memory, that the word you are looking for is not defined, that your modem is not working, and who knows what else.

## Metcalfe, Robert

Coinventor, at Xerox PARC, of the first local area network, and inventor of Ethernet.

He also invented the first laser printer and became founder of the high-tech firm 3Com. An all-around top techie.

> "The (computer) companies growing rapidly now are copycats that are not investing in applications, support, or new technology, so it leaves a net drain out of the industry. We need our seed corn. If all the sources of support and service and technology get killed, who is going to develop it?

## metropolitan area network (MAN)

A communications network within a city or suburb.

MANs are created when local area networks (LANs) outgrow their organizations. As businesses expand, they have a couple of options. They can lease a digital telephone line that links the local networks, but that is expensive and not specifically designed for data connections. Or, they can create a MAN.

The IEEE 802.6 committee is developing a standard designed as a metropolitan utility that will serve a large number of organizations across many miles. The standard, called Distributed Queue Dual Bus (DQDB), will likely be installed and administered by local telephone companies.

Another solution to the challenge of expansion is the fiber-distributed data interface (FDDI), which provides a backbone for a LAN across town and can gather traffic to feed the DQDB backbone. FDDI network adapters can be used as a local network connection within a building and then extended throughout a campus or throughout a town.

## MHS

✚ See **message handling system**.

## MHz

✚ See **megahertz**.

## micon

✚ See **icon**.

## microchip

Colloquial term for an integrated circuit—the proverbial chip.

Most microchips fall into these types: logic chips, which perform some or all of a processor's function; memory chips or RAM chips; computers on a single chip; analog-to-digital and digital-to-analog converters; special-purpose chips such as those in calculators and watches; logic arrays and gate arrays,

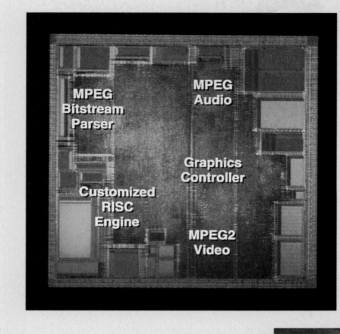

MPEG
Bitstream
Parser

MPEG
Audio

Graphics
Controller

Customized
RISC
Engine

MPEG2
Video

containing logic gates not tied together; and bit slice processors, used as building blocks of computer architecture.

## microprocessor

The central processing unit (CPU) consisting of a single microchip in all personal computers.

This powerful integrated circuit is also used in other applications, such as automobile engine control. Each year, faster microprocessors contribute to the increasing processing power of computers. One reason is that RISC microprocessors are replacing the slower CISC devices.

In 1985, Intel's 32-bit microprocessor—the state-of-the-art—could perform 4 million instructions per second (MIPS); in 1995, Intel's 64-bit Pentium chip does 149 MIPS.

✚ See also **transistor, transputer, and Moore's Law**.

Two views of a complex microchip from LSI Logic Corporation. The chip packs more than a million transistors into an area smaller than that of a postage stamp. It forms the heart of interactive, satellite and cable television set-top boxes, enabling up to 500 television channels to be viewed. Photos courtesy of LSI Logic Corporation.

## micro processor

Image of Pentium® chip courtesy of
Intel Corporation.

## Microsoft Disk Operating System (MS-DOS)

The ubiquitous operating system developed by
Microsoft for IBM PCs and compatibles.

It became the global de facto standard for PCs.

## Microsoft Windows

Bill Gates's best idea: an operating system for DOS-
based computers (IBM and compatibles) that uses a
mouse, icons, and windows.

Made by Microsoft, Windows "borrows" liberally
from the Macintosh operating system. It includes
the Mac staples just mentioned, and a graphical
user interface like the Mac. A user can open and
use more than one window at a time. The fourth
version of the system, Windows 95, which includes
Internet TCP/IP compatibility for the first time, was
launched in August 1995 with a $200 million world-
wide marketing campaign.

## microwave

A portion of the electromagnetic spectrum.

Communications satellites and earth line-of-sight systems (unobstructed view from transmitter to receiver) transmit at these frequencies.

Microwave transmission has 300 times the bandwidth of broadcast television. However, long-distance communication on the ground via microwave requires relay stations every 26 miles.

✚ See also **terrestrial microwave radio**.

## MIDI

✚ See **musical instrument digital interface**.

## mil

Domain name in the Internet system signifying a Federal military organization.

## MIME

✚ See **multipurpose Internet mail extensions**.

## millions of instructions per second (MIPS)

Measurement of the performance of a microprocessor, CPU, or computer system.

When engineers want to rate a piece of hardware, they give it a standard set of exercises to perform. The speed at which these are completed are expressed in MIPS. Once only a souped-up mainframe could reach a MIP or two; today's best PCs operate at more than 100 MIPS.

## minicomputer

A mid-scale computer, with processing power between that of a mainframe and a PC.

The minicomputer was made famous by Digital Equipment Corporation in the 1970s. Before that, most computers were mainframes, and were made by IBM. Mainframes fed dumb terminals that could do no computing on their own. "Minis" allowed the people in one department of a company (say, accounting, or sales) to have their own computing station, rather than having to slog through the wad of information on the mainframe. In time minis became connected with local area networks.

Today's minis can cost anywhere from $20,000 to $250,000. There is a lot of overlap in definitions, now, among minicomputers, high-end personal computers (or microcomputers), and low-end main-frames. Some people prefer the term *midrange*.

## Minitel

European videotex firm funded by the French national telephone company.

Wildly successful, Minitel provides train and airplane bookings, telephone directory listings, movie and theater schedules, private **chat lines**, and thousands of other information services to 6,500,000 **terminals** throughout France. What it cannot do, however, is tell Michael Eisner how to salvage EuroDisney, or investors how to dig themselves out of the Chunnel (the undersea tunnel between Britain and France that has drained both countries' resources).

## misc

In **Usenet**, one of seven world **newsgroup** categories.

Newsgroups that don't fit into the other six—comp, sci, news, rec, soc, and talk—are assigned to misc. (You can figure those out, right? Okay, the answers —backward—comp = retupmoc; sci = ecneics; news = swen; rec = noitaercer; soc = laicos; talk = klat; misc = suoenallecsim).

## mnemonics

Short-hand clues used to remember something.

Example: Roy G. Biv stands for the proper order of colors in the spectrum (or rainbow): red, orange, yellow, green, blue, indigo, violet.

The term originates from the Middle Ages and the Renaissance, when metaphysical memory schemes were devised for structuring large bodies of knowledge. In the context of a **user interface**, an **icon** may be a mnemonic for a document, a function, or a whole **program**. When programming with low-level languages, multi-letter mnemonics describe instruction sets.

The Hollywood flop *Johnny Mnemonic* was a screen adaptation William Gibson's book by the same name.

## mode

Particular set of rules that define a certain way of operating.

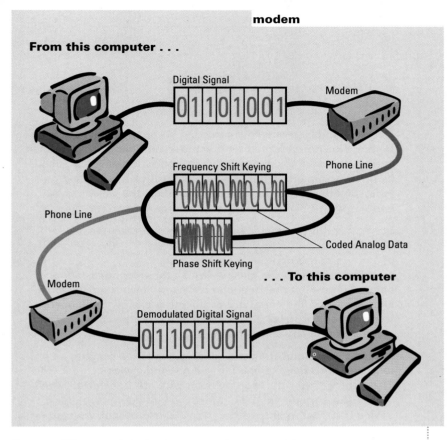

modem

**From this computer . . .**

Digital Signal

Modem

Frequency Shift Keying

Phone Line

Phone Line

Coded Analog Data

Phase Shift Keying

**. . . To this computer**

Modem

Demodulated Digital Signal

On your PC, you might be in text mode, or graphics mode.  If you are working late, you might be in waking mode or sleeping mode.

## modem

Device that converts digital computer signals to analog signals and vice versa for transmission over the telephone network.  Stands for *mo*dulator/ *dem*odulator.

The modulator part of the modem changes (modulates) the 1s and 0s into tones that are carried by the network.  The demodulator converts the tones back into 1s and 0s at the other end.  Modems can be self-contained units or cards plugged in to the inside of a computer.

+ See also **acoustic coupler** and **modulation**.

# Why A Modem?

To put it simply, modems are needed because the telephone system was not designed for computer communications. When you speak into a telephone handset, your voice is transformed by microphone into a fluctuating electrical current carried on a wire. The fluctuations in the current mimic the caller's voice, and—at the receiving end—are transformed back into sounds.

But that is not the way computers communicate. These machines use on-and-off pulses to indicate bits, the basic units of digital information. By a process called modulation, a modem transforms the pulses—which the telephone cannot handle—into the tones a phone can carry. Incoming sound signals, sent from the computer at the other end of the line, are transformed too, back into the digital pulses the computer can recognize. That's *demodulation*.

Modems communicating with each other at the sending and receiving ends have to obey the same modulation protocol. That protocol sets the rate at which data are transferred, and other necessary parameters. Most modem buyers look for a device that conforms to either the V.32bis protocol, which offers communication speed up to 14,400 bits per second (bps), or the newer V.34 protocol, which can operate at 28,800 bps.

Handy though they may be, modems are much slower than direct computer connections, such as a local area network. Within a computer, digital signals travel side by side, rather than single file—as they do through a modem. Because of this, it is painfully slow to transfer data-intensive graphics, or to receive them from the Internet. However, transfer of text is efficient with such services and programs as E-mail, Telnet, file transfer protocol, Archie, and Gopher. In the future, modems may be rendered obsolete by either the high-speed digital ISDN telephone system or the National Information Infrastructure.

## moderated newsgroup

Any newsgroup, in Usenet, where the postings are sent first to a coordinating manager, who screens them for appropriateness.

This gives the content more consistent value—in cyberslang, a higher "signal-to-noise ratio"—than that in unmoderated newsgroups. It also allows moderated newsgroup subscribers to avoid, for the most part, flame wars, mail bombings, and the like. To post to a moderated newsgroup, send your message via E-mail to the group moderator. If it doesn't run, the moderator will explain why. For addresses of moderators, access the newsgroup net.answers for the List of Moderators for Usenet.

## modulation

Process of altering a wave of energy so it can carry a signal.

Amplitude modulation—the AM of AM radio—imprints a signal by changing the amplitude of a wave. Frequency modulation—FM—alters a wave's timing. Pulse modulation, used widely for digital communication, translates a wave into a series of pulses.

## monitor

Television-like piece of hardware on which your computer displays information.

It may be a CRT or an LCD.

✦ See also **screen**.

## MOO (MUD, Object-Oriented)

Elaboration of a multi-user dungeon on-line game, in which you play against others from around the world.

It uses object-oriented programming (OOP) to bring more dimension to the otherwise text-based game. LambdaMOO is a popular and addictive MOO, originally started as an experiment at Xerox PARC in 1991. The programming language, built into the game, has much in common with C++. MOOs, unlike the more combat-oriented MUDs, readily make available the programming tools to players, even new users. MOOs may have a future in professional circles, as a fun way for researchers, scientists, or other groups of people who share the same interests to meet and discuss their ideas.

## Moore's law

Principle holding that at any given price level the performance of semiconductor technology doubles every 18 months.

It is named for Gordon Moore, cofounder of Intel. According to Moore's Law, for example, the density and speed of commercially available microprocessors will double every 18 months, and sell for an ongoing, constant price.

## morph

Transformation, by computer animation software, of one image into another.

By morphing, you can create a video clip in which a woman's face smoothly and gradually changes to a man's, or a cat changes into a dog.

Morphing is done by interpolating changes between two images. For example, you, as the animator, link key points such as eyes, nose, and mouth between the first face and the second, and then the computer mutates the first into the second. You can change one abstract form into another. Or, you can play all-powerful witch and rapidly age your little brother Daniel by blending his baby picture with an adult mug shot. Maybe that of David Letterman.

+ See also **computer graphics**.

## Mosaic

Software program that allows you to read and explore the Internet's nifty World Wide Web with armchair ease.

Distributed as freeware, Mosaic runs on Windows, Macintosh, and certain UNIX systems. Developed by the National Center for Supercomputing Applications, Mosaic may be the Internet's killer application. Netscape is a newer version of Mosaic.

## motherboard

Primary printed circuit board, onto which a computer's CPU, microprocessor, and RAM are attached.

## motion picture experts group (MPEG)

A group that meets quarterly under the auspices of the International Standards Organization (ISO) to generate standards for digital video and audio compression.

MPEG-1 and MPEG-2 are video compression standards, which define a bit stream of compressed video and audio optimized for transmission at a rate of 0.5–1.5 Mbps.  The video standard is no better than a home VCR's fairly low resolution, but the audio standard demands the clarity of a CD.

To play back MPEG-compressed video in real-time, you need a fast microprocessor and, preferably, a disk array for storage.  To view an MPEG-encoded file (which customarily will be indicated by the .MPG extension in its directory), you will also have to have a MPEG-compatible viewer—a decoder program that displays the video through a monitor and plays the audio through a sound card.  Some MPEG viewers are in the public domain (check the Internet), or available as shareware.

### mouse

A hand-held device for controlling the cursor on a personal computer screen.

It is used by pushing the little thing around on a desktop.  The cord connecting the mouse to the keyboard is the mouse's tail.  When turned upside down, the mouse becomes a trackball.

The mouse, in common use now, is facing new competition from small rubberized plastic switch/levers on the keyboard, and glidepoints—a miniature version of the monitor's screen that responds to the touch of a fingertip.  Is there no end to the rat race?

And as for the plural, most go with "mice."

### MIPS

+  See **millions of instructions per second**.

### MPC

+  See **multimedia personal computer**.

### MPEG

+  See **motion picture experts group**.

### MS-DOS

+  See **Microsoft Disk Operating System**.

### MSO

+  See **multiple system operator**.

## MUD

+ See **multi-user dungeon**.

## multi-cast

To transmit information in both directions among several participants at one time, as in teleconferencing.

+ See also **broadcast**.

## multi-cast backbone (M-Bone)

A **network** that permits multi-casting (two-way transmission between multiple sites), but with a limited receivership.

Still an evolving technology, M-Bone will allow you to send video in real-time or to do **videoconferencing** over the Internet. The M-Bone makes up for a major weakness of the **TCP/IP** protocols, the technical foundation of the Internet—their unsuitability for real-time video and audio. Because they tolerate delay to ensure accuracy of file delivery, audio and video arrive with irritating gaps and pauses.

The M-Bone experiment would upgrade those protocols, but requires an alternative backbone of specially equipped workstations and modified long-distance links. Even with those, M-Bone video transmission would be at three to five frames per second, far slower than the 15 or more frames per second needed for the illusion of smooth action.

Operative since 1992, the M-Bone is available on a limited basis; only 1,500 of the Internet's 70,000 networks could carry it as of early 1995. The M-Bone received worldwide attention when it was used for the first major cyberspace concert broadcast, by the Rolling Stones.

*"I wanna say a special welcome to everyone that's, uh, climbed into the Internet tonight and, uh, has got into the M-Bone. And I hope it doesn't all collapse."*

— ***Mick Jagger,***
singer

[Peter H. Lewis, The New York Times News Service, "M-bone exercises shaping things to come," *The Commercial Appeal (Memphis)*, Sunday, 12 February 1995, Final Edition, Sec. Business, p. 3C.]

## multimedia

The ultimate computing experience, a combination of two or more media—such as text, still pictures, **video**, and **audio**—presented in an **interactive** setting.

Multimedia is most frequently provided on your own PC with a **CD-ROM**. The content is **hypermedia**; you determine the direction of your involvement with a controller.

© Peter Hoey/Spots on the Spot!

▶ ▶ ▶ ▶

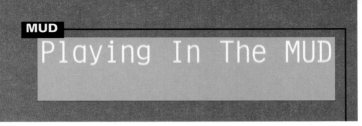

# Playing In The MUD

MUDs were originally designed so that Dungeons and Dragon players could role play in real-time with other players around the world. Their collective goal was to become a wizard, without having to play the physical version of the game, which often entailed getting lost in the steam tunnels underneath college campuses, and to find worldwide opponents. The first MUD was MDI, written by Richard Bartle and Roy Trubshaw in 1979.

Each user takes control of a computerized persona or character, and proceeds to walk around, chat with other characters, explore dangerous areas, solve puzzles, and even create rooms, descriptions and items, not unlike a season's worth of *This Old House* episodes. What changes, from game to game, is the environment.

Ten years after the original combat-oriented MUD was created, along came TinyMUD Original, the first of a family of games that emphasizes social interaction over combat. TinyMuds created the use of flags which turn rooms into havens where no character may be killed. There are also many MUDs that are even further afield and are instead oriented toward academic purposes and various kinds of experimentation. One long-standing MOO-styled MUD has been used for teaching physics, and there are others for scholars conferencing on the latest findings in molecular biology and genetics. The majority of the educational MUDs are in the social sciences, computer science, or humanities.

The basic MUD types are as follows:

○ Combat-oriented MUDs.
   Combat is an inherent part of the MUD culture. The Internet Yellow Pages' description of one such game, Nightfall MUD, suggests "...adventure through strange

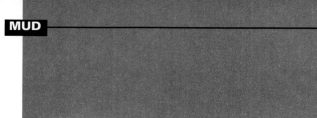

lands solving puzzles, killing monsters and selling treasures on your way." This is hardly unique.

○ TinyMUD and other socially oriented MUDs. These have a different focus, either on role-playing social interaction, or conversations with friends.

○ Miscellaneous MUDs.

The "look" of a MUD is determined by the software of the game and the database that describes the world. Differences occur because two games with very similar software may function with different databases. A MUD world is built with a variety of objects, which the players manipulate with commands such as "take ax" or "look book."

Whatever the environment, the players answer to the gods—the people who own the database—who are the administrators. In most MUDs, wizards are present, too, and barely distinguishable from gods. In some games, wizards are players who have won the game, and then created new sections of the game. Wizards are very powerful, but they must still follow a set of rules, or face the wrath of the gods. Like Dwayne Andreas dictating to the world's farmers, gods can do whatever they want to whomever they want whenever they want.

To start to play, you can Telnet to a MUD's Internet Protocol Port, using the MUD's network address and port number. However, Telnet may not be the preferred way of interacting, since it does not provide text wrapping. Consequently, if someone says something while you are typing out a line, it will make a mess out of your line, making it hard to see what you are typing and hard to keep track of what is going on. A better option is to select a client program providing a front end to the MUD. A number of MUD servers have evolved. Servers keep track of the database, the current players, and the rules, while running large programs.

Servers can be found at FTP sites.

Combat-oriented MUDS generally use these servers: MUD, AberMUD, LPMUD, DGD, DikuMUD, KMUD, YAMA, UriMUD, Ogham, CircleMUD, AmigaMUD.

Social-oriented MUDs servers include Tiny MUD, TinyMuck v1.*, TinyMush, TinyMUCK v2.*, TinyMUSE, TinyMAGE, MUG, and TeenyMUD.

Miscellaneous MUD servers include: UberMUD, MOO, LambdaMOO, SMUG, and UnterMUD.

To get a character, you may have to register. Some MUDs have this policy to cut down on abuse of privileges. Registration may be done by sending mail to the administrator. Others will let you create your own character. In either case, try to remember that MUDs are not a right, and that access is granted out of trust. People usually have to pay to use processing time on the large, expensive computers that MUDs often run on, and you are being given a special deal.

Once you (and your character) have been accepted into the game and you have logged in with a password, playing the game is a breeze. You may move through the universe of the MUD simply by keyboarding your character's actions and thoughts and using the game's commands. However, it is best to type *help* and *news* to become familiar with the game's commands before you proceed. Most MUDs have extensive help menus, providing instructions and directions. The *WHO* command will give you a list of the characters that are logged on. Thankfully, MUDs have a core of commands. For example, many use *look* and *go* as the basics for interacting and moving around. Commands prefixed by the @ symbol (generally) allow you to change the database. Commands such as @describe, @create, @name, @dig, and @link allow you to expand the universe, change it, or even, perhaps, destroy it.

How does a game session progress? Here's one player's report:

"I've logged on to my favorite server (TinyMUD) to play my favorite game (Purgatory Mush, based on The WhiteWolf Game,

Vampire of the Masquerade). I'm a vampire, assigned by the game's staff, and have been given a handful of quotas to make my virtual-based objects. These things or objects are the only Purgatory Mush items in my control. In this game, every object is equal to one quota—what a normal character is worth—and you need one object to exit. Of course, I have a mission, a covert action. Typically, missions can vary from capturing another character to getting another character to withdraw from a particular situation.

"My vampire and I head to our favorite hangout, the date club, where the werewolves, hunters, wizards, and gods pass through, waving and chatting with each other. It's a good place to make contact, to observe and be observed. But it isn't the right time to engage in heavy-duty action, the setting's not right. I have to get myself psyched to perform; conducting a mission can take a lot out of you. Even though my vampire is another persona, the actions and outcomes of encounters can be very emotionally affective. The nature of the mental imagery and the fact that it is real-time interactivity creates a very powerful environment. Another player cries out in cyberanguish that he is being abused by other characters. He takes a time out, to regain his balance."

In a MUDdy world, netiquette rules. Players hate rude and inappropriate behavior, and especially ignorance. "The jury is still out on whether MUDding is 'just a game' or 'an extension of real life with gamelike qualities,'" notes one MUD FAQ writer, "but either way, treat it with care." Another MUD caveat: They are time and space sponges. Some players have abandoned the "real world" and spend up to 80 hours a week in their MUD. They can eat up a network (not to mention your phone bill). Even if they are not CPU-intensive, most MUDs can take up a fair amount of disk space—anywhere from 10 to 90 megabytes—which may impact other users on the network.

## multimedia personal computer (MPC)

Complete, out-of-the-box system that gives the consumer 16-bit audio, 24-bit color, at least a 200-megabyte hard disk, 8MB of RAM, and the most essential ingredient, a CD-ROM drive.

## multiple system operator (MSO)

A cable television company that has more than one franchised cable system.

The big companies such as Time Warner, TCI, and Continental each have hundreds of systems.  Kind of like the kid with all the marbles.

## multiplexer (MUX)

Hardware that permits two or more signals—data or voice—to be transmitted over the same circuit, whether it's a telephone line, microwave link, or television broadcast.

A multiplexer (analog or digital) enables transmission across a network to be more efficient and economical than transmission without this device.

## multiplexing

Transmitting several signals from several sources simultaneously via hardware known as a multiplexer.

Multiplexing increases time and cost efficiency.  The two types are frequency-division multiplexing (FDM) and time-division multiplexing (TDM).  FDM uses several frequencies on the same channel to transmit different messages.  TDM divides a channel into time chunks and assigns each to a specific signal source.  The TDM multiplexer temporarily stores information to send all at once when the line is free.

In cyberspace, the term has also come to describe a person's ability to handle many tasks and projects at once, without going crazy. Housewives must wonder what the big deal is: Hey, from 5 to 6 p.m. they can cook, clean the kitchen, change the baby, do the laundry, and soothe hubby's ruffled ego all at the same time.

## multipurpose Internet mail extensions (MIME)

A protocol for sending graphics and other complex data sets by E-mail.

## multi-sensory environment

An interactive environment designed to stimulate the senses for a completely enveloping experience.

It uses devices such as projected immersive displays—extremely wide screen—and feedback linked to your position in space.

✦ See also **location-based entertainment (LBE)** and **virtual reality**.

## multi-sync/multi-scan monitor

A video display that accepts different signals such as National Television Systems Committee (NTSC) composite video or Red, Green, Blue (RGB) displays.

It automatically adjusts to the correct timing and number of scanlines for the format played upon it.

## multi-user dungeon or multi-user dimension (MUD)

Text-based, role-playing game such as Dungeons and Dragons that many people play simultaneously, on-line.

Players acting out their imaginary characters' lives have become so addicted to MUDs that their real lives have little other social interaction. Part improvisation, part conversation, participating in a MUD can seem like living in a virtual world with whomever else is simultaneously on-line.

Understanding the geography and language of a MUD takes some time, and a newcomer is vulnerable to dirty tricks by old-timers. As you become savvy to the ways of a MUD, you can alter your on-line environment using text description. Your MUD persona can be killed in the course of events on-line, a potentially devastating experience for someone who has spent 50 hours a week in a given character role.  Currently, MUDs are only text, but they are beginning to involve graphics.  In the not-so-distant future, they will probably include video displays and, later, virtual reality.

✚ See also **MOO**.

## musical instrument digital interface (MIDI)

Hardware and protocol that allows the sound from a musical instrument to be input to a computer.

Many electronic keyboards are equipped with a MIDI plug.  When the music is played, it is stored in the computer.  Later, the musician can manipulate the notes and the quality of the sound.
The altered result can be played back and recorded.  MIDI enables musicians to use keyboards to simulate many types of instruments and create special effects.

✚ See also **digital audio, sequencer,** and **synthesizer.**

## MUX

✚ See **multiplexer.**

Narly

## nanosecond

One billionth of a second, a measurement often used to describe the speed with which a computer carries out an operation.

A millisecond, by contrast, is a thousandth of a second.

## narrowband

(1) Lines or circuits able to carry data up to 2,400 bits per second. (2) Sub-voice-grade channels only capable of carrying up to 200 bits per second. (3) In cellular radio, splitting FM channels in order to gain more channels and greater capacity.

## narrowcasting

Sending specialized television programming via cable networks to select audiences, targeted more precisely than is possible with broadcasting.

## National Center for Supercomputer Applications (NCSA)

Research center at the University of Illinois' Champaign/Urbana campus.

Mosaic, the program that lets everyday people use the Internet, was developed there.

## National Information Infrastructure (NII)

Prototype of the information superhighway, which would link computer users nationwide over high-speed lines.

The political tech topic of discussion since 1993, when President Bill Clinton assigned a task force to look into it. One committee is examining key telecommunications issues. Another is overseeing the development and application of information technologies. And yet another is addressing critical information policy issues.

Other groups are examining the issues of security,

intellectual property rights, invasion of privacy, fraud, and breakdowns of the system—that is, what to do if the infrastructure fails in parts of the country because of weather or sabotage. Those who are thinking even bigger speak of the GII (for the Global Information Infrastructure).

## National Institute of Standards and Technology (NIST)

Major standards-setting body of the U.S. Department of Commerce. Formerly the National Bureau of Standards.

Among other things, NIST works closely with the National Security Agency in the design and planning of encryption technology for voice, data, and video transmissions and interception. In 1988, NIST and industry groups established the North American ISDN Users Forum, to develop standards that would enable competing services and products to be compatible.

## National Science Foundation (NSF)

Huge federally supported organization that funds a wide range of research, primarily at universities.

Through 1995, NSF underwrote NSFnet, a high-speed network that formed the original backbone of the Internet.

✚ See also **Advanced Research Projects Agency (ARPA), Arpanet,** and **Defense Advanced Research Projects Agency (DARPA).**

## National Telecommunications and Information Administration (NTIA)

Agency of the U.S. Department of Commerce, charged with the development of communications policy and innovative programs.

NTIA places an emphasis on telephone standards.

## National Television Systems Committee (NTSC)

Committee of the Electronics Industries Association and developer of NTSC—a color broadcast standard since 1953.

NTSC is the prevalent television format in the United States and Japan. It consists of 525 scan lines, a field frequency of 60 Hz, a broadcast bandwidth of 4 MHz, line frequency of 15.75 KHz, frame frequency of 1/30 of a second, and a color subcarrier frequency of 3.58 MHz. The format was designed to be backward compatible with black-and-white television. Because color is encoded as a phase component of the television signal, color can drift and vary from monitor to monitor. Wags like to say that NTSC stands for Never Twice the Same Color.

+ See also **phase alternate line, sequential couleur a memoir (SECAM),** and **television standards**.

## natural language

Human-speak.

Only a decade ago, many software programs required you to know some number of codes and other odd commands. As it progresses, however, more and more software provides a natural language interface. You tell it what you want it to do in plain English and it does it.

+ See also **language**.

## navigation

Finding your way around in cyberspace.

Just as ships' captains need to navigate the waters to find their ports of call, computer users must navigate through software packages, CD-ROMs, on-line databases, or whatever resources are present.

A well-designed interactive program is easy to navigate. Usually, there is a main menu that is always accessible, offering a way of knowing where you have been and where you might be heading. The Internet is so vast that navigation software, such as Mosaic, is essential—and an enormous success.

## NCSA

+ See **National Center for Supercomputer Application**.

## net

(1) These days, used widely to refer to almost any local or national network. (2) Friendly name for the Internet (usually capitalize as Net). (3) Top-level domain name assigned to an Internet administrative organization; it follows the last dot in the site's address, as in *info.net.* (4) Something to catch fish in.

## net.deity

An individual who is something of a celebrity on Usenet.

Doesn't have quite the status of a net.legend, however, who punctuates his or her notoriety with frequent bits of wit and a sense of style.

## net.legend

In Usenet, an individual who's made a major contribution, such as Brian Reid, creator of the alt. hierarchy of newsgroups.

## net surfing

Searching the Internet—for fun, not profit.

Not quite the national pastime—yet—but a recreation growing at a wild pace. Some surfers will look at the high-resolution graphics library of paintings and drawings at the Smithsonian Institution site. Others may prefer the alt.sex.movies catalogue of porn stars.

## netiquette

Etiquette in cyberspace.

No, you don't have to study Emily Post, but if you don't behave, you will be flamed by your on-line counterparts.

## NetWare

Operating system for local area network communications manufactured by Novell.

NetWare is the link between the hardware and the users on the network. It "packages" requests in a series of packets for transmission across a network.

## network

To link together related computers—and the system that results from doing so.

Just as highways connect local roads, a network connects local computers, creating a web of machines and the twisted-pair, coaxial, fiber-optic, and satellite connections that link them. A network may be as small as a local area network on one floor of a building, or as large as the Internet, a global network of networks.

If computers are the brains of a new world Information Age, networks are the arteries and veins of the beast, pumping information from place to place. The information superhighway promises to be the network that binds together all other networks, from the local to the global.

*"The timid turn truculent, shrinking violets issue impassioned declarations, and sticklers for propriety show an alarming lack of discretion.... Would you commit yourself to paper so cavalierly?"*

— *writer*
**Ellen McCooey**
[Ellen McCooey, "Dialog Box," *Windows*, August 1994.]

NetWare screen capture courtesy of Novell.

# Netiqutte:
# How To Behave In
# Cyberspace

Users on the Internet often think of themselves as "citizens" who are visiting, working in, or effectively living within what Electronic Freedom Foundation chief Esther Dyson has termed "a giant and unbounded world of virtual real estate." As such, their thinking goes, they—and not outside agents such as politicians or government agencies—are responsible for their behavior. And the standards are already being set.

Redundancy, histrionics, commercialism (except where specifically encouraged), profane language, and long-windedness are all traits that cyberspace citizens abhor. Their distaste can take the form of flames (personal insults, or violent verbal expressions of disapproval); mail bombs (a staggeringly huge amount of E-mail delivered to your mailbox); or an all-out campaign to ruin you personally and professionally (say, by publishing your unlisted phone number). The twisted logic of netiquette, however, maintains that these actions themselves are in poor taste. So just behave and there won't be any problem.

Most breaches of netiquette result from ignorance or laziness. Newsgroups tend to publish a file of frequently asked questions (FAQs) and their answers, and strongly urge (we do not "demand" or "insist" in cyberspace) any newcomer to read the FAQs before joining in a discussion.

The following tips can bring you a long way to being a good guy or gal (and provide a bit of shelter from those flames):

○ Keep your voice down.
Typing IN CAPITALS is screaming in cyberspace. Good citizens don't shout. Caps are hard to read, distracting, even arrogant. If you really want to shout, fine, go ahead. But if you are looking for emphasis, place asterisks around your text. "No, you're wrong. Seeing Kevin Costner in gills *is* worth $7.50."

○ Avoid evangelism.
Rushing headlong into the enemy camp may have worked for Lawrence of Arabia, the National Football League's European division, and manufacturers of fat-

free ice cream. But declaring with ardent conviction
that aliens have operated on your torso is bad form.
Hindu newsgroup readers don't want to be told they
are bound for hell, and IBM newsgroup subscribers
don't want to hear that Macs and Amigas represent the
cutting edge.

○ When you have something to say, post it
succinctly.
The best messages are short and pithy, with provoca-
tive headers. If the message fills more than a screen of
text—if the reader has to scroll to read it—EDIT IT.

○ Hedge your bets.
Net abbreviations such as IMHO (in my humble opinion), YMMV (your mileage may vary), BTW (by the way),
and FWIW (for what it's worth) all can temper—and
make more succinct—your opinion on the topic of the
day.

○ Apologize.
Especially if the misunderstanding is with someone you
respect. Take responsibility for being unclear, restate
what you meant, and go on.

○ Respect each group's norms and mores.
Lurk—that is, read postings over several days—before
you post. Accepted behavior in one group may not fly
in another.

○ Respect a group's elder statesmen.
In every Usenet newsgroup and listserv mailing list are
luminaries who have justifiably earned reputations for
wisdom and experience. Don't go head-to-head with
someone like that unless you are very well-schooled.

○ Stick to the subject.
If the discussion is on, say, Disney movies, don't try to
steer it to the effectiveness of the drop pass in the Sega
Genesis NHL '95 game. As a corollary, don't send a

message asking, "Why doesn't anybody say anything about Pocohontas?" If you want to start the discussion, say something yourself. Be careful, because the group may have just concluded a long, bitter war over the portrayal of Native American culture in animation.

Don't post ads.
Or chain letters. Or business offers—unless the bulletin board was created for it. Never send junk mail to unwilling recipients.

Sarcasm and subtleties get lost.
Typed attacks lack body language and inflection. It is hard to soften a blow without these physical signals. It is also hard to write funny, which is why emoticons or smileys are so valuable. Other Net conventions used to communicate emphasis are underlines and asterisks, as in: "You thought OJ's performance in _Towering Inferno_ was *masterful*?" E-mail, which is confidential, is a better vehicle for criticism than bulletin boards are.

Neither betray confidences, nor make official pronouncements.
Make sure you know, by reading the "To:" and "Cc:" lines carefully, where your message is going. The message travels instantaneously, and cannot be retrieved.

Remember that the Internet is worldwide.
American values are just that—American. The French don't want to be lectured to about our First Amendment. They have got enough problems with Big Macs and EuroDisney.

Read FAQs.
This bears repeating. Look for a FAQ file first. A group's norms and folkways will be found here. Usenet FAQs, for example, are posted monthly on the file: news.answers. Listowners of LISTSERVs often will mail you the FAQs for the list.

## network operating system (NOS)

Rhymes with "boss"—a group of software programs that control the operation of a network.

Some of the programs manage the sharing of files and peripherals across the network. The machines they reside in are called servers. The programs that enable computers to use the shared resources are called clients. This arrangement enables you to access resources on other computers while your coworkers are able to access your computer (or printer, or modem).

## network services

All the nifty things you can use when you access a network.

These can be newsgroups, information retrieval systems, bulletin boards, and much more. Services may be public or private.

## network topology

Physical arrangement of a network.

The topology may be a ring of computers linked as if in a circle (a token ring); a bus—a central pathway that enables computers to get on or off like riders of a city bus system (as in an Ethernet); or a tree or star configuration, typically used with small groups of personal computers.

## neural network

Computer system running on software that does not have to always conform to predetermined rules, but can learn what to do from examples and feedback.

Pioneered in the 1980s by Carver Mead, neural networks are characterized by many different elements functioning simultaneously. This kind of processing follows a model of how the brain works, hence the name *neural*. Software can be programmed to emulate organic functioning, or a computer can run multiple microprocessors in parallel. Neural networks have important applications—among them speech recognition, financial analysis, database management, and signal processing.

## newbie

Someone who is new to the Internet.

Because the Net and its history are so steeped in technical expertise, anyone making what is deemed a foolish mistake, such as posting a message to the wrong newsgroup, risks being flamed. Some tips for success:

- Read up on the Net's many resources, such as Archie, FTP, the World Wide Web.
- Learn what is acceptable to post on the network you've logged on to.
- Be certain you understand the topic being discussed on a newsgroup in which you want to participate.
- Read the documentation for a multi-user dungeon (MUD) or internet relay chat (IRC) carefully before joining.
- Observe netiquette.

## news

One of seven world newsgroup categories on the Usenet, whose discussions focus on the Usenet itself.

## newsgroups

Special-interest discussion group found on the Usenet portion of the Internet.

Newsgroups cover thousands of subject areas. For details, see Usenet.

## NII

✚ See **National Information Infrastructure**.

## 900 service

Special services available over phone lines by calling a number with 900 in place of the area code.

You can get the latest sports scores, talk on party lines, and pay an exorbitant fee per minute for the luxury of doing so.

## 911 Service

✚ See **emergency response system (ERS)**.

## Nintendo

The king of video games.

This Japanese company became a worldwide name in the 1980s and early 1990s based on the vast popularity of its products. Although other companies had made dedicated game systems that plug into the home TV, Nintendo's was the first to deliver arcade-like quality. Nearly 100 million game consoles—and billions of dollars in game cartridges—have been sold worldwide.

Now Nintendo is making video game consoles that hook up to a modem and thus to different networks. Games involving multiple players at different sites became a reality in the fall of 1994, when Nintendo opened a games network called XBAND. Five trial cities—Atlanta, Dallas, Los Angeles, New York, and San Francisco—were supposed to serve as a beta test (test under realistic conditions), with the modems distributed through a chain of video stores. But buyers quickly learned they could order the modem directly from the manufacturer. With digital transmission, video game software may even be delivered via telephone lines.

> *"Before this, I had to go across town to my friend's house. Now I can play in my own home and he can play in his home. Plus anytime you want to play anybody in a different place at a different time, you can."*
>
> — *XBAND game player* **Leanear Lane**
> [Mike Snider, "XBAND network connects long-distance video gamers," *USA TODAY*, Wednesday, August 23, 1995, Final Edition, Sec. Life, p. 6D.]
>
> *"I think there's probably going to be a bunch of parents who are going to be quite upset when they get the bills."*
>
> — *XBAND game player parent* **Carol Lama**
> [Mike Snider, "XBAND network connects long-distance video gamers," *USA TODAY*, Wednesday August 23, 1995, Final Edition, Sec. Life, p. 6D.]

## NIST

✛ See **National Institute Of Standards And Technology**.

## node

Point where equipment connects with transmission lines.

When you want to connect to a network, you dial a local phone number. This call connects you to some regional computer that provides the physical link to the network. That computer (and site) is a node.

## noise

(1) Undesirable audio or video pollution that inter-feres with the clarity of the sound or image signal being transmitted. (2) Irrelevant commentary on newsgroup.

✚ See also **artifact** and **signal-to-noise ratio**.

## NOS

✚ See **network operating system**.

## notebook computer

Small, full-function personal computer weighing about five to seven pounds.

Kind of like a laptop, kind of not. Depends on the lap.

## NSF

✚ See **National Science Foundation**.

## NSFnet

✚ See *The Evolution of the Net*.

## NTIA

✚ See **National Telecommunications and Information Administration**.

## NTSC

✚ See **National Television Systems Committee**.

## object

Old English

In object-oriented programming, a component containing both data and instructions for the operations to be performed on that data.

## object linking and embedding (OLE)

Feature of the Microsoft Windows 3.1 and IBM OS/2 operating systems that lets you put dissimilar elements—such as text, graphics, and sound—from different programs into one document.

The objects (the different elements) are embedded in a host document but are linked to other locations. If a change is made to an object in another place, it will appear in the host document as well. OLE is a tool of great value for groups of people working together on networks.

✚ See also **groupware** and **workgroup computing**.

## object-oriented programming (OOP)

Using an object-oriented programming language to construct objects that make up a software system.

✚ See also **MOO**.

## OCR

✚ See **optical character recognition**.

## off-line

State of being unconnected to any network.

Rather than use costly on-line time to compose a letter or put together one's thoughts for on-line publication, it is better to do those things off-line. When you are done, go on-line to send it.

## OLE

✚ See **object linking and embedding**.

## Olsen, Ken

Founder, in 1957, of the Digital Equipment Corporation (DEC), pioneer in minicomputers and computer networking.

At the Massachusetts Institute of Technology (MIT) in the 1950s, Olsen built one of the first personal computers—the Whirlwind—a 16-bit machine with a cathode ray tube, light pen, and drum storage. At DEC, he stole a great deal of market share from IBM in the 1970s with the minicomputer. He dismissed the PC market in the 1980s and lost substantial market opportunities himself.

> "When the PC became active in the late '70s, we formally decided we would not pursue it because anyone can buy the parts at Radio Shack and make a personal computer.... We did the harder things; we did the harder network jobs. But now workstations and personal computers are important to us.... We may have had vision, but nobody, I mean nobody, had any idea."
>
> —*Ken Olsen*, 1992
>
> [Ken Olsen, interviewed by James Connolly, *Computerworld*, 22 June 1992, p. 4.]

*"There is no reason for any individual to have a computer in his home."*

—***Ken Olsen***, *1977*
["Sure Forecasts Gang Aft Askew," *The Plain Dealer*, Monday, 4 January 1993, Sec. Editorials & Forum, p. 7B. (Said by Olsen at the World Future Society meeting in Boston, 1977, and quoted by David H. Ahl in a 1982 interview).]

## ONA

✦ See **open network architecture**.

## on-demand publishing

Technology that permits the customer to compile custom texts from a publisher's offering into a single product.

Up to now, on-demand publishing has resulted in a physical book, though it is increasingly presented in digital format, such as a CD-ROM or floppy disk. On-demand publishing could be effectively administered on-line, producing customized material without the costs of paper and printing.

✦ See also **electronic books, electronic publishing,** and **Xanadu.**

## on-line

Being connected to another computer via a telecommunications link.

## on-line classified ads

The cyberspace version of the traditional newspaper ad, found to-date on only a few networks.

On-line classified ads—and on-line Yellow Pages—are in the earliest commercial stages. Classified ads, which change every few days, are currently highly lucrative for print media. Recognizing this, most telephone companies have embraced the on-line version of the classified section, including real estate and car dealer ads, as an adjunct to their Yellow Page service.

A disadvantage for the telephone companies is that they are unaccustomed to dealing with ads that change every day. On the other hand, they have a massive billing structure in place, and, by cutting deals with banks and credit-card companies, can enhance classified advertising with transaction-oriented services.

✦ See also **interactive advertising**.

## on-line forum

Portion of an on-line service that facilitates a certain kind of interaction, such as a discussion group for parents, or searches through a research library.

Forums are provided by on-line services such as AOL, CompuServe, and Prodigy. Other areas are maintained for special-interest groups, for a general library, to hold a conference, and to exchange messages. Each forum has a knowledgeable system operator (or sysop) who is available to show you the system if you need help, and who sometimes monitors the participants' netiquette.

## on-line magazine

A magazine that never sees a printing press, existing only in cyberspace.

You subscribe just as you would to a printed magazine, and you pay with cybercash—today, with your credit card; tomorrow, directly from your bank account.

✦ See also **electronic publishing**.

## on-line publishing

Work that is published directly to an on-line service or a wide area network—whether it takes the form of a magazine, daily or weekly newspaper, or individual article.

On-line publishing is immediate; when the contents are ready, they are sent directly to subscribers or viewers. No trees are killed, no postal delays are incurred. On the down side, there is only weak copyright protection, and it is hard for the publishers to make any money since advertisers are not yet willing to take the plunge.

Conventional publications, in particular daily newspapers, are increasingly offering their complete issues on-line—but sometimes with a time lag. You can choose what articles you want to read by clicking on a headline offered on the home page. Some moderate advertising is beginning to appear at the bottom of some pages. Mostly, these are vehicles to entice readers to subscribe to the hard copy.

**+** See also **on-demand publishing**.

## on-line services

Interactive storage and retrieval systems for the exchange of information, accessed by a computer and modem.

These systems may be open to the general public or limited to a closed group—usually employees of a corporation. America Online, CompuServe, Delphi, GEnie, and Prodigy are examples of commercial on-line services. They are, in effect, common carriers— utilities, such as the telephone company—that allow you to connect with information elsewhere, whether it comes from your branch office in Oswego, your sweetie in Peoria, a database in Manhattan, or a file server in Phoenix.

E-mail is one of the most common services offered by on-line systems. You send a message to another user's mailbox, and it stays there until that person logs on and retrieves it. Most offer a variety of databases you can tap into, also: news wires, stock tickers, sports scores, airline reservation information, and so on.

You access an on-line service by dialing a network access number. After giving the proper password, you embark on a journey facilitated by command keystrokes, menus, lists, and prompts. Finding information can take only minutes—or hours. After the data are found, they can be read on-line or downloaded into your computer to be read off-line.

**+** See also **electronic publishing, gateway,** and **Internet**.

*"Right now, most people can only use America Online when they're at home in their den. Well, that's not what it's going to take to create a mainstream phenomenon. But when you look ahead 10 years from now, probably most of our subscribers will be connecting to us several times a day,*

## on-line Yellow Pages

Commercial telephone directories delivered electronically.

A potentially lucrative business, because the printed Yellow Pages currently generate billions of dollars in revenue for the regional Bell operating companies (RBOCs). According to a study done by SRI, the (print) Yellow Pages are considered trustworthy, a source of information and not just advertising.

Although the telephone companies have dealt with competition in the print medium from other directory companies, they might find it harder to combat an on-rush of on-line competition from newspapers, magazines, and multimedia producers with on-line services attached to CD-ROMs. The telephone companies will eventually produce their own CD-ROM–based Yellow Pages with more graphics and interactive listings. Unlike a telephone book printed only once a year, an on-line service can be updated frequently to keep up with changes.

+ See also **on-line classified ads**.

## on-ramps

Ways to get onto the information superhighway.

Basically, any host computer that links your computer to the Internet.

## OOP

+ See **object-oriented programming**.

## open architecture

Flexible, open-ended computer system.

A design philosophy based on the principle that different operating systems should still share enough commonality that they can work together. Having been discussed in the computer industry for years, open architecture runs into snags when different manufacturers have to decide how to implement the idea.

Usually, engineers talk in terms of layers like word processing. At the bottom, layers are basic capabilities that each system would handle in the same way. As you go up in layers, there is less compatibility and more company-specific differences. These enable firms to produce products that still have distinguishing (and therefore marketable) features.

## open network architecture (ONA)

Public switching network that, as conceived by the Federal Communications Commission (FCC), would encourage companies to provide value-added services such as voice mail, E-mail, and automated telephone shopping.

The companies that provide these services would use the telephone lines provided by local telephone companies. However, because the telephone companies want to be value-added providers as well, the FCC is concerned that local telephone companies will have an unfair advantage over other businesses. The ONA concept solves this dilemma by obliging the local telephone companies to provide the same class of service to nonaffiliated value-added companies as they provide to their own internal value-added divisions. Thus, the telephone company's architecture is "open" and the playing field is level.

## open systems interconnection (OSI)

Internationally accepted standard developed by ISO to allow communication between different information systems made by different vendors.

The goal of OSI is to create an open systems networking environment where all systems are interoperable. Most communications protocols today are based on the OSI model.

## operating system (OS)

Software that manages the basic resources of a computer.

The operating system allocates main memory, schedules tasks, determines how information is received from the keyboard, controls how material is moved to the screen and to the printer, and presents a default interface to the user between applications. The capabilities provided by the operating system and its design philosophy influ-

**OSI**

# The Battle Over Computer Network Design

The open systems interconnection reference model was developed by committee in the early 1980s when no one anticipated that the ARPAnet's Internet architecture would become the foundation of a global computer network. Consequently, OSI is not a particularly useful for the Net's design, because it does not address the unique problems of inter-networking, or connecting physically incompatible networks. Indeed, when ARPAnet officials tried to argue to the OSI committee that the standard had to be altered to accommodate on-line networking, committee members rebuffed them. To this day, Internet experts will cite the Net's own architecture as the most important standard, rather than OSI.

At the center of the OSI model is a seven-layer pile, termed a protocol stack. Although the layers are independent, they are collected into upper and lower groups. The first four layers—the lower group—concern themselves with getting a message from one point to another across the network. The last three layers—the upper group—deliver services to users.

The lowest layer is the physical medium—the cables and wires—through which the network signals travel. Above the physical lines lies the data-link layer, which addresses the

problem of transmitting data from point to point without them turning into gibberish. Protocols at the data-link level do this by putting data into packets, whose signals may then move from a computer through a telephone line to a server, or from a local area network over a T-1 leased line to a backbone. Each jump poses a new data-link problem. On the Internet, address resolution protocols and SLIP/PPP protocols make sure data get to a specific computer identified by its Internet address.

The network layer, third in the stack, routes messages from one point to another, although its Internet protocol doesn't worry about whether the data are actually received. That is done by the fourth layer, transport, which manages the data transmission using three separate protocols.

The upper-layer group—the session, presentation, and application layers—make certain that the user can access a local network; either compress, encrypt, decompress, or unscramble the data (if necessary); and send or accept the file in the appropriate format. Data moving out from the computer are said to be "going down the stack," while incoming information moves "up the stack." All simple enough—kind of.

ence the programming style and technical culture associated with the computer. MS-DOS, UNIX, OS/2, Windows, and the Mac's System 7 are operating systems.

When Microsoft's Windows 95 operating system reached the marketplace, supporters said it would both streamline and enhance the capabilities available on IBM PCs and compatibles. Cynics said Microsoft was simply copying (and playing catch-up) with Apple's Macintosh operating system, and at the same time rolling out a superb vehicle for selling the enhancements the system needs to run properly on most older computers.

## open systems interconnection

**Application Layer**
defines standards for application
& communication services

**Presentation Layer**
defines file formats,
file access formats

**Host Process**

**Session Layer**
makes/maintains logical
connections

**Transport Layer**
controls the delivery of information

**Network Layer**
handles data routing and addressing

**Data Link Layer**
defines data frames and ensures
reliable transmissions

**Communication
Subnet**

**Physical Layer**
handles cabling and communications medium

## optical character recognition (OCR)

Technology able to scan, and thus digitize, an entire book even if it was printed in the 19th century with an archaic font.

The ultimate challenge to OCR is to understand handwriting. Programs that do this must first be capable of understanding the idiosyncrasies of penmanship. When that is accomplished, you will be able to scribble a note on a pad with a computerized pen and see your handwriting reproduced as clean-typed text.

✚ See also **pen interface**.

## optical fiber

Glass filament that makes up fiber-optic cable.

It may be either single or multi-mode. Single-mode fiber is thinner, more efficient, and more expensive. It also has more bandwidth than multi-mode.

## optical memory

Computer memory that is stored in an optical medium, such as a compact disk, and is read with an infrared laser beam.

Most optical memory is read-only (ROM); you cannot manipulate the data on it. Magneto-optical memory is a particular kind of memory that is both readable and writeable with a laser beam.

## OS

✚ See **operating system**.

## OSI

✚ See **open system interconnect**.

## overlay

Layering of text, graphics, or video on top of other graphics or video on a display.

# packet to pulse-code modulation

## packet

Chunk of data sent over a network.

When you transmit or receive anything over a network, it is broken up into packets. Data are divided before they are sent, and regrouped when received. In addition to the actual data, each packet contains the address of where it's going, and where it came from. That way, even if the packets are sent by different routes, they can be put back together in correct order once they have arrived. E-mail is sent on the Internet by packet switching.

The packet is composed of a stream of characters that consists of a header, the information being sent, and an error-checking sequence. The header gives the destination address, the sender address, and any other address used for relaying the packet. The error-checking sequence ensures that the data received are the data that were sent.

## packet assembler/disassembler

Hardware that enables a terminal not equipped for packet switching to get onto a packet-switching network.

The PAD converts ("assembles") data and the destination address into packets for transmission. Upon arrival, the PAD strips ("disassembles") the address from the packet and passes the data to the recipient.

## packet internet gopher (ping)

A program used to test for the presence of destinations in a packet-switched network.

It does so by sending an Internet control message protocol (ICMP) echo request, and waiting for the replying "ping."

## packet radio

The transmission of data via portable units that communicate over radio frequencies.

The transmissions are divided into packets as they are sent. It's a packet-switching scheme using the AX.25 version of the international X.25 protocol.

## packet switching

Sending discrete units of information across a network to a remote destination.

**packet switching**

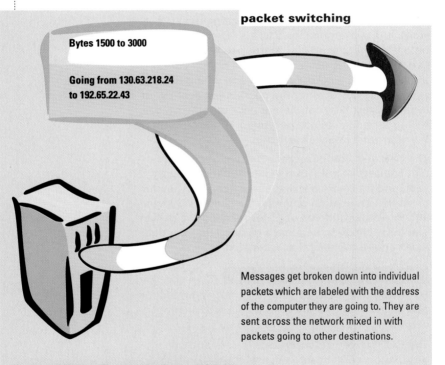

Bytes 1500 to 3000

Going from 130.63.218.24
to 192.65.22.43

Messages get broken down into individual packets which are labeled with the address of the computer they are going to. They are sent across the network mixed in with packets going to other destinations.

**Form of Data Transmission: TCP/IP**
(Internet Protocol)

## paging

Sending a message to a person whose exact location is not known.

Paging systems range from announcements over loudspeakers in airports to phone calls that are automatically sent to a beeper carried by the person who's to be paged. These beeper systems are functional in most large cities. The beeper itself is a tiny receiver that usually displays the telephone number of the caller, so the party who has been paged can call back. Some beepers can display messages a few characters long.

## PAL

+ See **phase alternate line**.

## parallel interface

Method of connecting peripherals, such as printers, to computers by sending data in synchronous parallel flows, which is less common but faster than serial interfacing.

## parallel processing

An architecture for computers in which many instructions are carried out simultaneously.

The basic premise behind early computers was that the computer would process instructions in series—one at a time, but very quickly. This serial architecture forms the basis for almost all current computers. But by the late '70s and early '80s alternative architectures began to be theorized and built. The leading option is a parallel processor, which processes many instructions simultaneously, although each one is processed more slowly. For certain problems that rely on many variables, or require the comparison of many factors, such as a weather prediction, this parallelism gives a faster answer. Some of today's supercomputers are built as parallel processors.

+ See also **neural network** and **transputer**.

## parameter random access memory (PRAM)

The battery-operated memory that keeps track of settings on a computer, such as clock time and what peripheral is connected to which port.

## password

Personal secret code that lets you access a program or log on to a network.

Once a password is entered, the system checks to see if it is on the list of authorized words. If so, you're in like Flynn. Passwords are not necessarily an effective defense against crackers, however; a good guess and security is breached. A survey by the Computer Emergency Response Team indicates that 80 percent of network security problems are caused by people choosing passwords that are too easy to guess.

Some ways to design an effective password:

- Don't use any part of your name.
- Avoid personal information such as phone numbers.
- Don't limit the password to numbers, but do mix numbers and letters in a memorable way.
- Skip well-known acronyms or industry terms.
- Don't use numbers or letters in the sequence in which they appear on a keyboard.

## pay-per-view

Special-event programming that the viewer can select—if he or she pays the extra charge for watching.

Events can range from several hours of operatic performance by Luciano Pavarotti to a less-than-two-minute fight between Mike Tyson and Peter McNeeley at a Las Vegas casino.

✛ See also **video-on-demand**.

## PBX

✛ See **private branch exchange**.

## PC

✛ See **personal computer**.

## PCI

✛ See **peripheral component interconnect**.

## PCM

✛ See **pulse-code modulation**.

## PCMCIA

✛ See **Personal Computer Memory Card International Association**.

## PCS

✛ See **personal communication service**.

## PDA

✛ See **personal digital assistant**.

## PDN

✛ See **public data network**.

## PDS

+ See **personal digital system**.

## pen interface

Technology enabling you to enter information into a computer by writing with a special pen directly on a computer screen.

The primary limitation of this technology is the difficulty software has in interpreting handwriting. Even with ever-improving optical character recognition, pen-based computing works best when users only need to use the pen to check items off a list, or sign a form on a graphics tablet.

+ See also **personal digital assistant and personal digital system**.

Photo courtesy of Apple Computer, Inc.

## peripheral component interconnect (PCI)

High-speed bus connection commonly used between parts of a computer (like a video capture card and a central processing unit) and the peripheral devices linked to it, such as a printer or modem.

## persistence of vision

The human ability to perceive quickly changing still-pictures as motion pictures.

The human eye takes approximately 1/15th of a second to capture a single "picture" of everything in its visual field and transmit that information to the occipital cortex of the brain. Fifteen times a second, the brain receives these discrete reports and synthesizes them into an image of the world. Because there is a built-in latency of 1/15th of a second during this transmission and interpretation process, images recorded on the human retina are said to "persist" for a brief interval.

This persistence of vision gives rise to a second phenomenon, known as flicker fusion: If a succession of still pictures is shown to the human eye at 15 frames per second or faster, the sequence of stills will be fused or smoothed out by the brain and perceived as continuous motion.

+ See also **animation**.

## personal communication service (PCS)

A system that tracks an individual's location and routes incoming telephone calls accordingly.

Cellular telephone carriers have offered a version of personal communication service for years. A major

# Stars, Apples, And Clones

Strictly speaking, the first personal computer was the Alto—later the Star—developed at Xerox PARC in 1973. The subsequent Altair MITS was advertised on the January 1975 cover of *Popular Electronics*, and 4,000 were sold within three months.

In 1977, Apple Computer introduced the Apple II. It became a best-seller in 1979 when VisiCalc, the first spreadsheet program, hit the market and could run only on the Apple. IBM did not enter the personal computer business until 1981, when it introduced the PC. It quickly established a de facto standard. IBM did not keep its specifications proprietary, so "clones" soon appeared—computers that could run IBM PC software, but were made by other companies. The personal computer business never looked back.

In 1982, Sun Microsystems introduced the first commercial workstation, a high-powered, memory-laden PC designed to run on a network. The Sun workstation ran UNIX software and was popular among scientists and engineers who appreciated its number-crunching capacity.

In 1984, Apple introduced the Macintosh, which offered a much more friendly and easy-to-use interface based on icons, windows, and a mouse. The interface attracted many new users who had been put off by the need to enter obscure commands to use the PC. It also had great appeal to designers and graphic artists because it was more visually oriented. The Macintosh, and Apple's introduction of the laser printer, paved the way for desktop publishing.

In the 1990s, personal computers are as powerful as the mainframes of the 1970s and minicomputers of the 1980s. Desktop PCs are now hooked into networks, where distributed computing and workgroup computing are new business paradigms. These concepts enable people to solve problems together by working on material shared over the network.

auction of an additional spectrum for a cheaper version of PCS garnered billions of dollars for the federal government and presages a massive growth in the wireless market.

We are on the verge of creating a revolution as dramatic as the introduction of the telephone itself, in which everyone will be able to reach everyone instantly, no matter where anyone is located. These systems have grown from one-way paging and messaging to two-way carriers offering voice and data transmission.

## personal computer (PC)

Computer for a single user, designed to operate independently of any other computer or network.

© Paul Schulenburg/Spots on the Spot!

Originally intended for home and small office use, PCs now are everywhere, and they are now commonly linked in networks, too.

## Personal Computer Memory Card International Association (PCMCIA)

Association of computer companies that is defining international standards for the size and capabilities of memory cards and smart cards—little units the size of credit cards that can be inserted into different computers and machines.

The aim is for the cards to be used interchangeably in different personal digital assistants, laptops, and video games. A PCMCIA card may hold extra memory, a miniature hard drive, or even a wireless network interface.

✚ See also **personal digital system**.

## personal digital assistant (PDA)

A portable computer, complete with modem, that is small enough to be held in one hand and operated with the other.

A "palmtop" PDA has a small screen—about five inches by seven inches—that is just big enough for a page of your address book or a short "to-do" list. Slightly larger PDAs with 8.5-by-11-inch screens are ideal for doctors making rounds, scientists doing fieldwork, or delivery people keeping track of their tender.

A doctor equipped with a PDA that has an FM wireless link to a server can assign a prescription, find out if there are any conflicts with other medications the patient is taking, and wire it into the pharmacy, all in a few seconds.

+ See also **cell-net** and **personal digital system**.

## personal digital system (PDS)

A personal digital assistant, distributed by IBM, with PCMCIA memory and smart card slots plus a cellular telephone.

Smart cards extend the functions of the PDS to include sending faxes, listening to radio, and even taking pictures.

## personal identification number (PIN)

A password, often four digits long, that enables you to access a database and interact with it, as when withdrawing money from a bank account at an automatic teller machine.

## PGP

+ See **Pretty Good Privacy**.

## phase alternate line (PAL)

Color television broadcast standard throughout Europe with the exception of France (where SECAM rules).

+ See also **National Television Systems Committee (NTSC)** and **television standards**.

## Photo CD

Introduced by Eastman Kodak, a system for processing ordinary exposed film into digital imagery.

A special lab at Kodak scans the images on a developed roll of film and stores them as high-resolution files on a compact disk. Existing slides or prints can be transferred to a CD as well. Photo CDs are inexpensive and yet offer high quality. Using a Photo CD player (also sold by Kodak, of course), images can be viewed on a television screen or computer monitor.

The photo CD system has the potential to reinvent the photography industry, for two reasons. One, CD-ROM photographs can be easily manipulated. If Aunt Harriet's face was darkened by a shadow, it can be lightened. A flower can be cut from the rose bush in the photograph and pasted onto her wide-brimmed hat, too. Second, Photo CDs are proving valuable as a storage medium for photographs. Their life span is around 50 years, about as long as

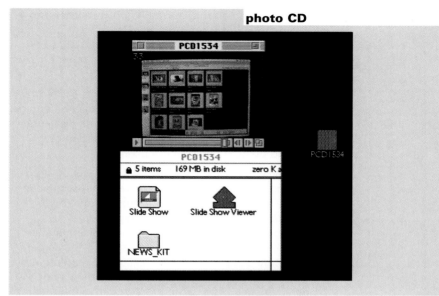

Screen capture courtesy of Kodak.

negatives last, but they are less fragile, more compact, and easier to access and view.

A standard Photo CD disk stores up to 100 photos
from any number of recording sessions. The Photo
CD presages the day when consumers will store all
snapshots in digital photo albums.

## picon

✚ See icon.

## PIN

✚ See personal identification number.

## ping

Slang for *packet Internet gopher.*

## pirating

✚ See copyright.

## pixel

Abbreviation for picture-element, the tiniest element
on a display screen.

A screen is made up of phosphors or liquid crystals
arranged in a grid. There is a minimum-sized point
of light these elements can project. This picture
element, a circle or square, is the basic building
block of an image shown on the screen. A typical

computer screen may have 640 pixels across and 480 down. The color and intensity of each pixel can be controlled; by changing the characteristics of each of the thousands of pixels on a screen, an entire image is formed.

On a black and white monitor, a pixel is either black or white. On a color monitor, a pixel may be any of hundreds or thousands of colors. On digitally controlled systems, images can be touched up or altered by manipulating the pixels.

One way to measure picture resolution is by the number of pixels used to create an image, relative to the screen size. Some monitors allow you to change the resolution of the image display by enlarging or shrinking the pixel size. For instance, an Apple 20-inch monitor can display a full screen at 832 by 624 pixels, or it can sacrifice resolution by blowing up each pixel and creating a display of 640 by 480 pixels. The same monitor can exhibit its highest resolution of 1152 by 870 pixels by squeezing the pixels to a smaller and thus more precise size. The price: It saps more of the computer's processing power.

## pixel aspect ratio

The ratio of the horizontal side of a pixel to its vertical side.

The aspect ratio of a square pixel is one to one. Though the square pixel is common, some systems have different-shaped pixels that must be taken into account in the preparation of any display. Odd-shaped final images result from ignoring this relative sizing.

## platform

Collection of basic hardware, software, and standards on which a company builds its many computers or computer-operated devices.

It is the common foundation on which different houses are built. In the auto industry, it's the bare-bones chassis, engine type, and electronics on which different car models are built.

Computer manufacturers make their platforms proprietary so that consumers will not "mix and match" components from other manufacturers.

In practice, platform can be used to describe either hardware or software and is often used to refer to operating systems; for example, a " UNIX-based" platform.

Proprietary information involves closely guarded secrets, whose release (and the timing thereof) can dramatically influence a product or technology's market share. In the 1980s IBM let the platform for the PC become public. Companies that made cheaper clones captured a large share of the market. However, in doing so, they made the PC operating system—MS-DOS—dominant, and IBM benefited along with everyone. Apple didn't license manufacturers of clones and suffered. Because more software and CD-ROMs were written for the DOS format, IBM and the others grabbed most of the market share. Apple is now declaring a truce in the long-standing platform war with DOS machines by offering hybrids—computers with both types of microprocessors, operating systems, and ports.

✚ See also **cross platform**.

## point of information (POI)

Use of an electronic kiosk to provide information to a visitor in a public place such as a museum, historic landmark, or shopping mall.

Prior to the development of the kiosk, most information at these kinds of sites was provided by a guidebook, tape recorder, or (gasp!) a human. Interactive multimedia kiosks allow information to be continuously updated. With this capability, the point of information system has important implications for retail shopping. Some believe the catalog and the cashier will become obsolete when there is a point-of-information terminal in every home.

✚ See also **point of purchase**.

## point of presence (POP)

A POP is a location of an internet server, i.e., internet service providers such as Netcom or UUNET talk about their POP's (location of their servers).

A POP is also a physical location within a local access and transport area (LATA) where a long-distance telephone carrier meets the network of the local telephone company.

A long-distance carrier may have more than one point of presence within a LATA, and the POP may support public and private, switched and non-switched services.

## point of purchase (POP)

A kiosk or vending-type machine in stores and shopping malls that can display products, give current pricing, and complete a transaction for purchasing an item.

All you do is walk to a window to pick up the product—and, of course, pay the bill.

✚ See also **point of information**.

## point-to-point protocol (PPP)

A protocol allowing a personal computer to connect to the Internet with just a modem and a regular telephone line.

It's like Serial Line Internet Protocol (SLIP), but with better error correction. These dial-up links are less expensive and slower than the more direct Ethernet or token ring connections.

### point-to-point protocol (PPP)

**Point-to-Point Protocol (PPP)** transmits data over phone lines. It operates the same as SLIP but is slightly faster. PPP is based on ISO 3309 protocol, which is incorporated into ISDN, X.25 and other protocol suites. With ATM, octets are transmitted with 1 start bit, 8 data bits, and 1 stop bit.

**Octets** are 8-bit quantities, often referred to in networking as "bytes" because some computers are designed to use bytes of some length other than 8 bits.

| Octets 1 | 1 | 1 | 2 | n | 2 | 1 |
|---|---|---|---|---|---|---|
| Beginning Flag (Start Bit) | Address (Set to FFH, the allstations address) | Control (Set to 03H for unnumbered info) | Protocol (ID's the higher layer protocol in use) | Data/Information (Higher layer information with default max length of 1,500 octets) | Frame Check Sequence (FCS) | Ending Flag (Stop Bit) |

**IP Datagram**
The packet into which the Internet Protocol places the segments delivered by the TCP.

## POP

+ See **point of presence, or point of purchase**.

## port

(1) Socket or outlet on a computer where a cable connection is made to peripherals (like a printer or modem) or to another computer. (2) Number assigned to a particular service, such as E-mail or Telnet, at a host computer. (3) Sweet wine from Portugal.

External sockets are usually serial ports or parallel ports. Serial ports allow a single stream of data to be input into the computer, and parallel ports allow a multiple stream of data in to the computer.

+ See also **small computer systems interface (SCSI)**.

## portable computer

© Christoph Hitz/Spots on the Spot

Miniature personal computer, between three and seven pounds, that includes a space-saving hard disk and an LCD monitor. Also called a laptop or notebook computer.

Many have modems and CD-ROM drives as well. They are powered by batteries that are recharge-able with AC current or even portable solar panels. A laptop offers the user considerable freedom. You can work on your commuter train, or on an airplane, or on safari in Africa—until your batteries run out. Battery power is a critical bottleneck, constraining performance and blocking further product miniaturization.

## posting

An electronic mail message sent to a Usenet newsgroup.

Posting is like tacking up a message on the wall, for all to read. The only difference is that once it's up, you can't take it down. Postings have headings that indicate the writer's identity, the subject matter, a synopsis of the contents, and keywords.

Postings are meant to be read by a newsgroup's public. Anyone can join a newsgroup and read postings. Friendly advice: Read a newsgroup for a period of days before posting; it will give you a better feel for the direction of the discussions. And don't post a query until you have first reviewed the

# The Great Debate In Cyberspace

To eavesdrop, or not to eavesdrop, that is the question.

With a sysop's ability to read and forward other people's E-mail, privacy is an issue on any network. Encryption is a common tactic against unwanted monitoring or "wiretapping." The Clipper chip—a piece of hardware that would enable encryption but also allow the government to listen in on any electronic communication—became a controversial issue because many computer users see it as a threat to their privacy.

With increasing awareness of crackers' capability to pry into the recesses of corporate vaults, people are concerned about the vulnerability of supposedly confidential information. Businesses deal with these threats by erecting firewalls between the privately and publicly accessible parts of their networks.

Privacy has also become an issue as marketing strategists refine techniques of tracking consumers on-line. As long as records of digital cash transactions and remote services are available, entire personal profiles may be generated and used for marketing or other purposes.

✦ See also copyright.

newsgroup's FAQs (or frequently asked questions).
Otherwise, brace yourself for appearing to sound
foolish.

## POTS

Acronym for "plain old telephone service."

POTS means just that—a telephone connected to a
standard line. No bells or whistles like call-waiting
or call-forwarding.

## PPP

✦ See point-to-point protocol.

## PRAM

✦ See parameter random access memory.

## Pretty Good Privacy (PGP)

System for encrypting electronic messages, avail-
able free on the Internet and sold commercially by
ViaCrypt.
✦ See also encryption.

## primary rate interface (PRI)

The basic services an ISDN central office will bring
to the user, providing voice, data, or video communications.

The primary rate interface is the ISDN equivalent of
a T-1 circuit. It operates in the United States at
1.544 megabits per second.

## privacy

The right not to be monitored.
✦ See also Digital Telephony Act 1994, encryption, intellectual
property, and key escrow.

> *"Are you happy with strong encryption the government can't decode?"*
>
> — ***Ester Dyson*** in
> Wired, *1995*

> *"It's inevitable. It's not even a question of, 'Are you happy or unhappy.' It's like the question, 'Am I happy that a terrorist might someday be able to rent a truck and have a tactical nuclear weapon?' It's inevitable. That being true, how do you deal with it? If you have adequate reason to believe the group is genuinely dangerous, then you may be able to get a court order blocking encryption, saying this particular group for these reasons cannot use encryption. They will then, of course, promptly evolve into a new group. My reaction to this whole*

## private branch exchange (PBX)

Private telephone switching system that links the many telephones in a large operation such as a hotel, business, or government office.

It's a cabinet of switches purchased from commercial suppliers that is installed on the premises.

All the lines within that operation are handled through the PBX's switching console. Some corporations have set up PBXs that serve various buildings on a site, bypassing the local phone company. Some also link offices in distant cities by having their PBXs communicate via satellite, bypassing the long-distance telephone carrier.

## private network

A network of offices linked by phone lines that are controlled by the organization's own private or leased switching facility.

It's having your own phone company.

+ See also **virtual private network**.

## program

The set of instructions for an automated system or a computer that dictates how it performs a particular job.

A source program is written by a person in a high-level language. Another program, called a compiler, turns the source program into a low-level language that the computer can understand and use.

+ See also **applications** and **software**.

## programmable read-only memory (PROM)

A memory chip whose information can be read repeatedly, but never changed ("written").

## programming

Act of writing instructions for a computer so that it will perform a specific task.

Programming encompasses developing an algorithm, writing code, and then testing and debugging the program.

## projected reality

Quasi–virtual reality system that incorporates a performer's movements using simple feedback

It does not use the complex gear of sensors and head-mounted displays of truly immersive virtual reality.

## PROM

+ See programmable read only memory.

## proprietary

When a company owns and controls a set of standards.

+ See also platform.

## protocol stack

Group of protocols, in hierarchical layers, which control the operation of a network.

Examples are Transmission Control Protocol/ Internet Protocol (TCP/IP) and open systems interconnection (OSI).

## protocols

Rules that different computers use to communicate and work with each other.

Protocols describe how the packets of information that are sent from one computer to another are to be broken down for the trip and how they are to be reassembled at the receiving end. TCP/IP is the international language that is spoken by computers on the Internet. When we drive our cars, we follow protocols too: We drive on the right side of the road, stay within (or at least close to) certain speed limits, stop at red lights, and drive in certain directions on on-ramps and off-ramps. Otherwise, we as data packets collide and destruct.

## public data network (PDN)

A network for the transmission of digital data in packets (cells of information) over high-speed channels.

Public data networks are cheaper than dialing directly on switched voice lines. They are also used to access databases and services that are inaccessible by dialing direct. Tymnet and Telenet

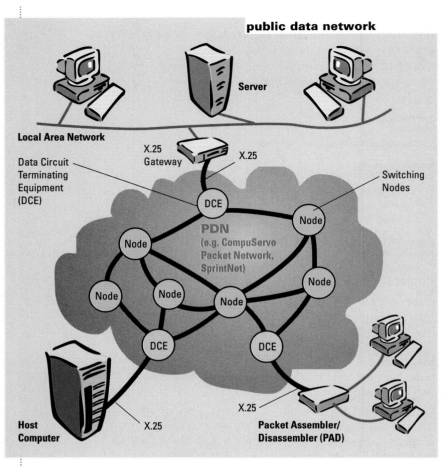

## public data network

**Server**

**Local Area Network**

X.25 Gateway

X.25

Data Circuit Terminating Equipment (DCE)

Switching Nodes

DCE

Node

**PDN**
(e.g. CompuServe Packet Network, SprintNet)

Node

Node

Node

Node

Node

DCE

DCE

X.25

**Host Computer**

X.25

**Packet Assembler/ Disassembler (PAD)**

are two PDNs in the United States. Most industrialized countries have at least one PDN, often owned by the government.

## public domain software

Software for which there is no copyright.

It may be used and copied without paying any fee. Caution: Just because a file is available on the Internet, and shows no indication of being copyrighted, it is not necessarily in the public domain. The copyright law says the work belongs to its author unless the author has specifically given up the rights.

## Public Utilities Commission (PUC)

State government agency that regulates and monitors the rates that can be charged by utility companies, including telephone companies.

## pulse-code modulation (PCM)

Translation of analog voice signal into digital form.

PCM makes the transmission of voice convenient because it can travel on a line with other kinds of digital information. PCM is clearer—with less static—and less expensive than analog transmission. This modulation is also used for recording digital sound onto tape. Hi-8 videotape can record both a PCM audio track and a regular analog video track.

With PCM, the amplitude of the voice is sampled 8,000 times a second and then encoded as binary data. At the receiving end, these data are "reconstituted" and then amplified to their original level.

✚ See also **adaptive differential pulse-code modulation (ADPCM), compact disk-digital audio (CD-DA), digital audio,** and **modulation**.

# Q

Quixotic

## quantize

Step in the process of converting an analog signal into a digital signal.

This step measures a sample to determine a numerical value, which is then encoded. The three conversion steps are sampling, quantizing, and encoding.

✦ See also **analog-to-digital converter**.

## QuickTime

Apple's widely used multimedia function, which allows text, sound, video, and animation to be combined and used in one file.

Useful for audio-visual presentations, a QuickTime production can include a short video segment, voice-over narration, and simple interactive commands. QuickTime movies are fun, brief spots of moving images, but not full-screen full-motion videos.

## QWERTY

✦ See **keyboard**.

Remedy

### random access memory (RAM)

Computer memory is called random access when the central processing unit (CPU) can directly retrieve or store information on any part of the memory.

In other words, the CPU does not have to start at the beginning. It can retrieve or store the information anywhere in the memory at the same speed.

✚ See also read-only memory (ROM).

### raster

Process of horizontally scanning a cathode ray tube (CRT) screen with a beam to create an image.

✚ See also pixel.

### raster image file format (RIFF)

File format for projecting images with grayscale values.

### RBOC

✚ See regional Bell operating company.

### read-only memory (ROM)

Storage medium that only allows access to the information written to it; the information cannot be altered (and is not lost when power is turned off).

Operating systems for computers are stored in ROM. Music stored on compacts disks is also an example of ROM.

### read/write media

Storage systems—either optical, electromagnetic, or magneto-optical—where information can be written to and read from.

Prime example: a computer disk.

### real soon now (RSN)

Trendy Net phrase used to imply that something is supposed to happen, but probably will not unless the gods, fate, and the weather permit.

For example, Marlon Brando will do an exercise video with Richard Simmons real soon now.

### real time

Actual time in which an event takes place.

When you watch a tape of a baseball game, you are watching something that already took place. When you watch the game live, you are watching it in real time. This applies to activity on networks as well. If you open your E-mail box and get a message from foo, foo wrote it in the past. If you get on a chat line, however, you will see foo's comments appear on the screen as he types them—that is, in real time.

### real-time animation

Animation that is generated as you are watching it.

Flight simulation programs where you see the landscape appear below your fighter plane and computer aided design (CAD) programs that allow you to walk through a house you have designed both use real-time animation to create their immediacy. The angle of view of these synthetic environments is defined by the position of the viewer, which must be programmed into the real-time animation program. With ideal real-time animation, the computer generates images as fast as you can look around.

In a virtual reality system, real-time animation is displayed in stereoscope on the dual screens of a head-mounted display.

### real-time operating system (RTOS)

An operating system that provides coordination and synchronous playback between the various elements in a multimedia or virtual reality application.

To appear seamless, audio, video, and any user interactions must be perfectly synchronized.

The trade name of the operating system at the heart of the Philips CD-I appliances is RTOS.

### real-time video (RTV)

Compression function of digital video interactive (DVI).

With RTV, the video images are compressed in real time. Relatively low resolution is required for this to work.

### reality engine

Computer firmware that creates the sights and sounds of a virtual reality environment.

A reality engine includes graphics and sound processors that can generate real-time visual and aural stimuli that make a computer-synthesized reality convincing. Silicon Graphics Inc. sells a fast graphic workstation trade-named Reality Engine.

### rec

The recreational category of newsgroups on Usenet.

All you'd ever want to know and hear about cartoons, science fiction, Star Trek, cooking, cars, humor, sports, pets, and movies.

### Red, Green, Blue (RGB)

Primary color system used in computer, television, and video applications.

An RGB image has higher quality than a composite or broadcast video signal, because the RGB color signal is not first encoded and then decoded before activating the phosphors on the display screen. It is therefore the display procedure of choice.

✛ See also **National Television Systems Committee**.

### reduced instruction set computer (RISC)

A microprocessor that requires only a small number of operating instructions to perform all its duties.

Because these microprocessors are simpler than complex instruction set computer chips, they are also easier and cheaper to manufacture. Their fast processing has made them invaluable for multimedia applications and personal digital assistant technology. RISC computers figure heavily in the convergence of video and telecommunications and have begun to replace the slower CISC technology in the newest computers. The Motorola Power PC chips are RISC.

## refresh rate

(1) Number of times per second an image is repro-jected a on CRT screen. (2) In active memory chips, the number of times per second they must be reen-ergized to maintain the data they are keeping.

For computer graphics, refresh rate is controlled by three factors: the speed of the microprocessor, the speed of the hard drive (or whatever storage medi-um) from which information is read, and the resolu-tion and size of the image being displayed.

## regional Bell operating company (RBOC)

Telephone companies established by the 1984 divestiture of AT&T.

There are several RBOCs that cover the United States, and each of them owns two or more Bell operating companies—your local phone company. The seven original RBOCs were Ameritech, Bell Atlantic, Bell South, NYNEX, Pacific Telesis, SBC Communications Inc., and U.S. West. The tele-phone companies owned by SBC Communications Inc. still operate under the name Southwestern Bell.

+ See also **AT&T Consent Decree**.

## regulations

Rules imposed by public authorities that attempt to create an even playing field for businesses and to ensure they maintain a degree of public account-ability.

Authorities include the Federal Communications Commission (FCC), the Federal Trade Commission (FTC), and the state public utilities commissions, among others. In the 1980s, regulations restricting competition in the telecommunications industry began to come under scrutiny. The seminal event was the breakup of AT&T in 1984, a court decision founded on antitrust regulations designed to pre-vent monopolies. Soon thereafter, the FCC began to loosen the regulations that limited the profit a tele-vision station or cable TV system could make; among other changes, the regulators no longer lim-ited commercials or required public affairs and chil-dren's programming.

In 1992, in response to a struggling economy, the FCC deregulated the radio airwaves, allowing freer ownership of multiple stations. Arguments for and against further deregulation began to focus on the question of balance between profitability, competition, and the free marketplace on the one hand, and freedom of noncommercial expression, public service, and accountability. That debate climaxed in 1995, as the Telecommunications Act moved through the U.S. House of Representatives and the Senate.

The telecommunications bill, which had not received the support of the White House, mirrored the trend toward further telecommunications deregulation through converging telephone, broadcasting, and computer industries. Presaging a competitive free-for-all, the legislation included dropping most cable television rate regulation, allowing cable TV carriers to sell information services, permitting local telephone and cable companies to compete, and freeing long-distance carriers to sell local telephone service. Further deregulation is expected.

## relational database

A database that contains cross-referenced entries.

Each entry is described by several different traits, so that you can search for groupings of these characteristics using Boolean operators.

## remote host

A host you access via Telnet, FTP, or a search engine such as Gopher or WAIS.

## remote sensing

Taking an image of the earth's surface from a plane or satellite, and digitizing it so it can be transmitted to computers down there on the ground.

Remote sensing was originally used by the military for surveillance. Today, sensors that take ultraviolet and infrared images are used to show the extent of deforestation, cloud cover, urban sprawl, and geological features several meters below the earth's surface.

## remote services

Services you can access through a distant computer.

Some examples: When you get money from your bank account at an ATM machine, you are using a remote service. Telemedicine enables you to access your doctor's advice remotely. Home shopping is a remote service offered on cable TV. The future home shopper may have remote tailoring—clothes or shoes made to order based on personal measurements taken by an interactive fitting capability. **Virtual reality** technologies could play a significant role in future remote services from **interactive video** games to virtual parties.

## Remotely Operated Vehicle (ROV)

Vehicle operated through remote control.

Used to be those great toy cars and planes; now the military may use them for surveillance and even bombing. Businesses use them in factories and warehouses to transport materials, supplies, work in progress, and the finished product.

## repeater

The amplifier in a **transmission** line that boosts the **signal** so that it is carried further.

## repurposing

The belief that preexisting television programs, movies, photographic archives, and books can be reengineered into successful **interactive** products.

The belief is that by adding supplemental graphics and audio, a high-impact interactive product can be created. This is usually an illusion of the owners, who are hoping to find profits in new **media**. Some think repurposing just siphons creative resources and money from the harder, but ultimately more rewarding, work of creating new entertainment and educational experiences.

## request for discussion

Posting on **Usenet** that is sent to the group news.announce.newsgroups, proposing the creation of a new **newsgroup**.

Follow-up postings will list pros and cons, and—if the positives seem to outweigh the negatives—the proposer may issue a call for votes, followed by a cyberelection to decide if the newsgroup is a go.

## resolution

Clarity and sharpness of an image.

For printers, resolution is measured in **dots per inch (dpi)**. An inexpensive ink-jet printer may manage 300 dpi—already pretty sharp—while some personal laser printers do 1,200 dpi.

The resolution of monitors is measured in pixels per square inch, which may range from 64 to 96. Resolution of an NTSC television monitor varies from 260 to 400 horizontal lines per frame.

✦ See also **sampling rate**.

## resource discovery tool

A program that helps you find stuff on the Internet.

Well-known tools include Archie (which searches directories), WAIS (which looks into databases), Gopher (which lets you browse through the Net), and Mosaic (which helps you navigate the World Wide Web).

## RGB

✦ See **Red, Green, Blue**.

## RIFF

✦ See **raster image file format**.

## RISC

✦ See **reduced instruction set computer**.

## Rivest-Shamir-Adleman (RSA)

Popular algorithm for encrypting an on-line message.

RSA Data Security is a company that sells RSA-based cryptography products.

## robotics

Science of making robots—machines run by computers to do mechanical tasks.

Commonly used on factory assembly lines, robots are appropriate for tedious and dangerous jobs, and those requiring very high precision. They are employees who do not require health insurance or pensions, and never talk back. A superior robot, operating with artificial intelligence, would be able to see, recognize patterns, understand natural language, and make decisions. Robots are no longer limited to heavy industry, however; they are finding use in police work, medicine, and other fields.

*"The three fundamental Rules of Robotics.... One: A robot may not injure a human being, or, through inaction, allow a human being to come to harm.... Two: A robot must obey the orders given it by human beings except where such orders would*

## ROM

+ See **read-only memory**.

## router

Combination of hardware and software that work together to move digital traffic from one network to another.

The job of the router is to know where packets of information are headed, to make sure they are

**router**

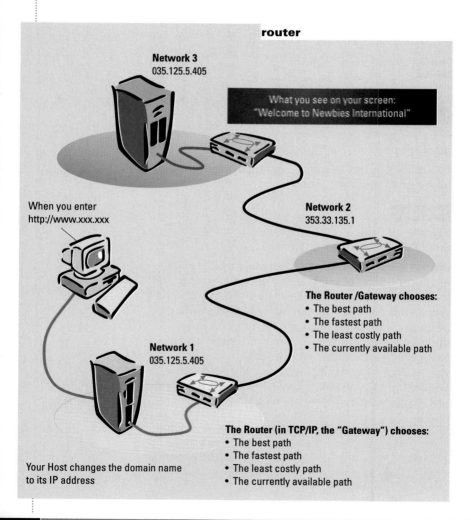

**Network 3**
035.125.5.405

What you see on your screen:
"Welcome to Newbies International"

When you enter
http://www.xxx.xxx

**Network 2**
353.33.135.1

**The Router /Gateway chooses:**
• The best path
• The fastest path
• The least costly path
• The currently available path

**Network 1**
035.125.5.405

**The Router (in TCP/IP, the "Gateway") chooses:**
• The best path
• The fastest path
• The least costly path
• The currently available path

Your Host changes the domain name
to its IP address

addressed correctly, and to send them on their way
by the most efficient route possible.

✚ See also **gateway**.

## ROV

✚ See **remotely operated vehicle**.

## RS232

Electrical standard for a serial interface between a
computer and its peripherals, set by the Electronic
Industries Association.

✚ See also **parallel interface** and **small computer systems
interface (SCSI)**.

## RSA

✚ See **Rivest-Shamir-Adleman**.

## RSN

✚ See **real soon now**.

## RTOS

✚ See **real-time operating system**.

## RTV

✚ See **real-time video**.

Stagecoach

### sampler

A device that takes many short sequential recordings—usually around 16–20 bits each—of an audio signal in order to create a single digital sound.

With a device known as a sampler player, these sounds can be assigned to different keys on a synthesizer keyboard and then played back. Sampler libraries are popular with musicians composing modern music.

### sampling rate

Number of times per second an analog signal is measured and converted to digital form.

For example, pulse-code modulation, the most common conversion scheme, samples voice 8,000 times a minute. The higher the sampling rate, the better the representation of the analog information.

### satellite communications

Communications using satellites that act as relays.

The satellites pick up signals from earth, amplify them, and return them. The signals are broadcast via microwave frequencies. Signals are received by earth stations or personal satellite dishes. Satellite communications are used for telephony, geo-positioning, meteorology, data transmission, and television. Some satellite broadcast television is encrypted so that only subscribers can receive it.

Satellites have differing capabilities. Traditionally, geostationary earth orbit satellites (GEOS) have been used for most purposes. But constellations of both low-earth orbit (LEOS) and medium-earth orbit (MEOS) satellites are scheduled to be launched before 2000. LEOS and MEOS will enable palm-sized satellite receivers to be used for worldwide telephone communications, and will eliminate the transmission delay of GEOS that gives some international calls an echo.

## scalable

The ability to easily be made larger or smaller—
sorry, doesn't work for weight watchers.

This term applies to the economic viability of a new
product as much as it does to strictly technical prop-
erties. For example, if a great new local area network is developed, and the prototype can serve five
terminals, the relevant business question is: "Can it
serve 100?" If the response is yes, then the system
is said to be scalable—and worth pursuing. If the
answer is no, the technology might be brilliant but it
will not make any money.

## scan

(1) In a television or computer CRT, the rapid journey of the scanning spot back and forth across the
inside of the screen to form scan lines. (2) In interactive media, a mode of play in which the machine
skips over several disk tracks at a time, displaying
only a fraction of the frames it passes. (3) In data
capture, the use of a scanner to convert a document
or photograph into digital data that can be stored in
a computer.

## scan conversion

The process of translating the raster format of one
television standard to that of another.

For example, converting NTSC video into phase
alternate line video.

## scanner

(1) A hardware device that captures an image
(much like a copy machine) of a document or photograph, and then digitizes it so it can be stored in a
computer's memory. (2) Portion of a machine such
as a fax machine that captures an image and converts it to a form ready for transmission.

Desktop scanners offer low resolution in the range
of 300 to 600 dpi. Fax machines contain scanners
that determine the brightness level of each pixel to
be transmitted.

## sci

A category in Usenet's world newsgroups that
includes all newsgroups related to the sciences.

### screen

Area of display on a monitor.

It is the glass you look at on your computer or TV. The screen is the physical interface between the user (you) and the information generated by the computer or television.

Screens are also useful for letting cool summer breezes waft into your beachfront condo on the Riviera.

### script

Segment of a program written in a scripting language such as Lingo or Hypertalk.

### scripting language

A high-level language that offers neophyte programmers a chance to develop their own hypermedia programs.

Simple commands allow the programmer to link elements, create pointers, and alter the sequence of events that flow from a user's actions. Macromedia Director is a popular software program for multimedia creation, using Lingo for its scripting. Hypercard uses Hypertalk.

### SCSI

✤ See small computer systems interface.

### search

(1) Instructing a database or network service to look for a particular entry, usually described with a keyword or phrase. (2) In interactive video systems, to request a specific frame, identified by its unique number, and move directly to that frame.

To facilitate on-line searches, several keywords may be linked together and qualified by the use of Boolean operators such as *and, or,* and *not.*

### search engine

Software that helps you locate files on a network.

Popular search engines for Internet are Archie and Veronica. Given the mind-boggling rate at which information is being dumped on the Internet and the World Wide Web, a browser is an indispensable aid.

✤ See also file transfer protocol (FTP).

## search time

(1) The amount of time taken to process a request and retrieve an item of information from a database. (2) In an interactive system, the amount of time it takes to request a specific frame and to arrive at that frame.

## SECAM

✚ See **Sequential Couleur à Mémoir**.

## secure http

Cryptographically enhanced protocol for World Wide Web communications and networking.

## Sega

Japanese video game company that, together with Nintendo, dominates the worldwide video game market.

Sega, like Nintendo, manufactures proprietary video game consoles that can only play Sega games. In 1993, Sega released mega-CD, a new format of CD-ROM. The company also provides interactive entertainment for PCs, portable game systems and location-based electronic theme parks.

Logo and photo of *Sonic* courtesy of Sega Corporation.

## sensenet

Mythical network that assumes the convergence of humans with telecommunications and other electronic devices, allowing direct digital connection.

As portrayed in science fiction, a network linking humans might be possible by implanting electronic devices in everybody's brain and body sensors that provide two-way tactile sensation. What fun!

✚ See also **cyberpunk** and **cyberspace**.

## sensor

Device embedded in virtual reality "clothes," such as data gloves, data suits, or head-mounted displays, that gives feedback to a computer about the movement and position in space of the person wearing the device.

✚ See also **biosensor**.

## sequencer

Computer or computer program that enables you to record, edit, and manipulate musical notes that are entered through a musical instrument digital interface (MIDI).

The sequencer acts like a word processor for music.

## Sequential Couleur à Mémoir (SECAM)

Television broadcast standard in France, the Middle East, and most of Eastern Europe.

SECAM is based on the sequential encoding of primary colors in alternating scan lines.

✦ See also **television standards**.

## serial interface

Computer port that converts the parallel arrangement of data to the serial form—bit by bit. Also called the serial port.

This is necessary for data transmission.

✦ See also **parallel interface** and **small computer systems interface (SCSI)**.

## Serial Line Internet Protocol (SLIP)

Dial-up protocol that allows Internet users to access advanced functions, such as the World Wide Web.

✦ See also **point-to-point protocol (PPP)**.

## server

Computing system in a network that shares its resources with other computers.

A server may be a PC, a workstation, or a mainframe computer. A file server is a computer that stores applications programs or files created by them. A print server enables computers on a local area network to access a common printer.

✦ See also **client-server**.

## set-top box

Hardware that sits on a television set and acts as the interface between your TV and the cable company.

Today's boxes are fairly primitive, compared with the capabilities of those in the near future. The set-top box of the next decade or two will allow two-way transmission of data and promises to be every person's on-ramp to the information superhighway.

As televisions, computers, and telephones merge into one unit, the set-top box will be the link between the individual and the outside world, providing video games, video dating, video-on-demand, and innumerable opportunities to shop, as well as the ability to vote in elections, search databases and libraries, and take advantage of distance learning. All that in a teeny little box!

## sex

The topic generating the most traffic, discussion, and controversy in cyberspace.

✦ See also **cybersex** and **virtual sex**.

## SFX

✦ See **sound effects**.

## shareware

Software that is copyrighted and freely distributed on the assumption that if you like it and use it, you will send the author a small payment.

Many valuable software utilities for the personal computer originate as shareware. If they prove popular, they are often incorporated into commercial software packages.

✦ See also **freeware**.

## shell account

Accessing the Internet through a shell—typically a minicomputer—instead of accessing it directly from your own computer.

Companies that allow employees Internet access typically use a shell, so they can monitor usage and do not have to bother with multiple connections or accounts.

## shouting

What you're doing when posting or sending E-mail written in capital letters.

Netiquette says, DON'T DO IT.

## signal

Information carried by waves of the electromagnetic spectrum.

There are five basic categories of signals in the telecommunications network: supervisory signals, information signals, address signals, control signals, and alerting signals.

# Everything You Wanted To Know About Cybersex
## (But Were Afraid To Access)

The cybersex subculture is alive and well—and reproducing like a superheated amoeba. No surprise here. In a culture bombarded with sexual messages and imagery, the ability to bombard back is irresistible for millions of net-heads. At last count more than a hundred Internet newsgroups were dedicated to aspects of cybersex, from the corny to the kinky. The total number of adult-oriented bulletin boards may number in the thousands, most of them homegrown from modest immodest beginnings.

Casual browsers of these bulletin boards will find a mixed bag of goods and services, to say the least. Cybersex can be as innocent as a World Wide Web version of Spin The Bottle—or as raunchy as a XXX-rated Marilyn Chambers film festival. It can be intimate, and it can be very public. Where love and lust meet on the Infobahn, anything goes and everything is possible.

Male users vastly outnumber females, as women tend to discover quickly upon signing up. Sexual harassment is a widely reported fact of cyberlife. Still, men own no monopoly in the province of electronic swingers, where bulletin boards designed by and for women are also beginning to proliferate.

First, some useful distinctions between cybersex, America's fastest-growing indoor sports, and cyberporn, one of its most controversial:

With cybersex, two or more individuals typically meet modem to modem through an adult chat line to exchange sexual fantasies in a game of can-you-top-this. Climax may be optional, but titillation is everything. Cybersex encounters are anonymous (usually), mysterious (you never know), and safe (compared to most forms of physical sex, though emotional trauma can be real).

Think of the experience as logging on to an interactive personals column, in which the descriptions ("WM, 52, seeks JWF

25–40 for walks on beach, Bach cantatas, light spanking") come alive at the tap of a keystroke. You have entered the world of hot chat.

Cyberporn is more a shopping mall than a singles' bar—a service keyed more to voyeurism than sex play. Customers can access (and download) everything from fetish games to hardcore pictures depicting acts of S&M, bondage, and incest. Netheads who are into women's underwear (literally or figuratively), can dial up  alt.pantyhose newsgroup. The home address alt.bestiality.barney will bring you colorful descriptions of erotic acts with purple cartoon dinosaurs. Very little is left to the imagination in services such as Amateur Action (billed as "the nastiest place on earth") and Graphic Impulse.

Pleasure Dome, a Virginia-based service with more than 3,000 subscribers nationwide, is an adult bulletin board system that gathers material from dozens of the top-rated boards and offers one-stop shopping for users. The board's inventory includes several hundred erotic picture files saved as graphical interchange formats, (or GIFs), adult messaging services, and specialties of the house catering to heterosexual, homosexual, and bisexual tastes. Pleasure Dome comes with built-in protections, too; potential users must fill out a lengthy electronic questionnaire before gaining access to the files and are flashed with stern warnings about underage usage.

In a culture showing signs of creeping conservatism, cybersex and cyberporn are drawing more and more political fire. Early in 1995 the U.S. Senate took up a bill that would make it illegal to transmit obscene or harassing data over any telecommunications device. The bill has been counterattacked by civil libertarians who oppose any effort to censor material. How far can cybersex go? As far as the human imagination can take it. After all, it is said that the most important sexual organ of all is the brain.

## signal-to-noise ratio (S/N)

(1) Ratio of usable signal to undesired signal being transmitted.

Usually expressed in decibels, this ratio measures the quality of transmission. The higher the S/N ratio, the better the quality of the signal.

(2) In cyberslang, the quality of discourse in a newsgroup relative to flames, insults, and newbie nonsense.

## signaling

Transmission of electrical signals between your telephone and the telephone company's central office.

Examples of signals are dialing and ringing. In asynchronous transfer mode transmission, signaling is used to establish, maintain, and clear connections.

### simple network management protocol

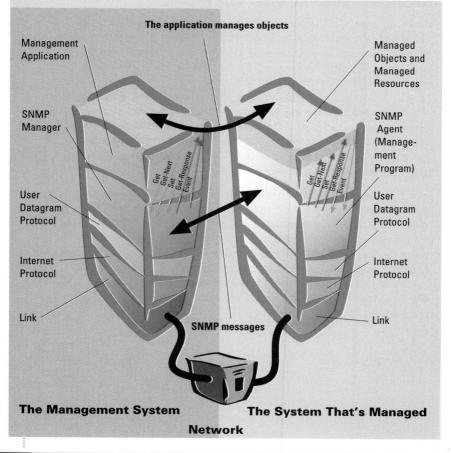

The application manages objects

Management Application

Managed Objects and Managed Resources

SNMP Manager

SNMP Agent (Management Program)

Get
Get-Next
Set
Get-Response
Event

Get
Get-Next
Set
Get-Response
Event

User Datagram Protocol

User Datagram Protocol

Internet Protocol

Internet Protocol

Link

Link

SNMP messages

**The Management System**

**The System That's Managed**

**Network**

## signature

Addition to an E-mail or posting on Usenet, indicating who sent the message and from where.

Signatures can have remarkable flourishes—ASCII characters collected to make a picture of, say, a spaceship. They can also become the bane of good netiquette. As a rule of thumb, don't let a signature file grow longer than 10 lines.

## simple network management protocols (SNMP)

Set of standards for network management software adopted by manufacturers of network equipment.

Using the SNMP architecture, small management programs called agents can monitor a variety of networked devices and gather data on their operation. Another program polls the agents regularly and downloads the data they have collected. It's all a way of making sure the network remains up and running.

## simulation

Software that models the dynamics of a real system, so it can create a computerized version of the real thing.

For example, biologists use computer simulations to approximate the living conditions of animals in a particular habitat, say the rain forest. By changing variables, they can then simulate what the effects of deforestation or pollution will have on the animal populations.

Real-time animated simulation is used frequently for fighter and airline pilot training; a virtual runway and flight forces are recreated in a simulator—a fake cockpit that moves and sounds like the real thing.

✚ See also **computer animation, computer graphics,** and **telepresence**.

## SLIP

✚ See **serial line internet protocol**.

## small computer systems interface (SCSI)

Pronounced "scuzzy," a port on the back of a personal computer, by which a variety of peripherals can be connected, usually with a SCSI cable.

✚ See also **RS232**.

## smart card

A microprocessor with several megabytes of memory on a small plastic device the size of a credit card.

## SMDS

✦ See switched multi-megabit data service.

## smiley

✦ See emoticon.

## SMPTE

✦ See Society of Motion Picture and Television Engineers.

## S/N

✦ See signal-to-noise ratio.

## snail mail

The U.S. postal system.

Need we say more?

## sniffers

✦ See cybercrime.

## SNMP

✦ See simple network management protocols.

## soc

Category in Usenet for newsgroups related to social issues or that encourage social interaction.

Soc newsgroups cover sexuality (bi- and homo-), feminism, religion, college life, human rights, and ethnicity.

## Society of Motion Picture and Television Engineers (SMPTE)

Pronounced "semp-tee," a trade association that sets standards for television and movies.

The acronym SMPTE is also used for a standardized frame numbering system adopted throughout the television and movie industries. It is used to locate exact frames on videotape. If you are shooting or recording video with so-called SMPTE time code, every frame is tagged with a signal that shows the elapsed time in an eight-digit order—hours: minutes: seconds: frames.

## software

Instructions telling a computer what operations to perform.

Everything that isn't hardware in a computer system is software: operating systems, programs, routines, subroutines, languages, and procedures. Without software, computers do little more than make good doorstops. Just as hardware is vulnerable to glitches, software is vulnerable to bugs and viruses.

✦ See also **firmware**.

## solid state

Processing signals by controlling electrons and magnetic and electric fields in a solid material.

There is no mechanical action. Integrated circuits are solid state devices. The original computers used vacuum tubes and moving parts. In the 1950s solid, semiconductor materials (such as silicon) were used to make transistors and resistors, which could process signals. These were wired to a printed circuit board to form a computer. Later, these same elements were miniaturized so they could be formed in one solid piece of semiconductor—an integrated circuit.

## SONET

✦ See **synchronous optical network**.

## sound effects (SFX)

Environmental sound in a movie or video, crucial to the dramatic illusion of reality.

Without the sounds of footsteps or clothes rustling as an actor moves, the illusion seems thin or weak. Typically, these sounds are added by foley technicians after the film or video is shot and edited. Natural sounds may be recreated or synthesized for heightened effect. Music is considered a separate part of the soundtrack from sound effects, though the two work together to create compelling dramatic effects.

## spamming

(1) Posting an unwanted, irrelevant message on scores of Usenet newsgroups. (2) Bombarding a MUD with massive amounts of information, which brings the game to a temporary halt.

# The Green Card
# Spam, And Others

Spamming is named after a skit acted out by Britain's wacky Monty Python comedy troupe (a cyberspace favorite). In the skit, undesirables were stoned with hunks of Spam, the processed lunch meat in a can produced by the Hormel Foods Corp. Spam jokes appear on the Internet frequently. But unlike the jokes, spamming is aggressive behavior far beyond the bounds of netiquette. It's basically the same as wandering from house to house and spray-painting your unwanted words on each person's front door.

It is fairly easy for a potential spammer to obtain a list of every Usenet newsgroup and public Listserv.list. Armed with these, and a reckless attitude toward the consequences, the person can write a little program that will mail the same message to every person on every group. Between early 1994 and the spring of 1995, three broadly targeted spams moved through the Usenet. One insisted that the end of the world was at hand. A second was pure advertising—a law firm broadcasting the availability of its professional services to any illegal aliens or foreign visitors seeking a Green Card. The third was a get-rich-quick scheme, the Net's version of a chain letter.

The law firm's spam got the most attention, and its defensive authors told the *Washington Post* that they considered the Internet to be "an ideal, low-cost, and perfectly legitimate way to target people likely to be potential clients." Most recipients felt differently, however. A consensus among newsgroup readers was that the Internet—with the exception of the World Wide Web—was an inappropriate venue for commercial messages. Most newsgroups' charters prohibit offers to do business, and the few that do allow transactions restrict them to individual buyers and sellers, not organizations. This is in keeping with the Internet's tradition of noncommercialism since its founding as ARPAnet.

There is also a cost involved in posting any message. One newsreader, "trn" (a newsreader is a program that enables you

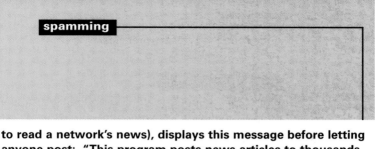

to read a network's news), displays this message before letting anyone post: "This program posts news articles to thousands of machines throughout the civilized world. Your message will cost the Net hundreds, if not thousands of dollars, to send everywhere. Please be sure you know what you are doing. Are you absolutely sure you want to do this?" Given that the spammers posted to more than 6,000 newsgroups, the cost of their unwarranted actions was substantial.

Equally annoying is the intrusion a spam has on the discussion at hand. Newsgroups are focused; when an outside message is posted, the disruption is often followed by a litany of complaints. The traffic increases further.

Here's what to do when you see a spam:

○ Don't reply.
The spammer won't read it anyway. He is not a newsgroup subscriber or regular reader. Your diatribe will only annoy other group members.

○ If you've got the time, respond by posting to the spammer's mailbox.
But don't be surprised if that account's already closed. Spammers are notorious for hitting and running.

○ If you are really furious, write to the administrator of the spammer's site.
Typically, this will be the postmaster@whatever.domain.

Warning: You might be tempted to send a mail bomb to the spammer's site that contains, say, all the entries from A to E in the *World Book Encyclopedia*. A mail bomb that is large enough can cause a site's server to crash, taking down every other user too. Resist this temptation: You may well lose your own privileges when your administrator finds out what you have done.

## spectrum

Continuous range of frequencies.

+ See also **electromagnetic spectrum**.

## speech recognition

Ability of a computer system to understand, convert into machine-usable binary code, and act on a command spoken in a natural language.

Speech recognition contrasts with voice recognition, the ability of a machine to recognize a particular voice. Voice recognition requires a training session between each man and machine; speech recognition does not.

The major problems faced by speech recognition systems are understanding continuous speech (as opposed to single spoken commands) and the difficulty of differentiating between voices, accents, dialects, and the intonations of any given language. The benefits of speech recognition can be seen in "hands off" situations such as car navigation systems. Eventually, speech recognition joined with automatic translation systems will enable us to telephone anywhere in the world and speak in our native language—while the receivers hear us in *their* language.

## speech synthesizer

A device that produces human speech sounds from input in another form.

The speech synthesizer takes a text word, determines the pronunciation by means of a phoneme index, correlates the appropriate signal from a table of correspondences, and "speaks" the word through an audio synthesizer.

## spoofers

+ See **cybercrime**.

## sprite

Image on a monitor that is moved around with a mouse or through keyboard commands.

It's your friendly local cursor. Rendered video game characters—such as Mario and Sonic the Hedgehog—are also sprites.

## SQL

+ See **structured query language**.

## SRAM

✦ See **dynamic random access memory**.

## standards

Agreed-upon specifications that allow different manufacturers to make compatible hardware or software.

Some companies make equipment that works only with their proprietary programs. They believe that by disregarding any attempt at standardization, they will be able to dominate more of the market and perhaps impose their own standard.

Because there is no international standard for television broadcast, U.S. television sets will not work in Europe and vice versa.

## start bit

✦ See **asynchronous transmission**.

## static random access memory (SRAM)

✦ See **dynamic random access memory**.

## stereoscope

A device that enables you to see an illusion of depth using two-dimensional images.

Stereo cameras shoot a pair of photos for every image (or frame) of a motion sequence from slightly different angles, using either a twin lens offset or a prism to split the beam of light. This pair of photos or video images is viewed, one image for each eye, with a stereoscope. Certain stereoscopic equipment, such as a head-mounted display, is used to create an illusion of 3-D virtual reality.

## still frame

Single frame of video or film frozen during playback; a single motionless image displayed on a CD-ROM or videodisk.

## stop bit

✦ See **asynchronous transmission**.

## storage

Holding data and software in an inert state, ready to be retrieved for use.

Storage media—forms of a computer's memory— are based on magnetic, optical, or magneto-optical technologies. Some storage media are permanent: Once they have been written to, they cannot be changed. Others may be erased and rewritten many times. The capacity—permanent or not—is the amount of space available on a particular storage medium.

An early and still widely used storage medium for personal computers is the floppy disk, a magnetic device that holds up to 1.4 MB of data. Hard disks, installed inside a computer rather than inserted into a drive, are also magnetic media and can hold several gigabytes.

## structured query language (SQL)

A standard database language used for creating, maintaining, and accessing relational databases.

## supercomputer

Very fast computer with enormous processing capability.

Supercomputers are reserved for problems that other machines cannot handle. Some use parallel processing, with dozens of central processing units operating at once. Like all computers, supercomputers get faster each year. In 1995, the benchmark for performance was more than 5 gigaflops (5 billion operations per second). Supercomputers serve as the raison d'être for the National Science Foundation's NSFnet, the original backbone of the Internet. The foundation determined that a high-speed connection between the country's supercomputer centers was important enough to fund their linkage through a 45-Mbps network.

## super VHS (SVHS)

VHS-based one-half-inch video format.

While VHS, the common household format, has 260 lines of resolution, SVHS can deliver 400 lines. To appreciate the sharper image, however, you need a television display offering 400 or more lines.

## SVHS

+ See super VHS.

## switch

A device that opens or closes circuits, completes or breaks an electrical path, or selects paths or circuits.

## switched multi-megabit data service

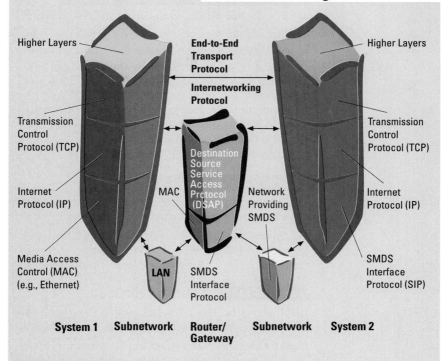

Higher Layers

End-to-End
Transport
Protocol

Higher Layers

Internetworking
Protocol

Transmission
Control
Protocol (TCP)

Transmission
Control
Protocol (TCP)

Destination
Source
Service
Access
Protocol
(DSAP)

Internet
Protocol (IP)

MAC

Network
Providing
SMDS

Internet
Protocol (IP)

Media Access
Control (MAC)
(e.g., Ethernet)

LAN

SMDS
Interface
Protocol

SMDS
Interface
Protocol (SIP)

**System 1     Subnetwork     Router/          Subnetwork     System 2**
**                             Gateway**

## Using SMDS with Internet Protocols

A switch may be mechanical, electrical, or electronic. In telephone parlance, a switch is a central switching office that routes all local calls — just look for the low-rise building with no windows found in every city and town.

### switched multi-megabit data service (SMDS)

A switching service that connects local area networks over the public telephone network.

### switching

Connecting you, the caller, to them, the party being called.

### synchronous

Processes that are synchronized or timed to a master clock.

A computer's central processing unit is timed to its internal clock. Timing is everything when audio and video are combined in multimedia.

## synchronous optical network (SONET)

A standard for public communications networks using fiber optics.

It was initiated by the regional Bell operating companies (RBOCs) and defined by the American National Standards Institute (ANSI). It allows networking of telecommunications products from multiple vendors. Providing data transmission rates from 51.84 Mbps to 13.22 Gbps, SONET will help create an infrastructure to support new broadband services and enhanced operations.

## synchronous transmission

Information sent over a telephone line by separating data by time, not by start and stop bits.

Synchronous transmission offers higher throughput—up to 9600 bits per second—than asynchronous transmission, but is also more expensive.

## synthesizer

Electronic machine, equipped with a keyboard, for creating and playing electronic music and sounds.

It was a seminal instrument in the 1980s for hundreds of foppish techno-pop bands from northern European cities. Early synthesizers were capable of only rough simulation of musical instruments. Now, synthesized music is often indistinguishable from the real thing. This leap in fidelity is due to the technology of sampling and MIDI interfaces. Any natural sound can be sampled and assigned to one of the keys on the keyboard.

For instance, you sample your friend playing a full scale of notes on her flute and enter those samples into your synthesizer. Then, at the keyboard, you can play the same notes, generating the same sounds. With further manipulation and fine-tuning by adjusting the "attack" and "envelope" of the individual notes with computer programs, your friend's notes can become those of Jean-Pierre Rampal. Or Jimi Hendrix. Or your tone-deaf sister.
+ See also **sampler**, **sampling rate**, and **sequencer**.

## system operator (sysop)

Pronounced "sis-op," it's the person who manages and monitors a bulletin board system, an on-line service forum, or a local area network.

Kind of like the school principal. If you have a problem, the sysop can solve it. If you *become* a problem, you can sit in the sysop's (electronic) office while he or she decides whether or not to suspend you for awhile.

This is the person you leave messages for when you cannot figure out how to navigate or send files. The sysop of a bulletin board must be a computer-dedicated individual, and interested in the special interests of his or her subscribers, since this job is often a labor of love.

✦ See also **multiple system operator**.

# T-1 carrier to twisted-pair cable

Times Roman

## T-1 carrier

A grade of telephone line connection.

It allows digital transmission. A T-1 carrier uses two pairs of twisted wires and can handle twenty-four voice conversations, each one digitized at 64 Kbps. A T-1 carrier is a superior phone line needed for heavy traffic. Network sites and servers need T-1 lines or better to link their services directly to the Internet. With more advanced encoding techniques, the carrier can handle even more channels. T-1 is the standard for digital transmission in the United States, Canada, Hong Kong, and Japan.

## T-3 carrier

A collection of 28 T-1 carriers; also called FT3.

The T-3 carrier runs on fiber-optic cable at 45 Mbps and is capable of handling 672 voice conversations or one state-of-the-art video channel.

## tariff

A public document filed by a regulated telephone company with the Federal Communications Commission or state public utilities commission.

The tariff lists the services, equipment, and prices offered by the telephone company to all potential customers. A tariff is not law; it is accepted by the FCC and PUC until challenged, usually in Federal court. If a telephone company subscriber violates the tariff, service is cut off.

When a court strikes down a tariff as unlawful or discriminatory, the telephone company refunds the money or removes the unnecessary equipment. Since deregulation, many telephone companies have violated their own tariffs—charging *less* money than their tariffs stipulate to get or keep customers.

## TAT

+ See **turnaround time**.

## TC/IP

+ See **Transmission Control Protocol/Internet Protocol**.

## TDM

+ See **multiplexing**.

## telco

Shorthand for the telephone company.

## telecommunications

(1) Science and technology of communicating over a distance by the electronic transmission of signals through telephone, telegraph, cable, radio, or broadcast media. (2) The transmission, reception, and switching of signals by wire, fiber, or electromagnetic means—used in the transmission of messages.

## Telecommunications Act of 1995

Legislation that allows regional Bell operating companies, cable television companies, and the long-distance phone companies to compete in each others' markets.

The act removes the significant obstacles to convergence by opening up the services and systems provided and maintained by each to the other.

## telecommuting

Commuting to work via modem, fax, or telephone, instead of by car or train.

Telecommuting has allowed many people to live in remote and beautiful places, disrupted only when a storm knocks out power or phone lines. It has also allowed many office-bound managers to get some work done at home, instead of remaining chained to the desk. Is that progress?

## teleconferencing

Technology that enables more than two people to participate in a conversation without being in the same room, whether by computer, telephone, or video.

+ See also **video conferencing**.

## Teledesic

Low-orbit satellite communications system, in which hundreds of satellite transmissions would blanket the planet.

The idea is to permit people everywhere to communicate over inexpensive handheld devices. To keep these small, the transmission power would reside in the numerous satellites. The cost of the system could be in the tens of billions of dollars. Deployment would not take place until some time early in the 21st century.

Teledesic was conceived by Bill Gates, chairman of Microsoft, and Craig McCaw, founder and former chairman of McCaw Cellular—now part of AT&T.

## telegraph

The earliest modern telecommunications system, which sent electric impulses down a wire.

In today's parlance, the telegraph delivered a maximum data transmission rate of 75 bits per second — basically, that was as fast as anyone could tap out dots and dashes. Invented by Samuel Morse in the 1830s, telegraph lines stretched from New York to New Orleans by 1847. Seven years later, more than 30,000 miles of telegraph lines crisscrossed the United States. The telegraph laid the foundation for the development of the telephone system and modern communications technology.

## telemarketing

The use of the telephone to conduct sales and marketing.

Incoming and outgoing telemarketing is generally run through 800 toll-free WATS numbers. Automated telemarketing is being developed using automated outbound dialers, voice processing technology, and automatic call distributors.

+ See also **automatic number identification**.

## telemedicine

Medicine practiced across a distance through electronic communications.

With teleconferencing, specialists in different parts of the country can compare EEGs, X-rays, and other medical data and work together to develop a diagnosis for a particular patient. Teleconferencing may introduce a new era of house calls: the patient's temperature, glucose levels, or EKG can be read by digital equipment at the home and transmitted via telephone lines.

By virtue of telepresence, a specialized surgeon at a big-city hospital will be able to participate in an operation on a patient in a small-town clinic. The surgeon might use equipment that conveys the tactile sense of operating while those motions would be mirrored by the robot physically performing the surgery.

Telemedicine dates to 1968, when a video camera linked the medical station at Boston's Logan Airport with Massachusetts General Hospital. Nurses at the airport could link with physicians at the hospital to conduct examinations, take blood samples, even review X-rays.

"Soon telemedicine developed an offspring, telepsychiatry," according to an interview with former Massachusetts General news director Martin Bander in the *Boston Globe*. He recounted a story about a nurse at Logan, who was treating a truck driver when she noticed a deep cut on the driver's wrist. She phoned the hospital and asked that a psychiatrist "examine" him on video. "Interviewing the truck driver over TV," Bander noted, "Dr. Thomas Dwyer quickly confirmed the nurse's observation [a suicide attempt]. In fact, the patient angrily threatened to commit mass murder. Referring to the infamous Texas Tower massacre, he snarled, 'I'm gonna do the same.' In a series of five

**telemedicine**

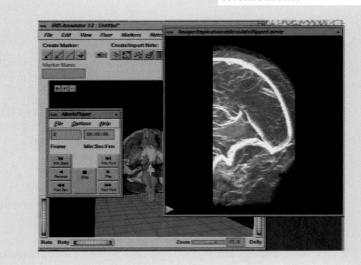

Photo courtesy of Peter Cahoon, MAGIC, University of British Columbia.

television interviews, Dwyer convinced him to drop his obsession and arranged for him to see another psychiatrist regularly."

## telemetry

Electronic measurement by remote control.

Telemetry has the potential to be applied in any cyberspace transaction that requires measurement. The National Aeronautics and Space Agency sent a spaceship equipped with telemetric devices to the surface of Mars. Closer to home, telemetry will be implemented when you order a pair of shoes on-line. Using telemetric sensing, the factory will measure your precise foot shape and size over your home video monitor before making your shoes.

## telephone

An appendage to your teenager's head.

Technically, an instrument that converts analog voice and sound signals into electrical signals that can be transmitted and received again as sound.

Socially, it is our connection to the world. Invented by Alexander Graham Bell in 1876, it was first used as a business tool. Its utility was quickly realized. By the turn of the century there were almost a million telephones in use.

Today there are more than a billion telephones in use. New transmission systems—microwave, satellite, fiber-optics—and the joining of computers with the telephone system have made the telephone system the backbone of the global information infrastructure.

## telephony

Pronounced "tell-*eff*-a-knee," translation of voice, data, video, or image signals into electrical impulses that can be sent long distances.

Derived from the Greek for "far sound," telephony has also come to mean the integration of the telephone with the computer. An example of this is the fax/modem.

## telepresence

The state of being projected to a remote location via electronic telecommunication.

Telepresence often refers to the use of virtual reality equipment to give a skilled person accurate remote control of a distant environment—for example, a surgeon operating on a remote patient.

✦ See also **telemedicine** and **telerobotics**.

## teleputer

As yet only an imagined product of the convergence.

It would be a hybrid tool that combines the functionality of telephones, televisions, and computers. The teleputer was first described by Jim Clark, founder of Silicon Graphics Inc., in a paper published in 1992.

## telerobotics

The use of robots for remote chores.

Through electronic remote control, robots can be ordered to do tasks dangerous for humans, such as cleaning up nuclear plant disasters or toxic waste spills. Robots can also act out actions of a remote operator, as in telepresent surgery.

✦ See also **telemedicine**.

## Telescript

An expert system, developed by General Magic, that employs intelligent agents (software programs) to do tedious secretarial chores.

A Telescript-equipped device can send agents to get specific information from any Telescript-speaking network. For example, Telescript can find the best price on a specific camera a customer has been wanting, and, if the client approves, take care of the paperwork and have it sent to the buyer's address. Telescript would eventually be linked through personal digital assistants as part of someone's account with the telephone company.

## Teletex

The international standard set by the ITU-TS for text transmission over a network.

## teletext

Text information (like subtitles) inserted into the normal television broadcast signal, but which is invisible unless decoded.

Certain television sets provide this decoding if the viewer desires. For example, people who are deaf or hard of hearing can receive subtitles when viewing television programs.

## television

The boob tube.

Television technology was developed by Philo Farnsworth in San Francisco in 1927, using trans-duction—the conversion of one form of energy into another. Philo's brilliant contribution was his invention of the scanning mechanism used to convert images to signals, and signals back to images, in both a TV camera and a television set. The scheme is still used in today's TVs and computer CRTs.

## television standards

National and international standards defining color-encoding methods, scanning rates, and other specs for commercial broadcasting.

There are three main television standards through-out the world: National Television Systems Committee (NTSC) in the U.S. and Japan; phase alternate line (PAL) in Europe; and Sequential Couleur à Mémoir (SECAM) in France, the Middle East, and the former Communist Bloc countries. Typical television sets can receive and play only one format.

## Telex

Worldwide switched message service consisting of teletypewriters connected to a telephone network.

Telex was the precursor to the fax, and is still popular and widely used overseas. It is, however, slow and inaccurate, because the system uses no error-checking procedures. Telex is being replaced by faster, more accurate forms of data communications, including fax and E-mail.

## telnet

A program that lets you log in to a remote host computer on Internet.

Telnet is actually a service you use to connect yourself to the hundreds of host computers on Internet—the places where you find other useful services that perform work for you. To run telnet, you type the "telnet" command followed by the name of the host you want to access.

## terminal

(1) Generic reference to your basic computer, keyboard, and display.

In the old days, a terminal was a "dumb" box wired to a mainframe computer; it provided access to the mainframe and displayed information, but could not perform any processing on its own.

(2) In the telecommunications world, the point where a telephone line is connected to other circuits in the network, or the point at which it ends.

## terminal emulation

Software that enables an intelligent computer device to mimic a dumb terminal in order to communicate with another computer.

Also, terminal emulator software is often equipped to allow a computer to connect with other terminals that use different protocols by "emulating" the terminal it wishes to reach.

## terminal madness

Sudden-onset psychosis suffered by multimedia developers (first noted by multimedia developer Peter Bloch).

It strikes developers who pioneer four new technologies in 10 years, don't make a dime, and suddenly realize they have to learn a new technology.

## terrestrial microwave radio

Radio transmitted on the superhigh frequencies of microwave.

Though microwave can carry more information than lower frequency radio waves, it can only be transmitted successfully in an unobstructed line of sight. Regular radio broadcasters make use of microwave relay stations to extend their signal.

## test posting

A posting on Usenet sent by a first-timer, or newbie, who isn't certain his message will appear.

If you are trying this, send it to either the groups alt.test or misc.test site. That's why they exist. Do not send it to a live newsgroup.

## text editor

Software that produces and edits text-only files but does not provide special formatting functions such as boldface and underlining.

### thread

On Usenet and other electronic forums, a message
and its follow-up postings.

To read threads on Usenet, use a threaded newsreader—named tin or trn—which organizes postings
by thread topic.

### time-division multiplexing

+ See **multiplexing**.

### time-of-day routing

A service created by 800 number providers, that
enables incoming calls to be routed to alternate,
predetermined locations at specified times.

### token bus

An architecture for passing information between
computers on a local area network.

A common line (the main *bus* route) connects all
stations physically. Data (*tokens*) are broadcast to
every connected station, but only the station with
the destination address responds. The token passes

## token ring

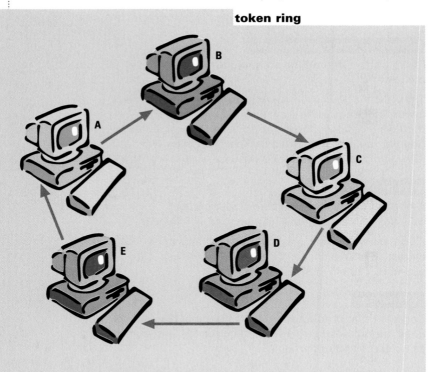

a maximum of data to a user, then goes and passes to the next logical station.

✦ See also **token ring**.

## token ring

A local area network arranged in a loop.

Before the computer sends data to any of the other computers on the ring, a token (a data packet that makes the rounds thousands of times per second) must be received by an attached terminal or workstation. Only then will the terminal or workstation start transmitting. A token ring can be wired in a circle or star configuration.

✦ See also **network topology and packet switching**.

## touch screen

A monitor that is sensitive to touch.

Icons or menus are placed at touch-sensitive areas, so you need only to touch a spot to activate what you want. You press the item on the screen with your finger or special pen, and the computer takes action. Touchscreens may be useful for people without mouse or trackball experience to access information from a point of information (POI) system.

They are not appropriate for prolonged work because of ergonomic limitations. They are handy in museums and airports, and for quick entering of orders at McDonald's cash registers.

## touch tone

The technology that makes the push-button phone possible.

When a key is pressed, a sound combining one high frequency and one low frequency tone is transmitted. There are also touch tones that the telephone company central office uses for signaling within the telephone network itself.

## tracking

A service, whether educational or commercial, that follows your progress on-line.

When a user is learning a new skill with distance learning or software, tracking keeps tabs on how fast he works and how many correct answers he gets on the first try. It's the silent teacher looking over your shoulder. This record can be reviewed to see how the student is doing and what needs improvement.

Tracking can also apply to on-line shopping. If a customer is in an electronic shopping mall, lingering over an item, his hesitation to buy may be tracked, so that next time he is on-line, the service will offer an appealing discount on that item to complete the sale.

Finally, employers can use tracking software to monitor the keystrokes or phone calls employees make.

## traffic

The amount of data being transmitted over a network.

Just as traffic jams occur on our asphalt freeways, too many people on the information superhighway at once can cause slowdowns of data transmission. The ongoing installation of fiber-optic cables across America will one day largely eliminate traffic jams.

## transistor

An electronic device that acts as a switch, or gate, and is the basic element of all integrated circuits...and thus computers.

The transistor, made of semiconductor materials, is actually a voltage and current regulator. Three Bell Laboratories scientists won the Nobel Prize in 1956 for its invention. Originally developed to improve AT&T's switching, transistors gave birth to the microelectronics industry.

The first transistor radio was introduced in 1965. Vacuum tubes in computers were replaced by transistors, and so began a long march to faster processing speeds, lower prices, and increased reliability. At one time, transistors cost nearly seven dollars apiece to manufacture. Now they are a fundamental commodity, costing only millionths of a cent in integrated circuits.

✚ See also **microprocessor**.

## transmission

Sending signals, whether audio, video, or data, from one place to another.

Transmission passes through a medium, which may be air, as in radio and satellite broadcasts, or any kind of wire or cable that can pass electromagnetic signals. Transmission facilities—the equipment used to assist the passage of the signal—include uplinks, downlinks, repeaters, multiplexers, and switching systems. Transmission may be degraded by the limitations of the media; there is an echo with geostationary-earth orbiting satellites (GEOS), and signal losses over long wires.

✦ See also **electromagnetic spectrum**.

## Transmission Control Protocol/ Internet Protocol (TCP/IP)

Primary protocols necessary for transmission on the Internet throughout the world.

The TCP/IP protocols were originally developed by the U.S. Department of Defense's Advanced Research Projects Agency to link multivendor computers across networks. Today TCP/IP protocols are also implemented over networks including Ethernet, local area networks, minicomputers, and mainframes.

✦ See also **open system interconnect**.

## transponder

The component of a communications satellite that receives signals from earth stations and retransmits them back to other earth stations.

Nearly 40 transponders per satellite may be used for relaying television, voice for long-distance telephone calls, or other data transmission, such as banking or business information. One transponder can relay one television channel without compression, or 10 channels with compression. Using polarization, two full—uncompressed—television signals can be handled by a single transponder.

## transputer

Reduced instruction set computer (RISC) processor known as a computer-on-a-chip because it includes memory and communication capabilities.

Multiple transputers are used simultaneously for parallel processing in some powerful computers.

## tricon

✦ See **icon**.

### Trojan Horse

A computer virus, named after the Trojan Horse of Greek legend, that at first looks benevolent and useful but really holds trouble.

A Trojan Horse is actually designed to break security or damage a system. An unsuspecting person brings a Trojan Horse into his computer system, puts it on his disk drive, and realizes its malicious intent only too late. For example, a virus was once distributed on software that displayed tantalizing pictures of naked women. While the viewers were absorbed in the pictures, the virus was destroying files on their hard drives.

### trunk

Heavy-duty communication line between two switching systems—the eight-lane freeway.

Trunk lines can connect switching systems between phone companies, and a single phone company's central office to private branch exchanges.

### Turing machine

Logic machine invented in theory by Alan Turing in 1936.

Though never built, the Turing machine was the prototype for a computer, a system that could function differently depending on what set of instructions—software—it was given.

The "Turing test" was Turing's proposal to determine whether or not a machine is intelligent. It goes like this: A computer and a person are in one room. A panel of judges is in another. The judges submit questions. Both the person and the computer type their answers. If the judges cannot tell which answer came from the person and which from the computer, the computer passes the test and is an intelligent machine. In his lifetime, Turing was primarily known for cryptography work that played a crucial role in World War II.

### turnaround time (TAT)

(1) In cyberspeak, the time it takes to get a response. (2) In batch-processing, the time taken to get back finished reports after turning in documents and files to be processed.

## twisted-pair cable

Bundles of pairs of twisted insulated copper wires, which form the vast majority of the telephone lines in the United States and elsewhere.

Twisted-pairs are slowly being replaced by fiber-optic and coaxial cable, both of which have much greater signal capacity.

✚ See also **copper cable** and **fiber-optic cable**.

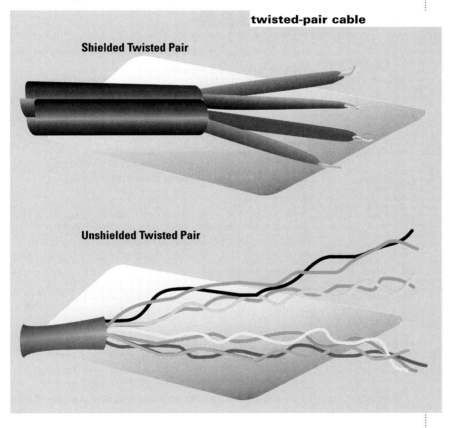

**twisted-pair cable**

**Shielded Twisted Pair**

**Unshielded Twisted Pair**

# U

## universal to username

Univers

## universal access

Concept that every person should have access to the information superhighway, a belief based on the idea of telephone universal service.

"Every person" means just that—regardless of geographic location, not to mention background, race, color, or creed.

## universal resource locator (URL)

The recognized scheme for naming a resource site on the Internet, originally developed for the World Wide Web.

A univeral resource locator—basically an address— includes words, abbreviations, and punctuation.  For example, http://www.mit.edu:8001/usa.html is the URL for the U.S. Weather Service's site for real-time weather maps.

The address http://hisurf.aloha.com/Find.html will send you to a site where you can have your name translated from English to Hawaiian.

## universal service

One of the original concepts behind the national telephone system—a vision that phone service would be extended to all residences at an affordable price, as long as a regulated monopoly was allowed to rise to deliver it.

The idea was conceived by Theodore Vail, the first chairman of the Bell System.  The federal government allowed AT&T to exist as a regulated monopoly; in return, it required AT&T to build a nationwide telephone infrastructure and to provide service to everyone—no matter how remote their location. AT&T was broken up in 1984, but the concept remains in local phone service, where the regional Bell operating companies still have a monopoly. Deregulation proposals in 1995 have threatened

that, too. Others—like cable television companies—
want to compete for the business.

✚ See also **universal access**.

## UNIX

Designed at AT&T's Bell Labs in the early 1970s, one
of the first and most important operating systems.

Because at the time AT&T was enjoined from entering the computer marketplace, it licensed UNIX to
universities at nominal fees. Consequently, many
students learned UNIX, and the federal government
adopted it as a preferred system. In the 1980s,
workstation giants such as Sun Microsystems
adopted UNIX as the preferred operating system.
IBM and DEC later introduced their own versions of
UNIX for workstations and minicomputers.

UNIX is very complex but very powerful. It allows
multiple programs to run simultaneously and multiple users to access a single computer. It is the most
commonly used operating system at nodes on the
Internet and in the telecommunications industry.

UNIX was never intended for public use, and will
never be widely used by consumers, because it is
saddled with complexity only programmers and
hackers can understand and appreciate. Its three
principals are as follows:

• It's comprised of many small programs, rather
  than a few large ones.

• Each program's output serves as input for
  another.

• The programs function by combining tools.

Because of the latter, UNIX is tough to use. Routing
a program's output from one program to another
for additional processing involves keying in compli-
cated commands. Steven Jobs' NeXT computer
addressed this by applying a graphical user interface to UNIX. However, Jobs' machine never found
a wide market.

The linkage between UNIX and the Internet will
grow less critical over time. As other operating systems include TCP/IP support, UNIX will become one
of many systems woven into the Internet's web,
rather than its principal driving force.

## unpack

To recover stored data in its original form, as they
were before they were compressed.

## upload

To transmit a file from a computer to a host system, via the telephone lines, satellite links, or whatever.

Upload means to transmit; download to receive.

## upstream

Direction of flow from a client to a server, or from a subscriber to a cable or on-line service head-end.

Many on-line shopping and entertainment services are planning only enough bandwidth for their upstream flow to allow for the customer's program choice and credit information.

✚ See also **downstream**.

## urban folklore

Myths, stories, apocrypha disseminated by cyber-space media, especially newsgroups on Usenet.

Tabloid newspapers and cocktail party gossip used to promulgate the existence of alligators in the city sewer system. Now the Internet is a princi-pal purveyor of these rumors and legends. Some urban folklore stories are deliberate fabrications, termed trolls on the Net. For a terrific overview of the subject, log on to the Usenet newsgroup, alt.folklore.urban.

## URL

✚ See **universal resource locator**.

## Usenet

Abbreviation for *user network*, an enormous and fast-growing network of newsgroups on the Internet.

Each Usenet newsgroup addresses a particular sub-ject area. It distributes timely postings (called arti-cles) to local sites, which in turn distribute them to as many as 30,000 subscribers. As with most of cyberspace, there are remarkably few rules and reg-ulations about participating. If there is one news-group among the thousands that catches your eye, you subscribe simply by requesting that your name and E-mail address be added to the newsgroup's list. If you want to post an article yourself you can do so, defining its distribution—to a particular region, country, or the whole world. The news may be sent directly via telephone lines or satellite, or indirectly via snail mail, on CD-ROMs, or via magnetic tapes to countries with inadequate telephone lines.

The Usenet preceded the Internet, having been founded in 1979 by grad students at Duke University and the University of North Carolina. As a result, it is not dependent on the Internet's TCP/IP network standards. Its protocols allow dial-up access sites to use an earlier program named UUCP, or UNIX-to-UNIX Copy Program.

Newsgroups on the Usenet are divided into two general categories: world newsgroups, which are distributed automatically to all Usenet sites, and alternative newsgroups. Within the former, one finds comp (for computers), news (about the news-groups themselves), rec (for sports and hobbies), sci (all the sciences), soc (social issues and socializing), talk (chewing the fat on the issues of the day), and misc (everything that doesn't fit elsewhere). Within the alternative category, the biggest—and most likely to preoccupy Congressional censors—is alt.

The anarchic tendencies of the Internet are best exemplified on the Usenet, which has no central governing body or ways of sanctioning abusers. Votes are taken to form new newsgroups, except within certain alternative newsgroup hierarchies, where almost anything goes (including the forma-tion of newsgroups without a vote). In certain newsgroup, especially in alt., there are lots of males, lots of foul language, lots of erotica, lots of harassment in the forms of flames, mail bombings, and the like. This is the Wild West of the Internet, and—within alt. newsgroups especially—it's best to watch your back.

Just the same, the alternative category is also home to biz (for business discussions and advertising), bionet (biology and the environment), ClariNet (daily news), and K12 (education).

To read any newsgroup, you need a newsreader—a program that lets you choose which group you want to peruse, and presents the current postings. The best newsreaders are those that follow threads, or certain subjects. Tip: if you want to contribute your own posting to a newsgroup, make sure you are familiar with netiquette, have read the group's FAQs, and understand what the current discussion has already covered.

## user access fee

Charge levied by some on-line services for accessing their databases or other materials.

It may be an hourly charge or a fee per item or chunk of data retrieved.

© Robert Neubecker/Spots on the Spot!

## user group

Casual association of people who get together in person or on-line to share information about hardware or software that they use in common.

Members of user groups pick up tips about the operation of systems and programs and occasionally, when necessary, lobby manufacturers as part of a consumer action group. There are user groups for Macintosh fans, Windows users, and many others.

## user interface

Part of computer program that handles the computer's interaction with the user.

The most sophisticated user interfaces are the graphical user interfaces, which employ icons and mice and allow you to choose by pointing and clicking.

## userid

✦ See username.

## username

The first part of your E-mail or Internet address.

The username in the address DonKing@frizzhair.alt is DonKing. (Yes, we made this up.)

# vaporware to VTR

## vaporware

New software that is announced long before it is ready to be shipped.

It's questionable, but it is standard marketing practice in the software industry.  Letting the word out builds anticipation before a company is ready to take orders, but many products never make it to market because problems crop up in development. Industry leaders defend the practice as a means of getting public feedback about a product's features. Hmm.

> "The widespread, market-driven practice the industry has been discussing is not in fact vaporware, but pre-disclosure.  Its purpose is to engage customers and the industry in a useful dialogue about products that help customers make better decisions and developers make better products."
>
> — From a "white paper" issued by **Microsoft** in 1995
> [Laurie Flynn, "Information Technology; The Executive Computer," The New York Times, Monday, 24 April 1995, Late Edition - Final, Sec. D, p. 4, Col. 1.]

## VCR

✦ See **videocassette recorder**.

## VDP

✦ See **video display processor**.

## vector graphics

Method for building images on a screen with straight lines—vectors—instead of a raster or stack of scan lines, as is done in television.

The advantage is that these images can be redrawn rapidly, which is useful in certain kinds of real-time animation and simulation.

✦ See also **bitmap graphics**.

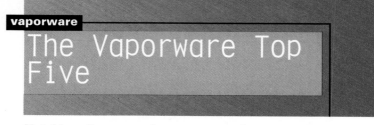

# The Vaporware Top Five

**Notable software products announced prematurely:**

○ Windows 1.0.

An operating system for IBM PCs and clones, which was to simulate the user-friendly computer screens Apple had designed for its Macintosh computers. Microsoft announced it in November 1983, and promised it for June 1984...then for June 1985. It was finally delivered in November of that year. It required most users to upgrade their computers, and was technically disappointing. Nonetheless, it became the IBM PC standard.

○ Ovation.

A novel operating system announced in 1983 by Ovation Technologies. It turned out to be nothing more than a mock-up. The company went belly-up before any software code was released.

○ 1-2-3 for Macintosh.

This spreadsheet program, already available for the IBM PC format, was announced by Lotus Development in November 1987. The program was not delivered until four years later; by that time Microsoft's Excel spreadsheet dominated the Apple Macintosh market.

○ File Server.

Software to coordinate computers linked together in a network at a large site such as a company or university. Apple announced it in January 1985, and delivered it two years later. By then, a start-up called Novell had established itself as the leader in networking software.

○ Windows 95.

Announced by Microsoft in February 1994, it wasn't released until 19 months later. It missed three target delivery dates along the way and became the butt of jokes. Microsoft compensated with a $200 million marketing campaign, and sold more than a million copies in the first week. We should all have Bill Gates' problems.

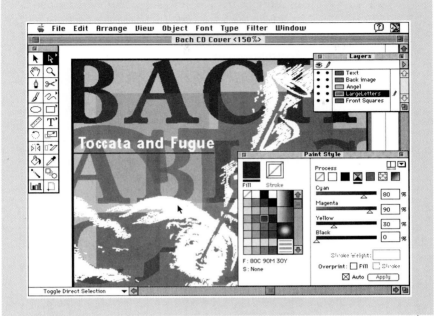

## Veronica

Stands for *very easy rodent-oriented net-wide index to computer archives*. Veronica is an agent that helps you conduct subject-oriented searches of Internet Gopher sites.

Veronica was developed in response to the overwhelming popularity of Gopher and the subsequent need for a search program that provided help similar to Archie's search functions for FTP files.

Tips: If a Gopher search pulls too many items, you can narrow your search with Veronica, using Boolean logic operators—"and," "or," "not." By beginning a search with Jughead, which looks for directory titles only, you will get a shorter list to begin with, and there is an excellent chance it will be more pertinent.

Screen capture of Adobe's Illustrator 6.0 for the Macintosh, a vector-based imagebuilding application. Logo and screen capture courtesy of Adobe Systems Incorporated. All rights reserved.

## VHS

✚ See **video home system**.

## video

System for recording and transmitting visual information.

The term *video* properly refers only to the picture on a computer terminal, television, handheld game, security camera, and the like. But in wider use it includes the audio and other signals that are part of a complete video experience.

## video camera

That infernal machine that sits on the shoulders of proud moms and dads everywhere: at the wedding, birthday party, prom, and Thanksgiving feast—in addition to such less-flattering circumstances as giving birth.

The camera encodes visual and audio information on a tape inside.

## video capture

Conversion of an analog video signal into digital form so it can be saved in computer memory and manipulated with graphics or other software.

A computer's video capture card—also called a frame grabber—accomplishes this by "capturing" the two fields that comprise a single video frame. Using a built-in compression chip, usually MPEG, the capture card takes a video signal and converts it to full-motion video (FMV). Once digitized, an image can be stored in a document or database, incorporated into CD-based applications, or transmitted over a network. A video capture card is the basic piece of hardware that enables desktop video.

## video display processor (VDP)

Set of integrated circuits (a chipset) used to decompress video in real-time in digital video interactive systems.

## video format

The way in which video information is encoded on a videotape.

There are several common video formats—1/2 inch, 3/4 inch, super video home system (SVHS), 8mm, and Hi-8. But the video home system (VHS) dominates the home market. The industrial and professional markets tend to use the other formats, plus U-matic, U-matic SP, and Betacam.

Until recently, broadcasters shunned all the formats in favor of television cameras, because image quality wasn't good enough for transmission. But now, fitted with time-based correctors and digital signal processors (DSPs), the industrial formats are being used more, especially for news gathering; it is much easier to negotiate a flooded street, crowded subway car, or fire-swept hillside with a handy camcorder than a bulky, heavy, power-hungry television camera.

## video game

A game played in an arcade or on a personal computer, dedicated console, or handheld unit.

## video graphics

Graphics covering a wide range of video techniques.

These include computer animation, chroma key, titles and logos, and a variety of electronically generated effects.

## video home system (VHS)

Dominant consumer videotape format—a half-inch tape packaged in cassettes of up to 160 minutes playing time.

VHS, first introduced by Matsushita and quickly endorsed by others, won the format wars with Sony's Betamax in the mid-70s. Prices dropped quickly.

+ See also **platform, video tape recorder (VTR), and videocassette recorder (VCR)**.

## video server

A server that stores video in one of several forms and disseminates signals on demand.

The video can be either in analog form, as in a videotape, or in digital form, as on a CD-ROM, or in a disk array. Still in development, video servers can be jukebox-like devices that stack hundreds of movies, or large computers with many large hard disks or optical disk drives. With video servers up and running, movies will be distributed over telephone lines, cable television networks, or via satellite transmission.

+ See also **video-on-demand**.

## video tape recorder (VTR)

Machine that encodes magnetic tape with audio and visual information from a video camera. When in cassette form, known as a videocassette recorder (VCR).

Video tape recorders, consumer and professional, can play only one format, such as VHS, though some may play more than one television standard, such as PAL and NTSC. Most videotape is manufactured in cassette form now. Broadcast-quality one-inch videotape, however, is still in reel-to-reel format.

## video wall

A wall of multiple rack-mounted video monitors or rear projection displays that together produce a very large image or combinations of images.

Video walls can be dramatic attention-grabbing devices for advertising or art, when a single image is spread across many adjacent monitors. Video walls can be fed from computer output or from real-time television signals. Software divides the image and routes the pieces to each monitor, and can create special effects.

## videocassette recorder

A machine that records and plays back video tapes containing movies, television shows, musical performances, and anything else your little heart desires. Hook it to your TV and make the popcorn.

## videoconferencing

A meeting held by people in different physical locations, in which all the people can see and hear each other on video screens.

By now most people have experienced teleconferencing—a three-way phone call is a simple example. Videoconferencing just adds the pictures. Participants see each other, live, on the screens. They can also view the same document at the same time on the screen, and even edit it together. Special rooms designed for videoconferencing come complete with effective lighting, speakers, a large video screen, suspended cameras, and microphones. Videoconferences are becoming favored by business executives because they eliminate the time and expense of travel.

A more informal, desktop video conferencing system is being developed, in which a small camera mounted on top of your computer captures you on video as you sit at your keyboard. These images would be transmitted between participants—say, coworkers in different cities. You could also hold up a graphic or blueprint in front of the camera so your associate could see it, and work together on common computer files shown on your terminal. Leave the camera off on a bad-hair day.

✚ See also **videophone**.

## videodisc

A form of information storage that uses thin circular platters of varying formats, played back by a laser on a video monitor.

Video, audio, and data signals may be encoded on the disk, usually along a spiral track. The most common videodisc is the LaserDisk, which can be formatted in a variety of ways. Favored for interactive video, constant angular velocity (CAV) disks are able to hold a perfect freeze-frame and can jump instantly from frame to frame. A 12-inch-diameter disk can hold up to an hour of video on each side, and is typically used for movies.

A videodisc has several assets: It doesn't wear with use, and its resolution is higher than videotape. As digital storage devices, videodiscs hold six gigabytes on a side. And, unlike CDs, they can be pressed on both sides. The player, however, is much more expensive than a typical videocassette recorder.

## video-on-demand

Technology that allows you to order a program for viewing in the home, from an interactive cable TV system or satellite communications system, or soon over telephone lines.

Arguably one of the allures of the information superhighway, video-on-demand requires the high bandwidth of fiber-optic cable, as well as efficient compression schemes.

A set-top box in most cable TV homes suggests the future of video-on-demand. Through that box, you can choose the channel you want. You can also get pay-per-view events. Video-on-demand is just the next step—custom-ordering each show you want.

Video-on-demand will not become a reality until storage media have been designed to hold the gigantic databases necessary to hold and dispense programming, fiber-optic lines become more widespread, and the technology to deliver the same movie at slightly differing times to hundreds, if not thousands, of purchasers is in place.

✦ See also **video server**.

## videophone

A telephone that transmits a video image of the speaker and displays it in **real-time** on a miniature built-in video screen.

This was theorized way back, and first attempted in the early 1970s as the Picture Phone. However, it was expensive and delivered poor quality video. With increasing sophistication of **digital** telecommunications, high-**resolution** video is now deliverable. Over telephone lines, a videophone plays an image at 10 frames per second, too slow for a continuous image. Nevertheless, with improving video **compression** techniques and the coming digitalization of telephone lines, the **transmission** of video in the normal course of a telephone conversation may become common.

✦ See also **videoconferencing**.

## videotex

A system that transmits **data** from a central computer to a home television set, either via **coaxial cable** or telephone link.

In **interactive** video-Teletex, you can order tickets, make reservations, send E-mail, and engage in live chats with people at remote sites.

✦ See also **Minitel**.

## virtual

Simulation of the real thing.

Virtual means "almost." Virtual appears before various computer-related terms today to indicate **simulation** technology that enables you to cross boundaries and experience something without needing its physical presence, as in **virtual sex** and **virtual theme parks**.

## virtual circuit

A reliable link between a user and an Internet site, even though the two are not communicating over a dedicated phone line.

Two kids talking across the alley with a string and soup cans have a "dedicated" line; it links only those "users" and no other conversation can break in. If they talked over a telephone, the phone system would route their conversation over all kinds of phone lines.

However, when your computer sends information to another computer over Internet, the network provides a virtual circuit; the data you send are guaranteed to be delivered in the exact order you sent them, without interruptions or noise, just as though a dedicated string was connecting the computers. The actual packets of information do indeed travel over different lines, but control software tracks and directs them.  This is made possible by the Transmission Control Protocol, which controls communication over the Internet.

## virtual circuit

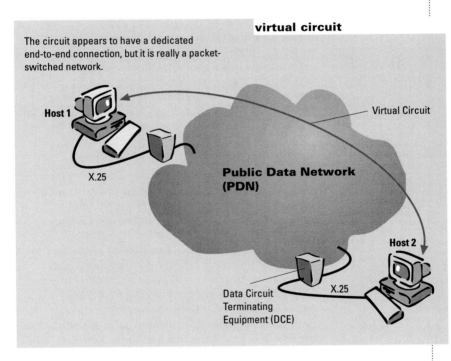

The circuit appears to have a dedicated end-to-end connection, but it is really a packet-switched network.

Host 1

Virtual Circuit

X.25

Public Data Network (PDN)

Host 2

Data Circuit Terminating Equipment (DCE)

X.25

## virtual memory

A program that temporarily simulates memory in a computer, so that several programs can run simultaneously.

## virtual private network (VPN)

A network where the transmission facility is leased by a company for its own use.

A VPN offers the appearance and functionality of a dedicated private network—but it is still controlled by the phone company.

## virtual reality (VR)

A world that exists only in **cyberspace**, but is made to look and sound real to a human being wearing special gear.

A virtual reality program delivers visual and aural stimuli to a person wearing a special helmet equipped with **graphics** displays and speakers. Once you put the **head-mounted display** on, you hear sounds and see 3-D graphics that make it seem you are physically immersed in another world.

**Sensors** in the helmet track your eye and head movements and feed the information to a computer. Without delay, the computer changes the environment in response; if you are standing at the edge of a cliff looking out into the air, and you move your head down, the computer pans the imaginary scene so it appears you are looking down the cliff—and will fall off if you step forward! By wearing special gloves, boots, and waistbands you can walk through virtual forests, climb virtual trees, even fly above the virtual hilltops. You will feel like you are moving, soaring, sinking, or spinning—all accomplished by only moving your body in place.

Virtual reality technology is based on four elements: sensors and display equipment, a reality engine, control software, and a geometry engine. Equipment such as head-mounted displays and **wired gloves** receive the virtual stimuli from the computer and send back positioning data. The reality engine then processes the visual, aural and, sometimes, tactile virtual environment in real time. The control software governs the interaction between the user and the virtual environment. The geometry engine holds the computer graphic information describing the three-dimensional nature of the particular virtual environment.

Implementation of virtual reality is still in its infancy. First developed by Ivan Sutherland in the 1960s at various U.S. university labs, it was subsequently fleshed out at the National Aeronautics and Space Administration and the Department of Defense for flight **simulation** training. Virtual reality entered the realm of video and **arcade games** in the early 1990s. Both tactile and olfactory senses have yet to be integrated into most virtual worlds. Some of the most

*"Virtual reality is electronic LSD."*

**— *Jaron Lanier*,**
*inventor of the Eyephone*
[G. Pascal Zachery, "John Lanier Develops Way For The User To Control And "Feel" Video Action—A Kind of Electronic LSD?" *The Wall Street Journal,*" 23 January 1990, p. A1.]

advanced virtual reality research is conducted at the University of Washington's Human Interface Technology Lab.

✦ See also **data glove, projected reality,** and **virtual sex.**

## virtual sex

Electronically simulated and stimulated sex.

With elaborate devices to monitor bodily motion and to deliver appropriate sensations, someday it will be possible to have sex with a virtual person or with a real person at a distant location through the sensory apparatus of augmented virtual reality.

How? A teledildonics suit, yet to be invented, would provide your entire body with tactile stimuli, and transmit your motions, skin temperature, and other physical traits back to the other person (real or computerized).

Why virtual sex? Of course, there are the kinky reasons. But it may also be desirable as a substitute for the real thing for people who are physically impaired, who don't want to be exposed to disease, or who are in long-distance relationships. Mates in Peoria and Peking (or on the space station!) could don virtual sex suits and engage via the telephone lines.

✦ See also **biosensor, cybersex,** and **sex.**

# The Virus Of Michelangelo: A One-Act Play

The most famous computer virus of all time had an equally famous name: Michelangelo. On New Year's Day, 1992, word began to spread that a destructive virus would strike nation-wide on March 6—the 517th birthday of Italian artist Michelangelo. It would be a time-bomb, remaining hidden until it suddenly went off on that date. Experts estimated that as many as 15 million personal computers were infected. Once unleashed, the virus would wipe out all the data on a computer's hard drive and replace it with random characters.

Such fear spread that sales of antivirus software soared and kept soaring through January and February. Cynics even charged that the entire scare was a scam perpetrated by makers of the software. The morning of March 6 was eerie at many corporations; managers told their staffs to keep their computers turned off, and everyone sat suspended in silence.

Many companies, government agencies, and individuals had discovered in time that their computers were contaminated, and had eliminated Michelangelo with antivirus software. Still, by day's end, about 10,000 PCs were stricken, according to estimates compiled later by the Computer Virus Industry Association. The damage was widespread; hundreds of computers were infected in offices of the State of California alone. These users learned the hard way the value of the advice given in every software manual: Make back-up copies of your data and applications before you find a problem—or a problem finds you.

## virtual storage

Storage space that a computer sees as internal, although it is actually at peripheral devices or locations.

## virtual theme park

Assortment of virtual reality and simulation games in one place.

These create an amusement park of consoles that take up little space but let the customer explore big virtual domains.

## virus

A software program that surreptitiously inserts itself into a computer, causing damage to the data or operating system.

Some viruses simply cause an unwanted message to pop up one time on your computer screen. Others can completely wipe out all the stored data and software on your system. Viruses usually infect data on your hard drive, or your operating system software (which controls how your computer handles its files).

Viruses embed themselves on floppy disks or programs on electronic networks or bulletin board systems. If you insert the disk into your computer or download a file from a network that contains a virus, it will burrow into your computer like a tick and stay there. The real dark side is that a virus, like its biological equivalent, replicates itself; once released into one computer, it can spread to thousands as disks or files are transferred.

Some viruses just sit and do nothing until your computer clock indicates a certain date, or until you initiate a certain procedure (like a car bomb, which goes off when you turn the ignition key). Viruses have become so common that many software companies sell virus-scanning software, a program you load into your computer that scans a disk or a file to be downloaded, searching for a virus before any data are transferred. Commercial disinfectant programs can remove a virus from a disk before it has a chance to make the rest of the system sick. Disinfectant programs, often distributed on the Internet for free, must be periodically updated, as new viruses are released into the world.

Tip: To protect yourself, always have a clean back-up of all your files on floppy disk, tape, or CD-ROM, so that if necessary you can purge your infected computer and start fresh from the backups. And equip your computer with virus protection software, which automatically scans your system—including its active memory—to make sure it is free from viruses.

✚ See also **Trojan Horse**.

## voice band

A communication channel that can transmit and receive speech, data, and fax. Also called voice-grade channel.

The voice band generally falls in the frequency range between 300 and 3,000 Hertz.

## voice-operated exchange (VOX)

Voice-activated circuits that control some tape recorders and all cellular telephones.

Walkie-talkie fans know that when you want to talk, you have to press a button to stop the incoming signal, so you can send your outgoing signal. Then you have to let go of the button to hear the other guy. This is a pain. The VOX in a cellular telephone does this for you; it tells the phone to transmit only when it senses you are speaking, and to stop trans-mitting and listen when you aren't speaking. GI Joe would have loved it.

## VOX

✚ See **voice-operated exchange**.

## VPN

✚ See **virtual private network**.

## VR

✚ See **virtual reality**.

## VTR

✚ See **video tape recorder**.

# WAIS to WYSIWYG

## WAIS

+ See **wide-area information servers**.

## WAN

+ See **wide-area network**.

## WATS

+ See **wide-area telecommunications service**.

## Watson, Thomas J., Jr.

President of IBM from 1952 to 1961, chairman from 1961 to 1971, and chairman of the executive board from 1972 to 1979.

He led the computer industry giant through a period of tenfold growth—increasing revenues from $650 million to $7.5 billion between 1956 and 1971. He helped establish American computer technology as the world's best. His father became president of the Computing-Tabulating-Recording Co. in 1914, and changed its name to the International Business Machines Corporation.

Tom Jr. served as U.S. ambassador to the Soviet Union from 1979 to 1981.

> *"When we got into computers, we were second to Remington Rand. They had the knowledge, the people. We were totally unprepared to do what we did over the next 20 years. We had almost no graduate engineers, no electronics engineers. But we made a kind of arbitrary decision to get a massive engineering organization up. We went from 2 percent of our budget spent on R&D to 10 percent in about four years, and we hired engineers like they were going out of style."*
>
> —**Tom Watson Jr.**, *former CEO of IBM*
>
> [Tom Watson, interviewed by Johanna Ambrosio, *Computerworld*, 22 June, 1992, p. 45.]

Walbaum

## wavelength

Length of one cycle of a periodic wave.

If you stand on the beach and measure the distance from one wave crest to the next, you will find the wavelength.

Wavelength has an inverse relationship to frequency—low wavelength means high frequency. For example, extremely low frequency (ELF) waves can have a wavelength of 6,000 miles long; very high frequency (VHF) waves have a wavelength considerably less than an inch.

✚ See also **electromagnetic spectrum**.

© Robert Neubecker/Spots on the Spot!

## wearable computer

Computing devices that may be worn on the arm or the waist, as a shoulder bag, as jewelry, or as any other accessory to your body.

Wearable computers are used by the U.S. Army emergency medical crews in Japan. If input/output (I/O) devices continue to get better and smaller, a personal digital assistant (PDA) may, in time, be an extension of your arm rather than a separate thing that must be hauled around in your briefcase.

## wetware

Flesh and blood, kindled by spirit.

Most everything in the world of computers falls into the categories of hardware or software. There is, however, a third essential category of computer: the human brain, known in cyberspeak as *wetware*. Not to be confused with "Waterworld" or Tupperware, both putatively the products of wetware.

## what you see is what you get (WYSIWYG)

Pronounced "wis-ee-wig," the ability to print out a hard copy that looks the same as what was shown on the screen.

This includes the same typefaces and the identical layout. WYSIWYG makes working with graphics and typefaces on a computer a more direct and satisfying experience. WYSIWYG is generally used in conjunction with high-level word processing or page-layout programs such as Adobe PageMaker or QuarkXPress.

## whatis

Command in an Archie server that produces additional information about a file.

If your search has discovered a file name that looks intriguing, but you are not certain is worth going into, a whatis query may give sufficient information for you to decide whether or not to call the file up.

## wide-area information servers (WAIS)

Pronounced "ways," browser software that retrieves information from databases throughout the Internet.

Unlike Gopher or Archie, which only search titles and descriptions, WAIS searches the complete contents of files and documents. A search request can be made using Boolean logic operators or plain English.

WAIS uses the grammar of the sentence structure of the request to rank its findings and decide which of the many items might be interesting to the seeker. Using "relevance feedback" to refine the search, you can choose several items from the list and ask it to find more along the same lines. WAIS works on UNIX systems; however, there are graphical user interface (GUI) programs available to make the hunting expedition easier if, like most of humanity, "you doesn't speak UNIX."

+ See also **World Wide Web**.

## wide-area network (WAN)

A network of geographically distant, perhaps international, computers.

These computers can be linked by dedicated telephone lines, satellite, or the Internet (the cheapest alternative).

## wide-area telecommunications service (WATS)

Discounted toll service provided by all telephone companies.

WATS comes in two types: out-WATS, which permits calling out at discounted rates, and in-WATS, where incoming calls are received at no charge to the caller (a typical 800 service). AT&T originated WATS but neglected to trademark the name, so it has become generic.

## wideband

Communications channel that is wider in bandwidth than a single voice band channel.

## window

Viewing area on your computer screen, separate from the rest of the screen.

Apple Computer invented it for its Macintosh computers in the early 1980s. Microsoft Windows' operating system, and many other programs, now use the same approach.

## Windows

✛ See **Microsoft Windows**.

## wired glove

A glove with position sensors used in virtual reality programs.

✛ See also **data glove**.

## wirehead

Mr. Fixit of the cyber age.

In the '50s there were motorheads, who spent all their time tinkering with their cars. In the '90s, especially in science fiction, there are wireheads who can lash together a computer from spare parts strewn around the kitchen.

## wireless network

A network that does *not* depend on cable to connect computers.

The connection is made over the airwaves via satellite communications or terrestrial microwave towers. With the advent of wireless networks, individuals who want to communicate no longer have to find a telephone or modem. They can enjoy truly portable communication. Wireless networks have helped give rise to groupware, whereby a number of computer users in different locations can work together on the same project.

✛ See also **cellular radio network**.

## Wiretap Act

Legislation passed in 1968, originally intended by Congress to preserve the personal privacy of communication.

The Wiretap Act prohibited people from listening in on other people's conversations—whether on a telephone or in person—without their consent. In 1986, this law was amended by the Electronic Communications Privacy Act to include electronic mail. Under the amendments, the Wiretap Act prevents a sysop from releasing E-mail to anyone except the intended addressee, though she may read it in the course of her duties. Though a court order may authorize reading E-mail that pertains to an illegal activity, the courts do not sanction a sysop's monitoring all E-mail.

Tip: If you want to ensure the privacy of your E-mail, use an encryption scheme.

✚ See also **privacy** and **password**.

## WMRM

✚ See **write many, read many**.

## woo woo tone

Telephone line tone that indicates the number is unavailable.

"Woo, woo, woo... We're sorry, your call cannot be completed as dialed. Please check the number and dial again... We're sorry, your call cannot be completed as dialed. Please..."

## word processing

Creating text documents on a computer or word processor.

It has almost entirely replaced the typewriter in modern offices. Examples of popular word processing programs are AmiPro, Microsoft Word, and WordPerfect.

## workgroup computing

People working on a common problem on the same local area network, though they reside at different places.

✚ See also **groupware**.

## workstation

High-speed personal computer, or minicomputer, loaded with memory and computing power and used for intensive tasks such as computer-aided design (CAD), engineering, and creation of computer graphics.

Photo courtesy of Sun Microsystems, Inc.

## world game

Computer model conceived by Buckminster Fuller, the visionary who coined "Spaceship Earth."

Fuller's proposal would develop a computer containing data on all the physical and human resources in the world. This "world game" computer would model different political, economic, and social strategies to discover how to make the world work best. The results would then be displayed on mini-Earth globes suspended 200 feet in the air over major cities around the world.

A World Game simulation was convened with Fuller's cooperation in 1970. It was a success, and it resulted in the founding of several companies and foundations. The World Game computer, however, remains a dream. Haven't seen one hovering over your house lately, have you?

## world newsgroups

Seven major newsgroups on Usenet.

The seven are comp (computers), news (about the Usenet), rec (sports and hobbies), sci (sciences), soc (society and socialization), talk (topics of the day), and misc (everything else). The current organization follows the Great Renaming of 1986.

## world view

Display of the three-dimensional view of an object or environment using the Cartesian coordinate system.

With three-dimensional computer graphics programs, you can twist and turn a creation in a world view to examine it from all angles. Neat stuff.

## World Wide Web (WWW)

The graphical lane on the information superhighway.

It's the hottest trend since the hula hoop. "The Web" offers text, graphics, sound, and video all in place on the Internet.

It is called the Web because its many sites are linked together. You can jump from one site to another by clicking on a highlighted word or "hot button" (a little graphic item). By clicking, you can roam from site to site. The World Wide Web is best explored with software programs such as Mosaic and Netscape. These serve as navigation guides for

"The World Wide Web is a printing press in the hands of the people. This is a new way to go out and tell the world about your interests and about yourself. You can soak up an awful lot of information on the Internet, but eventually you're going to say, 'Hey, I have something to say, too.'"

—*Michael Barrow*, Boston Computer Society

[Nathan Cobb, "Live from the Internet: It's me!; 'Home pages' let anyone claim a place in cyberspace," *The Boston Globe*, 7 June 1995, Sec. Living, p. 83.]

browsing.  While FTP and Gopher provide only tex-tual information, the Web is the first big step toward multimedia on the Internet.

Technically, the Web is a hypertext site. Commercial and nonprofit organizations, as well as individuals, can set up their own home page and link it with other sites of interest.  Businesses, from the Rolling Stones to Pizza Hut, maintain home pages on the Web as a way to generate customer interest—the first billboards in cyberspace.  So far, few businesses engage in financial transactions on-line, however.

Web presence is hardly limited to corporate giants. Setting up a home page is easy with hypertext transport protocol (http) software, which can be found free on Internet.  Hypertext markup language (HTML), the language used to design a home page, is simple enough that people without extensive computer experience can create a presence.

Amazingly enough, the Web got its start at CERN, a high-energy physics laboratory in Geneva.  There, Tim Berners Lee created the original software to help other scientists share information.  It became part of Internet in 1991, though its boom did not begin until the release of the browser program Mosaic two years later.  Because Web pages conve-niently organize information and make it instantly retrievable, it is immensely popular, embodying—in the opinion of many—the ideal model of public net-working.

## worm

A computer program that can replicate itself.

The most famous example is the 1987 "Internet worm," which shut down hundreds of computers nationwide.

## write many, read many (WMRM)

Optical storage disk that can be written to and erased, many times.

## write once, read many (WORM)

Optical storage disk for backup and archiving.

Information can be written to it only once, but can be read repeatedly.  The disk cannot be erased or reused.

## W3O

Also called W3C, an organization based at the Massachusetts Institute of Technology that sets standards for the World Wide Web.

## WWW

+ See **World Wide Web**.

## WYSIWYG

+ See **what you see is what you get**.

# Xanadu to X.25

## Xanadu

A hypermedia storage management system, still in its infancy.

Envisioned by Ted Nelson, Xanadu will give the public hyperlinked access to all the works of art, literature, and music in the world's libraries and museums, while handling copyright and royalty requirements.

## Xerox PARC

Abbreviation for Xerox's Palo Alto Research Center, the facility whose researchers have been responsible for some of the primary developments of the computer revolution.

These developments include the first prototype personal computer ("Alto"), the ubiquitous mouse, the user-friendly interface, object-oriented languages, bitmap graphics, and local area networks (including the Ethernet, the standard for businesses). Now researchers at Xerox PARC are continuing to invent the future, from innovative computing hardware and software to theoretical systems concerned with how people interact with networks and how networks can change the internal behavior of corporations.

Xerox PARC also presents one of the greatest ironies of the Information Age. Despite all the breakthroughs and brilliant research conducted there, and the handsome royalties and licensing fees Xerox Corporation reaps, the company has never managed to develop a hit product in the computer industry. It tried to commercialize a personal computer in the '80s and failed. The rest of the world, however, remains grateful, if not a little bewildered, that Xerox keeps the research going.

✚ See also **augmentation research center**.

Xavier

© David Wink/Spots on the Spot!

## Xmodem

A file transfer protocol (FTP) for transmitting text or data between modems.

It includes error correction. It was the first real standard, popular until Ymodem came along.

## X-series recommendations

Documents that describe data communication network standards.

These standards are published by the International Telecommunications Union, Telecommunications Sector (ITU-TS).

## X.25

Worldwide standard protocol for packet-switched data networks. X.25 is published by the International Telecommunications Union, Telecommunications Sector (ITU-TS). It is the common reference whereby mainframe computers, minicomputers, PCs, and a vast variety of terminals work together over private and public packet-switched networks, such as the Internet.

The standard specifies the interfaces between the devices and the network, and defines how data streams are to be assembled into packets as they cross the network. Until the early 1990s, the X.25 protocol dominated packet-switched networks. Now, systems are beginning to use the newer frame relay standard.

✚ See also **fast packet switching**.

# Yahoo to Ymodem

## Yahoo

An on-line guide to the World Wide Web.

It allows you to search for Web sites that hold information on a particular topic, and gives you the site address so you can access it.

Yahoo can be accessed by logging on to the Web and typing: http://www.yahoo.com.

## Ymodem

A file transfer protocol (FTP) for sending information between modems.

Faster than Xmodem, it became the state of the art—until Zmodem came along.

# zine to Zulu Time

Zapf Chancery

## zine

Any on-line magazine, usually written in ASCII text, with a focus on the esoteric, the bizarre, and the ephemeral.

Zine publishers—whose products have included titles like *The Neon Gargoyle Gazette* and *The Holy Temple of Mass Consumption*—may be supplanted by home page authors on the World Wide Web, who can cover the same editorial ground but add graphics and links to other kindred spirits.

## Zmodem

Currently the most capable of several file transfer protocols (FTPs) used to transmit information between modems.

## Zulu Time

✦ See **Greenwich Mean Time**.

Courtesy of *The Net* magazine

# Index